New Testan

Journey Through the Bible

VOLUME TWO

The New Testament

from

MATTHEW TO REVELATION

BY

Dr. Jerry Vines

To Bro. [illegible],
God bless you!
Jerry Vines

Journey Through the Bible
Volume Two
The New Testament - From Matthew to Revelation
by Dr. Jerry Vines

Jerry Vines Ministries • JerryVines.com

Published by
Free Church Press
P.O. Box 1075
Carrollton, GA 30112
FreeChurchPress.com

ISBN 9780982656174

Printed in the United States of America
by Lightning Source, Inc.

Unless otherwise indicated, all Scripture taken from the King James Version of the Holy Bible.

Cover Design by Jessica Anglea, www.jessicaanglea.com
Text Design by Debbie Patrick, www.visionrun.com

www.FreeChurchPress.com

This volume is affectionately dedicated to R. C. and Lois Mills. Their love and generosity made this book possible as well as many other projects for Jerry Vines Ministries. They are wonderful Christians who support many Christian causes.

PREFACE

When I was pastor of the wonderful First Baptist Church, Jacksonville, Florida, I led our people in a survey of the whole Bible. I remember with great appreciation their tremendous attendance and gracious comments.

Since then Jerry Vines Ministries has placed these 44 studies into a CD set. Thousands of Christians have used them to help them to better understand the books of the Bible. We have received overwhelming response from many believers.

These Old Testament and New volumes are edited from the CD set. They give an introduction, outline and survey of all 66 Bible books. Some of the books are combined into one study, thus the 44 studies.

The best way to use these volumes is to read them as you listen to the CD lessons (if you don't have them, get them!) Pick a book you want to study, listen to the CD lesson and follow along in the appropriate chapter in the book.

Our prayer is that these volumes will aid you in understanding and applying God's Word.

Jerry Vines
President, Jerry Vines Ministries, Inc.
Pastor-Emeritus, First Baptist Church, Jacksonville, Fl.
Past President, Southern Baptist Convention

Table of Contents

Study #20 Introduction to the New Testament
and The New Testament at a Glance ... 9
Introduction to the New Testament ... 9
The New Testament at a Glance ... 21
THE HISTORICAL BOOKS ... 23
Study #21 Matthew's Manuscript ... 25
Study #22 Mark's Message ... 37
Study #23 Looking at Luke ... 49
Study #24 John's Journal ... 59
Study #25 Acts Alive ... 69
THE INSTRUCTIONAL BOOKS ... 81
Study #26 Romans Road ... 83
Study #27 Considering I Corinthians ... 95
Study #28 Comfort from II Corinthians ... 107
Study #29 Guidelines from Galatians ... 119
Study #30 Exploring Ephesians ... 133
Study #31 Probing Philippians ... 145
Study #32 Considering Colossians ... 159
Study #33 Thrills in I Thessalonians and Truths in II Thessalonians ... 169
Thrills in I Thessalonians ... 169
Truths in II Thessalonians ... 177
Study #34 Teaching in I Timothy ... 181
Study #35 Triumphs in II Timothy ... 191
Study #36 Truths from Titus and Postcard to Philemon ... 203
Truths from Titus ... 203
Postcard to Philemon ... 209
Study #37 Heeding Hebrews ... 215
Study #38 Journey with James ... 227
Study #39 Promises in I Peter ... 239
Study #40 Progressing in II Peter ... 251
Study #41 Journey through I John ... 263
Study #42 Jottings in II John, Jottings in III John and Judgment in Jude ... 273
Jottings in II John ... 273
Jottings in III John ... 278
Judgment in Jude ... 281

THE PROPHETICAL BOOK...287
Study #43 Resting in Revelation..289
Study #44 The Old and New Testaments at a Glance 301

Journey Through the Bible

VOLUME TWO

The New Testament

Study #20
Introduction to the New Testament and The New Testament at a Glance

INTRODUCTION TO THE NEW TESTAMENT

OUTLINE

I. The Silent Years
Between Malachi and Matthew, 400 "Silent Years"
- **A. The History**
- **B. The Sects**
- **C. The Sanhedrin**
- **D. The Synagogue**
- **E. The Dispersion**

II. The New Testament Canon
- **A. The Name**
- **B. The Authors**
- **C. The Periods**

III. The Four Gospels
- **A. The Gospels as a Literary Work**
- **B. The "Synoptic" Problem**
- **C. Why Four Gospels?**

I. The Silent Years

A. The History

When you move from the book of Malachi to the New Testament, you will find yourself in an altogether different world. It is a totally different atmosphere. One of the things you need to be aware of is that we have about 400 years of history between the Old Testament and the New Testament. Think about that. It is longer than the United States has been in existence.

These years in Bible study are called the Silent Years. It is not that no one spoke during these years. Life went on, all kinds of activities took place, and history was being made. They are called the Silent Years because there was no new revelation from God during those 400 years. It is only when you come to the New Testament era and the ministry of John the Baptist and the inauguration of the gospel of Jesus Christ that God began to speak again. The writer of Hebrews in Hebrews 1:1-2 said, "God who at sundry times and in divers manners spoke in time past to the fathers by the prophets, has in these last days spoken unto us by his Son..." But for about 400 years, there was no new revelation from God.

Daniel 11 gives a general idea of what was going on among the people of God during that time. It gives some of the framework of sacred history or history as it relates to the children of Israel.

When you pick up your New Testament, after those Silent Years, you will discover that the New Testament is new indeed. It is a different world. When you close the Old Testament, you have Assyria, Babylon, captivity, and Persia. When you pick up the New Testament, you find yourself in the atmosphere of the Roman Empire. Alexander the Great came in these 400 silent years. But when you pick up the New Testament, you see the Roman Empire, you see things Roman. There is a new language being spoken. Hebrew is no longer the language. Rather, the language in the world at large, or in the Roman world, was the Greek language. In the Holy Land itself, the language being spoken was Aramaic. Aramaic is very similar to Hebrew, but it is not the same.

Also, there is a Greek version of the Old Testament at this time, the Septuagint. When Jesus referred to the Old Testament, He quoted from this version, as well as the writers in the New Testament.

Another thing you will notice is the Jewish temple is not the same. It is a different temple in the New Testament time. There are new places also. Cities are mentioned that were not previously mentioned. You will notice new customs, and there are synagogues that Jews will go to that you did not see in the Old Testament.

B. The Sects

There are a number of sects that are important because, as you study the Gospels especially, you will run into these particular groups. For instance, you will find the Scribes. As Jesus moved in and out of Jerusalem, there were the Scribes.

The Scribes were held in high esteem by the people. They were the interpreters and teachers of the Scripture. The Scribes as a group came into existence after the captivity. Ezra, for instance, was not only a priest, but he was also a Scribe.

The Scribes were bitterly opposed and adamantly against the Lord Jesus Christ. A sad thing had happened to these men who knew their Bible so very, very well. They had become so accustomed to their Bibles that they put more importance on their traditions than they did on the Scriptures. One of the things that has always amazed me about them is when the Wise Men came to Jerusalem because they had seen the star, they knew that the King had been born and wanted to know where He was. Herod brought in the Scribes and asked them where the Messiah was to be born. They knew exactly where, Bethlehem (Micah 5:2). Yet, there is no evidence they bothered to take a trip of five miles to go to Bethlehem to investigate and see if the Messiah they had been reading about in their Old Testament had been born.

Another group in your New Testament, especially in your Gospels, is the Pharisees. We have always talked about the Pharisees. If there is anything you do not want to be, it is a Pharisee. They were a group current in the times of the ministry of our Lord. The Pharisees were the literalists of their day. They were the ones who held to the strict letter of scripture. They were the separatist party, so to speak. They were probably the most influential of all the different sects or parties among the religious life of Israel. They believed in the supernatural. They believed in the resurrection of the dead. You might call them the conservatives of their day.

Do not get the idea that these Pharisees were bad people. They were not bad people. They were very moral people. In fact, they probably lived on a higher level morally than the average Christian does today. The problem was they had become legalists. They were living on this level, trying to prove and earn their standing with God.

The Pharisees really gave Jesus a hard time. In Matthew 23, Jesus has quite a passage about the Pharisees. If you want to really see where they were spiritually, read Matthew 23.

The third group is the Sadducees. Whereas the Pharisees were more the conservatives of the day, the Sadducees were the liberals of their day. They were the rationalists. They were the ones who put human intelligence above spiritual matters. They denied the supernatural, whereas the Pharisees believed in angels, the spirit world, and the resurrection; the Sadducees denied every bit of this. One of the funniest passages in the New Testament is when the apostle Paul was before the official gathering of the Jews (Acts 23). He knew some were Pharisees and some were Sadducees, and he knew they had constantly argued about the resurrection. Paul stood up and said he was there just because he believed in the resurrection of the dead. The Pharisees thought if he believed in the resurrection, he was all right. The Sadducees said no he wasn't. They got in a big squabble, and Paul just stood there and watched it.

Keep in mind that the Pharisees were the conservatives, the literalists of the day. The Sadducees were the rationalists or liberals. The Sadducees though were the priestly aristocracy. They were the wealthy, influential people.

The fourth group is the Herodians. They composed a group of people among the Jews who decided to cast their lot with the powers of Rome. They were the loyalists to the government of the day. Herod was the king at that time, and so they became known as the Herodians, the Herodian party. They opposed the Lord Jesus because they viewed Him as a threat to the political status quo. They did not want anybody rocking the boat or messing up the good deal they had. They were like being on the inside at the White House.

The Zealots were indeed the revolutionaries. They were the extremists. They were the little party among the Jews that was constantly plotting to overthrow the Roman Empire. Evidently, one of the disciples of our Lord had been a Zealot, Simon the Zealot. Matthew 10:4 and Luke 6:15 give us some indication Simon was probably a Zealot.

C. The Sanhedrin

The Sanhedrin was the supreme civil and religious body of the Jewish nation. It was the high court among the Jews. If you appealed a matter in Jewish political circles, then you went all the way to the Sanhedrin. The high priest was the president of the Sanhedrin. They had to have 23 in the Sanhedrin to have a quorum. They had the right to pass the death sentence, but they did not have the right to carry it out. The Roman Empire was in charge of Palestine and Jerusalem; keep that in mind. They allowed the Sanhedrin to do certain things, but they could just go so far. That is why when they tried Jesus and found Him guilty and worthy of death, they had to go to Pontius Pilate. They could not carry out a death sentence. They issued the death warrant, so to speak, for Christ, but they themselves were not able to execute. Jesus stood before the Sanhedrin. Stephen stood before the Sanhedrin. Peter and John stood before the Sanhedrin, and the apostle Paul stood before the Sanhedrin,

D. The Synagogue

If you had gone to sleep in the Old Testament and had awakened 400 years later, you would have been like Rip Van Winkle in America. In the Old Testament things had wrapped around the temple. But when you come to the New Testament, you find a new institution in Jewish life, and it is the synagogue. In the days of captivity when the Jews were away from Jerusalem and they did not have their temple as the center of their worship, in order to maintain the teaching of the Law and their Jewish customs, they organized synagogues for the purpose of instruction in the Old Testament Law. When you come to the New Testament, you will find the Lord Jesus as His custom was on the Sabbath day going up to the synagogue (Luke 4:16). We can be grateful for the synagogues because they kept the Law alive. The synagogue was also an early model or framework for the local New Testament church. If you go to Jerusalem today, there are synagogues everywhere. Just like many places here, down every road there is a church.

E. The Dispersion

When the Jews were allowed to return to Jerusalem after being taken into captivity, some of the Jews decided not to go back to Jerusalem. They had put roots down in these other places and decided they would stay there. In addition to that, the Jews, famous for their merchandizing and their trading, scattered out all over the Roman Empire selling their wares, and so they lived in all parts of the Roman Empire. Because of their contact with the more cosmopolitan culture, they were more liberal minded than the people who lived in the homeland. Greek was the common language, and these Jews felt the need for an Old Testament in Greek so they could read it. Some of their own children could not read Hebrew. So in Alexandria, Egypt, a group of 70 Jewish rabbis translated the Old Testament from the Hebrew into the Greek. It became known as the Septuagint, which means the 70. It is sometimes referred to as the LXX. Most of the Old Testament quotations in the New Testament are taken from the Greek Septuagint. That is why you will find slight differences sometimes in the way the New Testament reads a verse and the way the Old Testament passage reads it.

II. The New Testament Canon

A. The Name

The word *testament* means "covenant." We know that the Old Testament means the Old Covenant, the Old Agreement. The Old Testament was a covenant of law. The New Testament is a covenant of grace. Look at John 1:17, "For the law was given by Moses, but grace and truth came by Jesus Christ." This shows you the difference. The New Testament, the new agreement, is an agreement made in the blood of Jesus. When our Lord inaugurated what we call the Lord's Supper, He said in Luke 22:20, "This cup is the new testament in my blood, which is shed for you." The name of the New Testament means the new agreement. God's agreement with us is grace on the basis of the shed blood of the Lord Jesus Christ.

B. The Authors

As best we can tell, all the authors of the 27 books of the New Testament were Jewish with the exception of one, Luke. We are not exactly sure who wrote the book of Hebrews. We are not told specifically who it was, so the writer of Hebrews may have been a Gentile also. Six of the writers of the New Testament were eyewitnesses. This is important. Six of the authors of the New Testament were eyewitnesses; that is they themselves saw with their own eyes the information which they recorded. Matthew, Mark, John, and Peter, all disciples of Jesus, and James and Jude, the half-brothers of Jesus, were all eyewitnesses. The two other authors, Paul and Luke, were in close contact with those who had eyewitness accounts.

Luke was a physician, but he was also a historian. There is a tradition that he was also an artist. When you read the Gospel of Luke, you can see an artist painting beautiful portraits of the Lord Jesus Christ. In the first four verses of the Gospel of Luke, Luke very carefully explains how he went about composing his Gospel. He makes it very clear that he drew on eyewitness accounts.

C. The Periods

There are several periods of time in the New Testament era. The first one is the period of Beginning. It is the period when the Lord Jesus Christ comes and the basic Gospel events occur.

The second stage of the New Testament era is the Expansion period. After the resurrection, the Lord ascends back to heaven, the Holy Spirit comes down, and the New Testament church is brought into existence on the day of Pentecost. Then in the power of the Holy Spirit the missionary enterprise begins to expand the gospel. Preachers and teachers travel all over the Roman Empire. They are organizing churches from Jerusalem all the way to Rome.

The third period is what we call the period of Consolidation. It is the period during which the church becomes an institution. The doctrine of the church is fully established. Solidarity is built. The church begins to go through tremendous times of persecution. It is not that they were not persecuted from the outset, but the persecution intensified during this time. Also, there was a decline in spiritual life. That is always the tendency since all things earthly tend toward decline. That is why I do not believe in evolution. The tendency is not upward; the tendency is always downward. There has to be constant diligence and constant attention to the fundamentals of the faith and constant attention to the rudiments of the gospel that we do not allow declension to take place. It is just like a field. If you leave a field to itself, it will go to weeds. If you want a beautiful field of flowers, you have to be constantly cultivating it, constantly working it.

III. The Four Gospels

A. The Gospels as a Literary Work

The New Testament, and especially the four Gospels, is the essential document of our faith. The question is, are these documents trustworthy? What about these Gospels, Matthew, Mark, Luke, and John? If the four Gospels are true, if what is in the four Gospels is true, then to reject their message is fatal to the human soul. But if they are not true, then they are an exercise in futility. We have been wasting our time. The trustworthiness and the reliability of the New Testament, in particular the four Gospels, are very important.

There was a man named Simon Greenleaf who wrote a book entitled *A Treatise on the Law of Evidence.* I do not know if lawyers still refer to it or not, but for many years it was the basic law that set the principles of evidence and making determinations about whether evidence was true or not. Greenleaf, using the same laws of evidence he had set forth in his book for the legal profession, examined the testimony of the four Gospels. When he finished his examination, he came to the conclusion that the Gospels are absolutely trustworthy, that they were not lying about the Lord Jesus Christ for their testimony rang true. That was his conclusion from a legal perspective.

First Timothy 1:15, paraphrased, says this, "This statement is completely reliable and should be universally accepted." So the ring of authenticity is found in your New Testament. It has been examined; it has been scrutinized; there have been attempts made to discredit the New Testament. Yet, the New Testament remains a completely trustworthy document.

We have only four Gospels. Every now and then you will run across a hidden gospel or another gospel. One of the more familiar is the Gospel of Thomas, What about those gospels? You find out that they are fanciful in nature. They are kind of legendary and are written to bolster the view of some particular sect. They have things that are totally unnecessary to the life of our Lord. For instance, some talk about the fact that when Jesus was a boy He would make little birds out of clay. Then they would come to life and fly away. It is agreed there are only four that meet the criteria for reliability. They are the four Gospels: Matthew, Mark, Luke, and John.

Another thing you have to keep in mind is none of these four Gospels claims to cover all of the information or to be an exhaustive account. In one sense of the word, you really do not have a life of Christ, as such, in any of these documents. None sets out to give you the life of Christ in chronological order. That is not the purpose of these four Gospels. Each one of these Gospel writers selected the information that was out there to achieve the purposes for which he was writing his Gospel.

B. The "Synoptic" Problem

That brings me to what is known in New Testament studies as the "synoptic" problem. It is in quotes because I do not consider it a problem, but that is what it is referred to, the "synoptic" problem.

Three of the Gospels are called "synoptic" Gospels. Synoptic is made up of two Greek words: syn, which means "together," and optic, which means "to see." *Synoptic* means "to see together." Matthew, Mark, and Luke are called the "synoptic" Gospels because you will find a lot of the same material in each of them. Every New Testament student should have what is called a Harmony of the Gospels. That is a book that puts Matthew, Mark, and Luke side by side and then also includes the information that John includes but they do not. It allows you to compare and see.

In some places the three Gospels are identical word for word. In other places Matthew will include some things that Luke will leave out, but they are in general agreement in terms of the information that they include. That has caused some people to raise questions about those three Gospels. That is what they call the "synoptic" problem. If you were a school teacher and you gave an examination and got three test papers back that were almost identical, wouldn't you raise a little eyebrow? Wouldn't you get a little suspicious? They have concocted all kinds of theories about the "synoptic" problem. One of the primary things the liberals have to say is that Matthew and Luke copied Mark and a third source to put their Gospels together. They call that third source "Que" after the Latin word quelle, which means source. The only thing is no one has ever found "Que." No one has ever had a copy of Que. It was a figment of some liberal's imagination, if you really want to know. But that is one of the theories about how this came about.

Here is why you will find similarities in these three Gospels. The first thing you have to keep in mind is you have eyewitness accounts and that the Gospel was spoken before it was written. Another thing you have to remember is that the Jewish people were trained to memorize. There were Jews who memorized the first five books of the Bible. They did not have computers. They heard these sermons that Jesus preached, and they memorized them. For instance, when we study the Gospel of Mark, there is pretty good evidence that Mark wrote down what he heard from Simon Peter. It was the basic substance of his Gospel. You have to keep in mind that the New Testament is eyewitness accounts of those who actually heard what Jesus said and saw what Jesus did.

But here is the missing ingredient that liberals never seem to understand. We believe our New Testament was written by human beings who were inspired and led by the Holy Spirit. Second Peter 1:21 says, "Holy men of God spake as they were moved by the Holy Spirit." That is why you have these similarities.

C. Why Four Gospels?

Why are there some differences in the four Gospels? That brings us to Why Four Gospels? Each one of these four Gospels gives a unique presentation of the Lord Jesus because each has a distinctive emphasis. Each has a purpose in mind for writing his particular Gospel.

Matthew is written for Jews. If you are not a Jew, you can still get something out of Matthew. All of the Bible applies to us, but not all of the Bible is addressed to us. Or I can reverse it. Not all of the Bible is addressed to us, but all the Bible applies to us. Do you see the distinction? To say that Matthew was writing for the Jews does not mean that you and I cannot get anything out of it. Of course, we can. But it helps us to understand that his target audience was specifically the Jews. Then you will understand why he includes some things that none of the other Gospel writers includes. It will also help you to understand why he excludes some things. For instance, Matthew starts off his Gospel with a long list of names, a genealogy. He was writing to the Jews. It would be very important to the Jews to see the lineage, the family tree of Jesus, since Matthew is showing that Jesus is the Messiah.

As you read through Matthew, you will notice that Matthew ties the life of the Lord Jesus Christ to the Old Testament Law and prophets. He uses the word *fulfilled.* So Matthew is writing for the Jews to present Jesus the Messiah, the King of the Jews.

When you get to Mark, Mark begins at the baptism of Jesus. He does not even mention the birth of Jesus. Mark is writing for Romans. They were his target audience. That is why Mark explains a lot of Jewish customs and words. Matthew would not explain them because he was writing to Jews. They would understand. It is like a person coming from the North. When I use Southern talk around Northern people, I have to explain what I am saying. But around Southerners I do not. They know what I am talking about. When I say "plum nearly," Southerners know what I am talking about, but Northerners do not have a clue. So I have to explain it to them. Mark explains Jewish words and Jewish customs. He is writing for the Romans, and he is presenting the Lord Jesus as the Servant. That is why Mark is the Gospel of action. He goes from event to event to event. It is a Gospel of action.

Luke writes the third Gospel for the Greeks. He writes beautiful polished Greek. He sets forth the Lord Jesus as the perfect Man and emphasizes the humanity of the Lord Jesus Christ. Luke, the doctor, sets forth the Son of Man. That is why when you get to Luke 3, Luke has a genealogy that traces the line of Jesus Christ through the blood line through Mary. Matthew, on the other hand, in his genealogy traces the legal line through His legal father Joseph. There is a different emphasis there.

The Gospel of John is targeted to believers and to the world in general. John was writing to those who believe, but he was also setting forth Jesus as the Savior of the world. He presents Jesus as the Son of God and emphasizes the deity of Jesus. That is why John selects seven of the miracles of Jesus. Jesus did a lot more miracles than seven, but John selects seven of them and specifically says those seven are signs so that people might believe that Jesus is the Christ and that believing they might have faith in His name, John 20:31.

By the way, John is one of the writers of the New Testament who has a way of giving you a little key to unlock the door of his book. Sometimes he hangs his key on the front door, and sometimes he hangs it on the back door. For the book of the Revelation, he hangs it on the front door. Revelation 1:19, "Write the things which you have seen, write the things which are, and write the things which shall be hereafter." In the Gospel of John, he hangs the key on the back door, John 20:31: "But these things are written, that ye might believe." He also says Jesus did a whole lot more than what he included, but he included what he did so people might believe. When you are witnessing to people, one of the best things you can do for them is to get them to read the Gospel of John. The Gospel of John is specifically written to bring people to believe that Jesus is the Son of God.

THE NEW TESTAMENT AT A GLANCE

OUTLINE

I. Historical (5 Books)
   A. The History of Christ
   B. The History of the Church
II. Instructional (21 Books)
   A. Doctrinal
   B. Pastoral
   C. General
III. Prophetical (1 Book)

I. Historical (5 Books)

There are three main sections of your New Testament, just like the Old Testament. The first section is Historical: Matthew, Mark, Luke, John, and Acts. The first four books are called the Gospels and give us the history of Christ. The fifth book, Acts, gives us the history of the Church.

II. Instructional (21 Books)

The next 21 books of your New Testament are Instructional. Nine books are Doctrinal books. That does not mean you do not find doctrine in other books, that you do not find instruction in the Gospels; you do. But these books are primarily doctrinal. They are written to seven churches, and the doctrine of the church is unfolded in them. They are Romans, I and II Corinthians, Galatians, Ephesians, Philippians, Colossians, and I and II Thessalonians.

The next four books are called Pastoral or Personal. Those are written primarily to pastors. This would not necessarily apply to Philemon; but I and II Timothy are letters written to the young preacher Timothy, and Titus is written to the young preacher Titus. Then you have the little postcard to Philemon, which is one of the most exciting little books in the entire New Testament.

The next eight books of the Instructional section are called the General letters. All of there are letters. The General section starts with Hebrews and goes through Jude. They deal with General truth, General instruction.

III. Prophetical (1 Book)

The third section is the Prophetical section, and it has one book, Revelation.

The Historical Books

Study #21
Matthews Manuscript

MATTHEW'S MANUSCRIPT

When you open up your New Testament, the first book that greets your eye is the Gospel of Matthew. The four Gospels are not specifically biographies of the Lord Jesus, in that they do not necessarily begin with His birth and then go in chronological step-by-step order through the details of His life; but they do share about the life of Jesus Christ. Each has a point of view; they have a perspective; they have a purpose in mind.

Matthew is the kingly Gospel. It sets forth Jesus Christ as the King of the Jews and the King of the world. The primary target audience was the Jews. Mark, on the other hand, is the servant Gospel. We see Christ as the Servant. His primary audience or target was the Roman world. The Gospel of Luke sets forth Jesus Christ as the Son of Man, the perfect Man. Luke was writing primarily for a Greek audience. Then, the magnificent Gospel of John is a book that sets forth Jesus as the Son of God. It was written for believers and for the world at large.

The Bridge between the Old and New Testaments

Matthew, as the opening book, serves as a bridge between the Old Testament and New Testament. It ties the two Testaments together. Matthew carefully documents our Lord's claim to be the Messiah of the Jews. This is Matthew's purpose, and so this Gospel has a number of quotes from the Old Testament. It has about 129 quotations or uses of the Old Testament. Matthew references or quotes from 25 out of the 39 books of the Old Testament.

Matthew answers questions that the average Jew would ask concerning Jesus Christ. Another word for Christ is Messiah. That is what the word *Christ* means, the Anointed One. The Jews were looking for the Messiah. All through the Old Testament, it had predicted that the Messiah was going to come, so all through these centuries the Jews had been looking for their Messiah to come.

Jesus comes on the stage of human history. He appears in Palestine and declares Himself to be the Messiah, and the Christian church declares that He is the long-awaited Messiah. The Jews would immediately begin to ask certain questions: What about His ancestry? What kind of family line does this Jesus have if He is the Messiah? Does Jesus qualify? Others would ask these questions: What is His relationship to the Law and the Prophets? How does He regard the Law and the Prophets? It is evident when you read the Gospel of Matthew that Matthew's purpose is to show that Jesus Christ is the promised Messiah.

Its Author

Another name for Matthew in certain passages is the name Levi. Levi is the Jewish name for Matthew. Look at Matthew 9:9 and following: "And as Jesus passed forth from thence, he saw a man, named Matthew, sitting at the receipt of customs; and he saith unto him, follow me. And he arose, and followed him." This is Matthew, the author of this Gospel. Now we learn here that he was a tax collector. In some passages he is referred to as a publican, which can also mean tax collector. Matthew 9:10, "And it came to pass, as Jesus sat eating in the house, behold, many publicans [tax collectors] and sinners came and sat down with him and his disciples." It mentions many publicans and sinners.

You have to keep in mind that a tax collector in Palestine at that time would be a Jew who had basically sold out for money to the hated Roman Empire. Patriotic Jews had nothing to do with tax collectors. This would be a scandal right here. Jesus comes walking by and there sits Matthew at the tax collectors table. Jesus says follow Me; and he gets up and follows Jesus. That was scandalous for high patriotic Jews. Note he is called Matthew in Matthew 9.

Look in the second Gospel, Mark 2:14, "And as he passed by, he saw Levi, the son of Alphaeus, sitting at the receipt of customs, and he said unto him, follow me. And he arose and followed him." It is the same person, but here he is known as Levi; so Matthew and Levi are one and the same.

Matthew did a wonderful thing when he began to be a follower of the Lord Jesus. We are told in Matthew 9 and parallel accounts that he threw a big feast for his friends. Matthew 9:10, "And it came to pass, as Jesus sat at meat in the house [that is in the house of Matthew], behold, many publicans and sinners came and sat down with him and his disciples."

Matthew was so thrilled at his new found faith, that he had found his Messiah, that he wanted all his friends to know about it. That is a pretty good encouragement for us today when we come to know the Lord. One of the best places to begin to witness is among those you know. There is a tendency the longer a person is a Christian to become more and more around Christians to the point that if you are not careful your only friends are Christians. The Bible teaches we do not have fellowship with this world, but we are to have friends for Jesus' sake. Your circle of friends is a good place to go to win people to Christ.

Matthew is the author. He was a disciple of the Lord Jesus Christ because he answered the call to follow Him. A disciple is one who follows the Lord Jesus Christ. He was also selected as one of the original twelve disciples. Matthew 10:1 tells us Jesus called His 12 disciples; then in verses 2-4 it says, "Now the names of the twelve apostles are these; The first, Simon, who is called Peter, and Andrew, his brother; James the son of Zebedee, and John, his brother; Philip and Bartholomew; Thomas and Matthew, the tax collector; James, the son of Alphaeus, and Lebbaeus, whose surname was Thaddaeus; Simon, the Canaanite, and Judas Iscariot, who also betrayed him."

By the way, as you look at the different authors of the Gospel accounts, you will notice that God uniquely prepared each of them for the assignment to compose his Gospel. Matthew was good at figures; he knew how to be meticulous. It is another strong evidence to us of the accuracy and trustworthiness of what we find in this Gospel of Matthew.

Its Date

The Gospel of Matthew was written probably around A.D. 58, though no one really knows the exact year. Why do we say A.D. 58 and not A.D. 78? We do know that the temple in Jerusalem was destroyed in A.D.70. It is a matter of historical fact, of historical record. But when you read the Gospel of Matthew, there are a number of references to the temple. These references are made in ways that let you know when Matthew was composing his Gospel, the temple was still standing. For instance, Jesus predicted the fall of the temple, He predicted what would happen in A.D.70.

If Matthew had been writing after A.D. 70, then there is every reason to believe that he would have made reference in some way to this destruction of the temple and would have pointed out the fact that what Jesus Christ had predicted had indeed come to pass. Our best conservative scholars put the writing of Matthew's Gospel sometime around A.D. 58.

Now this is important because in earlier years, liberals used to attack the credibility of some of the books of the Bible on the basis of later authorship. They tried to put as much space as possible between the actual events and the writing down of those events, sowing seeds of doubt about whether or not the New Testament was reliable. All of our evidence now moves these books of the New Testament closer and closer to the historical occurrences of the material they give us. That is why dates are important.

Its Theme

The theme of Matthew's Gospel is that Jesus is the predicted Messiah of the Jews. He is the promised King of the Jews. He is the King of the world. Matthew shows in his Gospel that though Jesus is the predicted Messiah of the Jews, He was rejected by the Jews and was crucified. But not only was He crucified for the Jews, He was crucified for the whole world. He was buried, He rose again, He now is in heaven, and one day He is coming back to reign. That is the basic theme of Matthew's Gospel.

How does Matthew go about proving his point? If this is his purpose to set forth Jesus as the predicted Messiah, how does he go about this? He does it in a very unique way and in a way that would appeal to the Jewish mind and to those who were familiar with the Old Testament.

Imagine you had never read the New Testament before, and someone said here is a New Testament and I want you to read it. You pick it up and open it to

Matthew 1:1. Then you scan down and run into all kinds of names. You immediately become aware of the fact that you are dealing with a genealogy.

Genealogies are real popular now. I have been in the genealogical library of the Mormon Church in Salt Lake City. It is very fascinating. In fact, it is now on the internet, and you can access their massive records. We know that their purpose for these genealogical records is certainly inconsistent with what we understand the Bible to teach. They are doing it so people can trace their ancestors and be baptized for them. We do not believe there is salvation in any individual who is baptized on the behalf of someone else. But my point is genealogy is a big thing now. It was a big thing in the days of Jesus also. Again, one of the first questions they would ask about Jesus would be what about His ancestors? What about His genealogy?

Genealogies are a prominent part of your Old Testament. If you have read through the Old Testament, you know there are many genealogies listed. There is an interesting arrangement of the Old Testament Scriptures in the Hebrew Bible, the way the Hebrew is put together.

Now in our Bible, the last book in the Old Testament is the book of Malachi. In the Hebrew Bible, the last book is the book of II Chronicles, and in it you will find a lot of genealogies.

Matthew's Gospel would immediately get the interest of a Jew. Look at how it starts, Matthew 1:1, "The book of the generation of Jesus Christ [Messiah], the son of David, the son of Abraham." That would really get your attention as a Jew because here is a claim that Jesus is the Messiah and what is going to follow is going to prove that Jesus Christ is in the line of David and Abraham. Those were the two qualifications in terms of ancestral lines for the Messiah. He had to be in the line of David; He had to be in the line of Abraham.

By the way, this first verse uniquely ties the Gospel of Matthew to the Old Testament. Genesis 5:1, "This is the book of the generations of Adam." We learn about Adam in the book of Genesis. The first man. Tie that to Matthew 1:1, "The book of the generation of Jesus Christ [Jesus Messiah]."

The Old Testament, the book of the generations of Adam. The New Testament, the book of the generation of Jesus Christ. The apostle Paul uniquely ties these two genealogies together and Adam and the Lord Jesus together in I Corinthians 15:22, "For as in Adam all die, even so in Christ shall all be made alive." Do you notice the two things contrasted there? Adam and Christ. Death and life. Genesis 5 is the death chapter. I think about eight times in this chapter the little phrase *and he died* occurs. In Adam, all die; but in Christ, all shall be made alive.

Matthew 1:1 uses this word *begat* (or begot), Abraham begot, Isaac begot, Jacob begot, and so on. That is a reference to the generation of biological life. In Adam, all died. In Jesus Christ, all are made alive. The Old Testament is the death book that leads to the curse; the New Testament is the life book that leads to glory.

Do you see what Matthew is doing? He is tying the Old Testament and New Testament together. Then he is going down through this genealogy and showing the connection between the Lord Jesus and Abraham and David.

Matthew 1:2: "Abraham begot Isaac," and he comes right on down. In verse 6, "Jesse begot David." He has tied Christ to Abraham, and now he ties Christ to David.

Matthew has proven on the very first page of his Gospel that Jesus Christ is qualified to be the Messiah for the Jews. In fact, Jesus is the only one who can be proven to be the Messiah of the Jews. In A.D.70 the temple was destroyed and burned. When it was, all of the genealogical information was in it and all of it was burned and destroyed, so there is no genealogy today that any Jew can point to that will prove his right to be the Messiah of the Jews. The only one who can prove that he is the Messiah of the Jews is the Lord Jesus Christ. God has preserved it for you right in the pages of the Word of God, the Bible.

Did you know that this genealogy was predicted? In Isaiah 53, God predicted that someone would put down this genealogy. This chapter is one of the most remarkable chapters about the Lord Jesus Christ in the whole Bible. Someone has said it is just like Isaiah is sitting at the foot of the cross writing. Verse 8, "He [the Messiah] was taken from prison and from judgment; and who shall declare his generation?" The Old Testament prophet and the Old Testament ask the question who shall declare his generation? It is almost as if Matthew raises his hand and says he will.

I have studied these genealogies through the years, and this is one of the great Christmas messages. I have preached on the genealogy of Jesus at Christmas time. It is fascinating to see how it is arranged and to see the unique proof of the virgin birth of Jesus right here in this first chapter. Matthew 1:16 shows the virgin birth. "And Jacob begat Joseph, the husband of Mary, of whom was born Jesus, who is called Christ."

The "of whom" here refers to Mary. Jesus was not begotten of Joseph because you and I know as we find later on in the last verse of this chapter (verse 25) that Jesus was born of a virgin. So Matthew's purpose is to set forth Jesus as the Messiah. He does it uniquely by this introductory genealogy.

Its Key Word

I mentioned the fact that Matthew makes reference to many Old Testament scriptures. There is a word that occurs many times in the Gospel of Matthew, and it is the word *fulfilled*. Look at Matthew 1:22, "Now all this was done, that it might be fulfilled which was spoken of the Lord through the prophets, saying." Then you get a quotation from Isaiah 7:14.

Look at Matthew 2:15. It is talking about Jesus being carried down into Egypt, and it says, "And was there until the death of Herod, that it might be fulfilled which was spoken by the Lord through the prophet, saying, out of Egypt have I called my son." That is a reference to Hosea 11:1.

Note Matthew 2:17, "Then was fulfilled that which was spoken by Jeremiah, the prophet," and then he quotes Jeremiah 31:15. Look at Matthew 2:23, "And he came and dwelt in a city called Nazareth, that it might be fulfilled which was spoken by the prophets, he shall be called a Nazarene." This is in reference to Isaiah 11:1.

Matthew uses the word *fulfilled* to tie Jesus, the Messiah, to the predictions concerning the Messiah that are made in the Old Testament, in the Bible of the Jewish people. You can imagine what a Jew would be doing as he would be reading these things. He would be back and forth to his Old Testament.

The word *fulfilled* really is the key word to the Gospel of Matthew. Look for that word *fulfilled* in Matthew's Gospel.

Another reference in Matthew is "the kingdom of heaven." Thirty-two times in Matthew's Gospel, you will find reference to the kingdom of heaven, and it is evidently used in a special way by Matthew, in a way the Jews would understand.

The kingdom of heaven is a reference to this age in which you and I live, and it is a mixture of good and bad, true and false. The church exists in this kingdom of heaven, but the kingdom of heaven is something wider or larger. That is why in Matthew 13, there is a series of parables. In many of these parables, Jesus begins the parable by saying, "The kingdom of heaven is like."

Matthew 13:24 says, "Another parable put he forth unto them, saying, the kingdom of heaven is likened unto a man who sowed good seed in his field." Jesus talks about the man sowing and the wheat and the tares in the field. Matthew 13:31 says, "Another parable put he forth unto them, saying, the kingdom of heaven is like a grain of mustard seed, which a man took, and sowed in his field." It is a technical term that Matthew uses that the Jews could identify with.

Do not expect Matthew or the other Gospels to necessarily be in chronological order. Their material is arranged for a particular purpose in order to create a cumulative effect toward the thesis or point of view that the individual Gospel writer was trying to carry out and teach about the Lord Jesus in his Gospel.

OUTLINE

I. The Revelation of the King, 1–10
- **A. His Person**
- **B. His Principles**
- **C. His Power**

II. The Rebellion against the King, 11–13

III. The Retirement of the King, 14–20

IV. The Rejection of the King, 21–27

V. The Resurrection of the King, 28

I. The Revelation of the King, 1–10

The first main division is The Revelation of the King, chapters 1–10. Matthew is trying to show who Jesus is, what Jesus said, and what Jesus did. Matthew is revealing the Lord Jesus as the long-awaited Messiah.

A. His Person, 1–4

The first four chapters reveal His Person, who Jesus is. That is why you have the genealogy here. It is why in the latter part of chapter 1 and on into chapter 2 you have His birth. Then in chapter 3 you have the account of the ministry of John the Baptist and then the baptism of Jesus, Jesus coming to John the Baptist to be baptized of him. Then in chapter 4 you have the marvelous account of the temptation of our Lord. The first four chapters reveal the person of Jesus.

B. His Principles, 5–7

Chapters 5–7 are familiar to us. This is commonly known as the Sermon on the Mount. These chapters give us His principles or His teachings, what Jesus said. Of course, it is not all He said, but He lays forth the basic principles of life as a believer. He shows the connection with the Old Testament and His purpose, why He came.

Note Matthew 7:28-29, "And it came to pass, when Jesus had ended these sayings, the people were astonished at his doctrine: For he taught them as one having authority, and not as the scribes." There is a reason for that. The reason Jesus taught with authority is because He is authority. When Jesus spoke, it was God speaking, so there was astonishment on the part of the people.

C. His Power, 8–10

After Jesus' teachings, you move into the third part of this Gospel, His Power, chapters 8–10, what Jesus did. He did more than this, but Matthew selected about ten miracles in those three chapters. These miracles set forth the Messiahship of the Lord Jesus Christ.

II. The Rebellion against the King, 11–13

The second division of Matthew is the Rebellion against the King, chapters

11–13. Now Jesus' words and works among the Jewish people produced adverse results. He was not the kind of king they wanted. A lot of people at that time were looking for the Messiah to come, but they carefully selected the passages in the Old Testament they wanted Him to fulfill. They wanted Him to fulfill the passages that talked about His coming to rule and to reign. There are other passages in the Old Testament that talk about the Messiah and His coming to serve and to suffer. They did not like those passages. They were looking for the Messiah the King to come and get them out from under the bondage and under the heel of the Roman Empire. When Jesus came and did not do that, they got upset with Him. The leaders of the Jews especially rejected Him and rebelled against Him. In these chapters you will find controversy and rebellion starting against the things Jesus was saying and doing. That is why Jesus gives the parables in Matthew 13. He was showing the mixture of good and bad.

III. The Retirement of the King, 14–20

The third division is the Retirement of the King, chapters 14–20. This is not retirement like retiring from your job and buying a place up on the lake and going fishing. What I mean here is Jesus retreats or withdraws with His disciples to spend quality time with them to get them prepared for what is ahead. He had to get them ready for the cross. He had to prepare them for what was coming. In this section He begins to talk about the cross. Read Matthew 16:13. Jesus is with His disciples, and it is one of these retirement or withdrawal times; He begins to ask them some questions. In verse 13 He asks them who did the people say He was. In other words, what were people saying? The disciples had all the answers. Verse 14, "And they said, Some say that thou art John the Baptist; some, Elias; and others, Jeremiah, or one of the prophets." Then in verse 15, Jesus says, "But whom say ye that I am?" You remember we have the tremendous statement from Peter in verse 16, "You are the Christ, the Son of the living God." Remember Matthew's purpose?

Jesus all this time has been trying to teach His disciples one primary lesson, "Who am I?" So it is test time. Question, "Who am I?" Simon Peter raises his hand and says, "You are the Christ, the Son of the living God." They had learned lesson number one. Now, then, look at verse 21, "From that time forth began Jesus to show unto his disciples, how that he must go unto Jerusalem, and suffer many things of the elders and chief priests and scribes, and be killed, and be raised again the third day." That is the first time Jesus mentions the cross to them. He has taught them the first lesson, "Who am I?" Now He is going to switch to lesson number two: "What have I come to do?" And He starts talking about the cross.

Notice He also mentions the resurrection. In verse 21 He is going to be killed and He is going to be raised again. But that went right over their heads. They totally missed it. When they heard the word *killed,* that immediately grabbed them. They could not think of anything else except that. They totally missed that Jesus said He was going to be raised from the dead. Two other times in this section Jesus makes mention of His cross. Matthew 17:22-23, "And while they abode in Galilee, Jesus said unto them, The Son of man shall be betrayed into the hands of men: And they shall kill him, and the third day he shall be raised again. And they were exceeding sorry." He talks about the resurrection, but again it goes right over their heads. They are exceeding sorry.

The third time is in chapter 20:17, "And Jesus going up to Jerusalem, took the twelve disciples apart in the way [withdrawal], and said unto them, Behold, we go up to Jerusalem; and the Son of man shall be betrayed unto the chief priests and unto the scribes, and they shall condemn him to death, And shall deliver him to the Gentiles to mock, and to scourge, and to crucify him; and the third day he shall rise again." He mentions the resurrection again, but again it goes right over their heads. But He is trying to prepare them for His cross.

IV. The Rejection of the King, 21–27

The fourth division is the Rejection of the King, chapters 21–27. These chapters show how the Jews reject Christ as their Messiah, how the religious leaders officially reject Him and carry Him to the civil authorities. They engineer and arrange the death of the Lord Jesus Christ. In that section you have chapter 27. It talks about the crucifixion of our Lord Jesus, His dying on the cross not only for the sins of the Jews but for the sins of the whole world, for your sins and my sins.

V. The Resurrection of the King, 28

The fifth division is the Resurrection of King. This marvelous 28th chapter wraps up everything. The Lord is resurrected, He makes His appearances, and then He closes out in verses 18-20 with what you and I know as the Great Commission. The Great Commission is very clear: we are to go, make disciples, baptize, and teach. Jesus says He will be with us always, even unto the end of the world. Matthew concludes his Gospel by saying Amen.

Study #22
Marks Message

MARK'S MESSAGE

The first three Gospels, Matthew, Mark, and Luke, are known as the synoptic Gospels because they take a common view of the Lord Jesus Christ. We have the word *optic* which means "to see," and *syn*, which means "to see with" or "to see together." A lot of the material in these Gospels is parallel. You will find some repetitions. For that reason, some have theorized that they collaborated with one another. What they are though are eyewitness accounts of the life of the Lord Jesus, either by an apostle himself or by someone who was close to an apostle. For instance, Matthew, the writer of the Gospel of Matthew, was one of the twelve apostles and gives an eyewitness account. Mark, although not an apostle, had a unique relationship as will be explained.

Each one of the Gospel writers had a definite reason for including what he included and for excluding what he excluded. Each one selected his material for a distinguishing purpose, for a special reason. We do not have any complete account of the life of the Lord Jesus Christ in our Bible. John's Gospel makes it clear to us that if he had tried to put everything that the Lord did and said and the meaning of everything, there would not have been a way for all of the books of the world to ever include the material.

Its Author

The traditional position is this Gospel's author was John Mark. John was his Jewish name; Mark, his Roman name.

When you go to the book of Acts in particular and piece together the different references to John Mark, you find a rather amazing, unusual story. John Mark was a young man and his story is one of the thrilling stories in the New Testament. Acts 12 is the beginning of the information about John Mark. This background helps us to know how he came to this Gospel and why he writes the way he does.

Acts 12's setting is right after the miraculous delivery of Simon Peter from prison. He was in prison and was scheduled to be executed the next morning. Then the Lord released him from his chains and opened the doors of the prison. The Christians were praying for him to be delivered out of jail. When he was, they thought he was a ghost. They did not believe. God answered their prayers, and they did not believe it. We laugh at them, but isn't that the way we are at times?

Acts 12:12 gives us the first reference to John Mark: "And when he [Simon Peter] had considered the thing, he came to the house of Mary, the mother of John, whose surname was Mark, where many were gathered together praying." This is in Jerusalem, and a group of believers had gathered to pray for Peter in the home of Mary. There are different Marys mentioned in the Bible. This is not the mother of Jesus, but this Mary is known as the mother of John who was surnamed Mark. Again, John his Jewish name; Mark his Roman name. This let us know who his mother was. She was a believer, and her home was a place where believers gathered together for prayer.

Acts 12:25 is the second piece of information we know about John Mark: "And Barnabas and Saul returned from Jerusalem, when they had fulfilled their ministry, and took with them John, whose surname was Mark." This young man, John Mark, was selected to be with Paul and Barnabas on their missionary journey.

In Acts 13 is the commissioning of Paul and Barnabas for a missionary journey. Acts 13:5, "And when they were at Salamis, they preached the word of God in the synagogues of the Jews; and they had also John as their minister [helper or servant]." John had been taken to be their assistant. This is not uncommon today. Here is the picture: John Mark was a young Christian, he had a Christian mother, and he was selected by Paul and Barnabas to go with them on their missionary journeys.

They embarked on the journey and got to a certain point. Acts 13:13, "Now when Paul and his company loosed from Paphos, they came to Perga in Pamphylia; and John, departing from them, returned to Jerusalem." John Mark went back home to his mother. We do not know why. We do not know what the problem was, if he got homesick or if he was just young and immature. What we do know is he had started off on the trip and right in the middle of it, he went back to Jerusalem.

In Acts 15 Paul was ready to go again on a missionary journey. Some time had transpired, and Acts 15:36 says, "And some days after, Paul said to Barnabas, let us go again and visit our brethren in every city where we have preached the word of the Lord, and see how they do." He wanted to go back and retrace their steps to see how the people they had won to Christ were growing in the Lord. He wanted to see if the churches were prospering.

Acts 15:37 says, "And Barnabas determined to take with them John, whose surname was Mark." Notice the word *determined.* That is a strong word. In other words, Barnabas had his mind made up. He was going to take John Mark. He was not just suggesting, but he was demanding. Look at verse 38, "But Paul thought not good to take him with them, who departed from them from Pamphylia, and went not with them to the work." Barnabas said they were going to take John Mark, but Paul said they were not. You have two strong men here, two Christians. They loved the Lord, but they had a disagreement.

Acts 15:39, "And the contention was so sharp between them that they departed asunder one from the other." The word *contention* is a mild word in terms of the meaning of the word. What it means is they had a big argument. They had a falling out over John Mark. Barnabas probably wanted to give John Mark another chance because he was a young man. Paul did not want to. He probably did not want anyone who was unreliable. They had a parting of the ways. Notice again verse 39, "and so Barnabas took Mark, and sailed unto Cyprus." There is a reason that Barnabas wanted to help John Mark, and we will see that later; but Barnabas took John Mark and sailed to Cyprus. Acts 15:40, "And Paul chose Silas, and departed, being commended by the brethren unto the grace of God." Paul sailed in another direction, and what the early church now had was not one missionary party but two: Barnabas and Mark and their group, and Paul and Silas and their group.

A Methodist friend one time told me that we Baptists were amazing folks. He said when the Methodists have a fuss, it kills their church; but when Baptists have a fuss, we split up and make two churches that are bigger than the one we started with. My point is even good Christians, people who love the Lord, can have disagreements with one another. It is not a good thing, but God can, even in spite of it, if Christians are willing to do what they ought to do, put it back together and bless.

Let's see what happened. Paul writes in Colossians 4:10: "Aristarchus, my fellow prisoner, saluteth you, and Marcus, sister's son to Barnabas (touching whom ye received commandments; if he come unto you, receive him)." He was making reference to the young John Mark. We learn that he was the sister's son to Barnabas. Barnabas' sister was Mary. John Mark was Barnabas' nephew. It helps to know this to see why Barnabas had the attachment to John Mark. This was his sister's son.

Something happened by the time of II Timothy. As far as we know, II Timothy is the last book Paul wrote. In chapter 4 Paul talks about different people; II Timothy 4:10-11, "For Demas hath forsaken me, having loved this present world, and is departed unto Thessalonica; Crescens to Galatia, Titus unto Dalmatia. Only Luke [that is the beloved physician] is with me. Take Mark, and bring him with thee; for he is profitable to me for the ministry."

Do you see what had happened? Here was a young boy who had a bumpy start, but he made good. Does this say something for Paul also? Here was a man who was willing to give John Mark the second chance that Barnabas wanted to give him in the first place. This also tells us that even when we fail the Lord, God is the God of the second chance. He is not only the God of the second chance, but He is the God of the third chance, the fourth chance, and on and on. The young man who was given a second chance was the author of the second Gospel, the Gospel of Mark.

Another reference to Mark leads to why John Mark was selected to write the second Gospel. Look at I Peter 5:13, written by the disciple Simon Peter. "The church that is at Babylon, elected together with you, saluteth you; and so doth

Marcus, my son." That does not mean he was his flesh and blood son. The meaning is evidently Simon Peter won John Mark to the Lord; John Mark was one of Peter's converts. That is why he refers to him as his son.

There is strong tradition in the early church that John Mark became associated with his spiritual father, Simon Peter, and those who study these kinds of things notice a remarkable parallel between Simon Peter's sermon in Acts 10:34-43 and the Gospel of Mark.

Every New Testament book author was either an eyewitness or was closely associated with eyewitnesses of Jesus Christ. Peter's sermon in Acts 10 demonstrates this for us. I am confident you have a synopsis for Mark's Gospel from the notes of Simon Peter's sermon to the Gentiles in the house of Cornelius. Acts 10:37, "That word, I say, ye know, which was published throughout all Judea, and began from Galilee, after the baptism which John preached; How God anointed Jesus of Nazareth with the Holy Spirit and with power: who went about doing good, and healing all that were oppressed of the devil; for God was with him."

In verses 39 and following, Peter talks about the cross and the resurrection. Bible scholars have examined carefully this sermon and have compared it to the general outline of Mark's Gospel, and they have found out there is a close parallel. For instance, Mark begins his Gospel not with the birth of the Lord Jesus, but he begins with the baptism of John.

Then Mark talks about the Galilean ministry of the Lord, and he goes right on to the cross, the resurrection, and the ascension. A man named Papias, a historian in A.D. 120, which is pretty close to the New Testament era, said that Mark translated into Greek the Aramaic sermons which Simon Peter preached.

Simon Peter preached in Aramaic; the Lord Jesus spoke in Aramaic. It was the language of the people in Palestine at that time. With that little historical statement there is an indication to us that Mark wrote down the sermons of his spiritual father, Simon Peter, into Greek. Drawing from the sermons of Simon Peter, he composed, under the inspiration of the Holy Spirit, the Gospel of Mark. What you have is an account drawn from the information of an eyewitness.

Its Readers

Each one of the Gospel writers wrote for a specific audience. It is not that others would not read the Gospel, but each author wrote in order to reach a certain audience. It is clear when you read the Gospel of Mark that Mark was writing for Romans. He had Gentiles in mind. Matthew was writing for Jews. He had the Jews in mind. Mark, on the other hand, was writing for Gentiles.

Let me share why we know this. Number one, there are very few Old Testament quotations in Mark. They would not have had the impact on the Romans or on the Greeks that they would on the Jews. Second, unfamiliar words are translated in Mark. In other words, there are some words that Mark used that Jews would understand, but he was aware that Gentiles would not understand them, so he translates them for them. An example is in Mark 5, where Jesus raised the young girl from the dead. Mark 5:41, "And he took the child by the hand, and said unto her, Talitha cumi." That is Aramaic. Then notice what he does, he translates it, "which is, being interpreted, Damsel, I say unto thee, arise." He puts it in Greek.

Another reason is Jewish customs are explained. Mark 7:2, "And when they saw some of his disciples eat bread with defiled, that is to say, with unwashened, hands, they found fault."

Mark explained what it meant to have defiled hands. Defiled in what sense? In that when the Jews ate, they had to go through a ceremony of washing their hands all the way to their elbows. It is like when a doctor scrubs up. They had to be sure they were very clean. That would not make a lot of sense to Gentiles, so he explains it.

Another example is in Mark 15:42, "And now when the evening was come, because it was the preparation, that is, the day before the Sabbath." Every Jew would know what that meant, but Romans would not, so Mark explained it was the day before the Sabbath.

The fourth reason is Mark locates some places that would be unfamiliar to Romans. Mark 13:3, "And as he sat upon the mount of Olives, over against the temple." Mark identifies where the mount of Olives was located. It lets us know he was writing to people who were unfamiliar with Jewish words, Jewish customs, and locations in Palestine.

Its Book

The Gospel of Mark is the shortest of the four Gospels. Mark is called the Gospel of action. Mark focuses on what Jesus was doing more than what Jesus had to say.

Mark does quote Jesus and gives some of His sayings, but his focus, his primary emphasis, in this Gospel is activity, action. Notice a key word. Mark 1:10, "And *straightway* coming up out of the water." Mark 1:12, "And *immediately* the Spirit driveth him into the wilderness." Verse 18, "And *straightway* they forsook their nets, and followed him." Verse 20, "And *straightway* he called them." Verse 28, "And *immediately* his fame spread abroad."

Straightway and *immediately* are the same Greek word, and we do not understand why they did not translate it in a consistent manner. This one word occurs 41 times in the Gospel of Mark. It is an action word.

Mark is not only the action Gospel but also emphasizes the servant role of Jesus. He was coming forth to serve. Mark shows Jesus as He was on the move from place to place, meeting the needs of people.

The hands of Jesus are prominent in the Gospel of Mark. When you read through the Gospel of Mark, look for references to hands of Jesus. The hands represent service so you see the hands of Jesus involved in service.

Mark is the Gospel of our Lord's service and our Lord's sacrifice. You do not see any mention of the genealogy of Jesus or any mention of the birth of Jesus. Why should you if you are talking about a servant?

The first part of Mark is the plow part. The latter part is the altar part. The first part is service; the last part sacrifice. The first part is Jesus' ministry. The last part, His cross. In the first part of the Gospel of Mark you will find Jesus in His service posture; the latter part you see Jesus in His sacrifice, death, burial, and resurrection.

The key verse is Mark 10:45, "For even the Son of man came, not to be ministered unto [He came not to be served; that is what minister means] but to minister [to serve], and to give his life a ransom for many. In Mark's Gospel Jesus is serving and sacrificing.

OUTLINE

I. The Personality of the Servant, 1:1-11
II. The Proof of the Servant, 1:12-13
III. The Particulars of the Servant, 1:14–13:37
  A. Eastern Galilee
  B. Northern Galilee
  C. Judea
  D. Road to Jerusalem
  E. In Jerusalem
IV. The Passion of the Servant, 14–15
V. The Position of the Servant, 16

I. The Personality of the Servant, 1:1-11

The first division is the Personality of the Servant. It sets forth who this servant is and starts with the baptism, "The beginning of the gospel of Jesus Christ, the Son of God. Verse 2 is a quotation from the book of Isaiah and talks about John the Baptist. Then he goes to John the Baptist at the river Jordan and the Lord Jesus coming down to be baptized. When Jesus came out of the water, the Holy Spirit descended like a dove, and the heavenly Father spoke from heaven and said, "This is My beloved Son, in whom I am well pleased." He sets forth the Personality of the Servant in verses 1-11.

II. The Proof of the Servant, 1:12-13

The second division is just two verses, the Proof of the Servant, 1:12-13. It is the temptation section. He gives just two verses to this. "And immediately the Spirit driveth him into the wilderness. And he was there in the wilderness forty days, tempted of Satan; and was with the wild beasts, and the angels ministered unto him." Luke has an extensive account of the temptation of the Lord Jesus. The temptation proves though who Jesus is. It proves He is the Son of God. The purpose of the temptation of Jesus Christ was to demonstrate that as the Son of God, He could not sin.

When I was a boy, my dad was the manager of a furniture store. Right next to it was a Belk store. They had a special sale one time of unbreakable china. The floor of that store was made out of concrete. They had a man demonstrate the unbreakable china. He would stand there with a plate of that china and would let it fall, but it would not break. His purpose was not to try to make the china break; his purpose was to prove it would not break. The temptation of Jesus proves that the Lord Jesus was proved in all points like we are, yet without sin.

II. The Particulars of the Servant, 1:14–13:37

The third division is the Particulars of the Servant, Mark 1:14–13:37. It shows some of the details of His servant ministry. He started His Eastern Galilee ministry in 1:14, "Now after John was put in prison, Jesus came into Galilee, preaching the gospel of the kingdom of God." Galilee was in the north. Jerusalem was in the south. From Mark 1:14 all the way through Mark 7:23, Jesus was up in Galilee, Eastern Galilee.

Beginning in 7:24 through Mark 9:50, you have Northern Galilee. You have all kinds of things taking place in Jesus' ministry. Notice Mark 7:24, "And from thence [from Eastern Galilee] he arose, and went into the borders of Tyre and Sidon [that is on up north in Galilee; right up in the Golan Heights of today]."

Then Jesus went south into Judea, Mark 10:1-31. Look at verse 1, "And he arose from thence [Northern Galilee] and cometh into the coast of Judea by the farther side of Jordan." That is south. He was down in the area of the River Jordan, the southern portion, Jericho and other places.

Then look at Mark 10:32, "And they were in the way, going up to Jerusalem." Judea was south, but Jerusalem is on a hill. Any way you approach the city of Jerusalem, you are going up. So Jesus was going up to Jerusalem. Verse 33, "Behold we go up to Jerusalem." Then Jesus began telling them what was going to happen. He began talking about the cross and the fact that He was going to die and rise again from the dead. The Road to Jerusalem is through verse 52.

In chapter 11:1, Jesus was in and around Jerusalem: "And when they came nigh [or near] to Jerusalem to Bethage and Bethany at the mount of Olives." In chapters 11 through 13 you have events that take place just before the cross of our Lord.

IV. The Passion of the Servant, 14–15

The fourth main division is the Passion of the Servant, chapters 14 and 15. The events surrounding the trial of Jesus, the arrest, and the crucifixion of the Lord all tie together.

V. The Position of the Servant, 16

Mark 16 is the fifth division of the Gospel, the Position of the Servant, and deals with the resurrection and ascension of Jesus. Mark 16:19, "So then after the Lord had spoken unto them, he was received up into heaven and sat on the right hand of God." That is the Position of the Servant, the Lord Jesus. He is seated at the right hand of the Father. Verse 20 says, "And they went forth, and preached every where, the Lord working with them, and confirming the word with signs following. Amen." Jesus was the servant, and now His followers were serving also.

In some new translations, you will not find these last verses. I am not qualified to even go into these matters because they are matters of textual criticism and the comparison of the old manuscripts. I have been told that the manuscript evidence is about 50-50. The fact of the matter is, though these closing verses, verse 9 to the end, are not in some of the older manuscripts, everything you find in them is found somewhere else. They have the authentic ring of truth. If they are found somewhere else, I am going to err on the side of leaving them right where they are. But I did want to be honest to mention this and to let you know I really do not know enough about it. Not many people really do.

By the way, the New Testament is one of the reliable documents on the earth. There are over 4,000 portions of the New Testament in these ancient manuscripts. There are scholars who take these different texts and compare and study them to bring us the text of the New Testament. The fact of the matter is, when you look at over 4,000 portions of New Testament documents, there is not a half page of difference in any of them. That is incredible. There is no major doctrine in the New Testament affected by any differences in any of the ancient manuscripts.

You can approach the New Testament with complete confidence and know that what you have is an accurate account of what actually occurred. No other ancient document is as reliable. If you have four or five ancient documents for other writings, you are fortunate. The writings of Plato and Aristotle or other ancient writings do not have even close to the number of old manuscripts of their works like we do of the New Testament.

Read the Gospel of Mark, and you will see Jesus the Servant.

Study #23
Looking at Luke

LOOKING AT LUKE

Each of the four Gospels, while they are not primarily biographies of the Lord Jesus Christ, nor necessarily chronological accounts of the Lord Jesus Christ, does present our Lord from a unique particular perspective. Matthew presents the Lord Jesus Christ as the King. Mark presents the Lord Jesus Christ as the Servant. Luke places the focus upon the person of the Lord Jesus. He gives us a view of Jesus as the Son of Man, the human-divine One. The Gospel of John is what we call the heavenly Gospel. John places a special emphasis on the deity of Jesus Christ. Luke on the other hand places his emphasis on the humanity of Jesus; so, in the Gospel of Luke, you will see Jesus as the perfect Man.

One writer has said that the Gospel of Luke is the most beautiful book that has ever been written. Matthew tells us what Jesus said; Mark puts the emphasis on what Jesus did. Luke tells us about the Lord Jesus Christ. It is a beautiful book because it is about the beautiful life of our Lord Jesus Christ.

Its Author

Luke's method of writing gives us some insight into understanding the composition of the New Testament. It is generally believed, there seems to be no debate about it, that Luke indeed was the author of the Gospel which bears his name. He was a Greek and also a physician.

In Luke 1 a name is used that connects Luke with another New Testament book. Luke 1:3 makes reference to someone named Theophilus: "It seemed good to me also, having had perfect understanding of all things from the very first, to write unto thee in order, most excellent Theophilus." Luke was writing to Theophilus. The name *Theophilus* means "a lover of God." Theos or Theo is the Greek word God. Philus is where we get Philadelphia and means love. So Theophilus' name meant a lover of God.

We believe Theophilus was an actual person and Luke was writing for the specific purpose of sharing the life and teachings of Jesus with him. Notice Acts 1:1, "The former treatise [the former writing, the former book] have I made, O Theophilus, of all that Jesus began both to do and teach." We have two books written to this man named Theophilus, the book of Acts and then in the book of Acts he refers to a previous book, the Gospel of Luke. In the Gospel of Luke, he wrote, "I gave you what Jesus began both to do and teach." So we do know that Luke was the author of the book of Acts, and he was also the author of the Gospel that bears his name.

We know Luke was the traveling companion of Paul. Acts 16:10 shows this. Paul had sailed from Troas across the Aegean Sea into Macedonia. Notice what it says in verse 10. "And after he [talking about Paul] had seen the vision, immediately we endeavored to go into Macedonia, assuredly gathering that the Lord had called us to preach the gospel unto them." Paul picked up a companion, several of them probably, but we know he picked up Luke. Notice the word "we." These are what we call the "we" sections of the book of Acts. Sometimes the writer refers to Paul in the third person; at other times he refers to Paul and himself in the first person. Again, these are called the "we" sections of the book of Acts. Luke was a traveling companion of the apostle Paul.

We also know Luke was a physician. Colossians 4:14 states, "Luke, the beloved physician, and Demas greet you." Second Timothy 4:11 makes reference to him, "Only Luke is with me. Take Mark, and bring him with thee; for he is profitable to me for the ministry." Philemon 1:24 also mentions him, "Mark, Aristarchus, Demas, Luke, my fellow workers." Those three verses refer to Luke, and two refer to him as a physician. The verse in Colossians refers to him as the beloved physician. A Christian doctor is indeed a beloved person. If your doctor is not only your physician but also your friend, you are indeed a blessed person.

Luke was a traveling companion of Paul's, and he was a physician. Evidently,

Luke was Paul's personal physician as he traveled with Paul. It is an interesting thing to think about, but maybe Paul and Luke had known each other since college days. We do believe that Paul went to the University of Tarsus. We also know that university had an outstanding medical school. This is speculation; you can let your imagination come into play here, but it is interesting to imagine that maybe while Paul was a young student at the university and while Luke was in the medical school there, they became friends. Maybe it was this friendship that moved into this ministry together.

There are a number of medical terms in both Luke and Acts. In the book of Acts you will also see a number of nautical terms which he uses, which lets us know Luke had knowledge concerning the sea and life in the ships. There are some who speculate that maybe he was a ship doctor.

Its Style

Luke writes with the mind of a careful historian, the heart of a loving physician, and the beauty of a gifted artist. Some people believe that not only was he a doctor, but he was also an artist. Whether that is true or not, it is certainly true that the language he uses in the Gospel of Luke is some of the most beautiful language found in our New Testament.

The Gospel of Luke is beautifully written in polished literary Greek style; it is evident that the author of this book was well-trained. He was skilled in the use of the language. Now, on the other hand, when you read the writings of Simon Peter for instance, he was just an old rough fisherman and he wrote like one.

The Holy Spirit uniquely selected each of these writers. Though the Holy Spirit is the ultimate author of all the books of the Bible, the Holy Spirit used individuals and He did not obscure their personalities. When you read their writings, you see their personalities coming out. It is not reducing Scriptures to a human level to acknowledge this fact. But the beautiful thing is the Holy Spirit took these men who had been uniquely and providentially prepared to be these authors and used them to write the books that we have and for each to give a particular emphasis.

Luke teaches us something about the whole New Testament in Luke 1:1-4. Luke lays out his reasons for writing, and he shows us how he goes about it. It is almost like you are reading the preface of a historian's book and he is explaining to you his method.

In the introduction of the Gospel of Luke, he explains his methodology. Luke 1:1-4: "Forasmuch as many have taken in hand to set forth in order a declaration of those things which are most surely believed among us, Even as they delivered them unto us, who from the beginning were eyewitnesses, and ministers of the word; It seemed good to me also, having had perfect understanding of all things from the very first, to write unto thee in order, most excellent Theophilus, That thou mightiest know the certainty of those things, wherein thou hast been instructed."

Do you see what Luke says in verse 1? He was not the only one writing about Jesus. Many others had done this also, and we do know of three others: Matthew, Mark, and John. Then he says in verse 2 that they were eyewitnesses and ministers of the word.

Luke was saying he had researched this information and what he was going to give him was the result of his research after interviewing the eyewitnesses, the people who actually saw those things take place. Then he says they were now ministers of the word. They were preaching what they had heard.

Then in verse 3 Luke says it seemed good to him also. What he was saying was others had written before him; he had interviewed them; he had checked with them about what they had to say. Now it seemed good to him, having had perfect understanding of all things, to write to Theophilus *in order*, that is, in chronological order. He was writing what he knew in an accurate, orderly manner. Luke's Gospel, evidently, is more chronological than the others are. He puts his Gospel in more chronological order. We have already said not all of them did that, nor was that necessarily their purpose.

Notice Luke says he had carefully researched everything, he had interviewed the eyewitnesses, and he had listened to those who had ministered the word. In the middle of verse 3 there is something that is not apparent in your English version: "I have had perfect understanding." The word *perfect* that is used is where we get our word *accurate*, accurate understanding. "Accurate and exact understanding of all things from the very first" is what the English says.

That little phrase is the translation of a word that is translated "from above" in other places. For instance, in John 3, Jesus said to Nicodemus, "You must be born again." But we know that when He said, "You must be born again," it was a word that means you must be born "from above." Luke was saying he had an accurate understanding of all things "from above."

He was claiming that not only had he gathered all of the historical information, interviewed the eyewitnesses, and had done his work meticulously as a historian; but now Luke wanted them to know he got this information, "from above." The Holy Spirit had inspired what he was writing.

That is what gives our New Testament such stability and firmness because we have not only the writings of men here, but we also have the writings of men that were overshadowed, guided, and controlled by the Holy Spirit. "All scripture is given by inspiration of God, and is profitable for doctrine, for reproof, for correction, for instruction in righteousness" (II Timothy 3:16).

What we have here are the words of men inspired by God. That is what Luke was talking about. He wanted Theophilus to know why he wrote, what his motive was. His motive was so Theophilus "might know the certainty" of those things he had been instructed. Certainty means stability or firmness. He wrote that he might have stability and firmness in his faith. Luke was saying this Gospel was reliable.

Of course, by extension we take these statements right here and we apply them to our entire New Testament. There is not a book on the earth as reliable and as dependable as the Bible. The Bible is absolutely accurate and it is absolutely God's Word.

There is little story in this connection that primarily revolves around the book of Acts, but it revolves around Luke and his dependability and reliability as a historian. A man named Sir William Ramsay, who was an archaeologist and also an unbeliever, believed there were historical inaccuracies, in particular, in the book of Acts. If Luke was the historian who wrote down the book of Acts and there were inaccuracies there, he thought there would be inaccuracies in his Gospel also. His primary interest though was the book of Acts. He said Acts was shot through and through with historical errors because some of the information in Ramsay's day raised questions about the accuracy of some of these facts. So Sir William Ramsay made a trip to Asia Minor to prove the Bible incorrect.

When Ramsay got through with his investigation, he came to the conclusion that there was not one historical inaccuracy in the book of Acts, and as a result he became a Christian. Some of the greatest writings on the historical accuracy of the New Testament and the book of Acts, in particular, have been written by this great scholar, Sir William Ramsay.

Its Prominent Themes

The theme of the Gospel of Luke is the perfect humanity of the Lord Jesus Christ. He sets forth Jesus in all of His humanity. That is why Luke spends more time on the birth and boyhood of Jesus than the rest of the Gospel writers. In fact, Mark starts at the baptism of John when Jesus is at least 30 years of age.

Luke was a doctor, and he gives us more information about the birth of the Lord Jesus Christ than any other writer in the New Testament. There are two chapters that cover Jesus' birth and boyhood. Luke 1 has 80 verses, and Luke 2 has 52 verses, though it does go into other matters. Why does he belabor the point of the birth of Jesus? It is because Jesus was born of a virgin, Mary. Luke, as a medical doctor, knew that it was biologically impossible. Luke goes extensively into the virgin birth of the Lord Jesus Christ; for as a doctor he was making it very clear that the birth of Jesus Christ was not by normal biological processes, it was by a supernatural act of God.

When you get to the boyhood of the Lord Jesus, Luke makes some interesting statements when you keep in mind he was a doctor. For instance, Luke 2:52, "And Jesus increased in wisdom and stature, and in favor with God and man." Right there Luke takes up the four crucial areas of the growth and development of a child: wisdom (mental development), stature (physical development), in favor with God (spiritual development), and in favor with man (social development). Luke's purpose was to show that Jesus is the perfect man.

As you read through the Gospel of Luke, you will see the human touch all along the way. You will see Jesus in His compassion. You will see Him coming into this world to live among people, to love people, to help people, and to die on the cross for people.

Its Key Verse

The key verse is Luke 19:10, "For the Son of man is come to seek and to save that which was lost."

Luke has more to say about women than the other Gospel writers, and he shows the tenderness of Jesus with women. Women ought to love the Lord Jesus Christ because when Jesus came into the world, there was a totally different outlook toward women. Jesus came and you see His sensitivity and His great love for women. You will find beautiful paintings in Luke of the relationship of Jesus and children. You also will find more instances with Jesus and the poor in Luke than the other Gospels.

Luke places great emphasis on the Holy Spirit. He starts off in Luke 1 with the Spirit-filled family, the family of Zacharias. The angel tells Zacharias the fact that his wife Elisabeth was going to have a son, and his name was going to be John. He tells about the son in verse 15: "For he shall be great in the sight of the Lord, and shall drink neither wine nor strong drink; and he shall be filled with the Holy Spirit, even from his mother's womb." In scripture you have to follow truth to its culmination. You do not build a doctrine on one verse, but John the Baptist was going to be filled with the Holy Spirit.

We see John the Baptist's mother, Elisabeth, filled with the Spirit in Luke 1:41. "And it came to pass that, when Elisabeth heard the greeting of Mary, the babe leaped in her womb, and Elisabeth was filled with the Holy Spirit." Mary went up to Elisabeth's place and when Elisabeth heard that Mary was going to have a child and He was going to be the Savior of the world, the Bible says the babe leaped in the womb of Mary and Elisabeth was filled with the Holy Spirit.

Look at Luke 1:67, "And his father, Zacharias, was filled with the Holy Spirit, and prophesied, saying." Zacharias had not believed the angel and could not talk until his son was born. Then he was filled with the Holy Spirit.

Luke again emphasizes the Holy Spirit in Luke 4 when the Lord Jesus Christ began His ministry and quoted from the book of Isaiah. Luke 4:18-19, "The Spirit of the Lord is upon me, because he hath anointed me to preach the gospel to the poor; he hath sent me to heal the brokenhearted, to preach deliverance to the captives, and recovering of sight to the blind, to set at liberty them that are bruised, To teach the acceptable year of the Lord."

OUTLINE

Introduction, 1:1-4

I. The Savior's Coming, 1:5–4:13
- **A. Birth**
- **B. Boyhood**
- **C. Baptism**
- **D. Background**
- **E. Battle**

II. The Savior's Career, 4:14–21
- **A. The Work in Galilee**
- **B. The Way to Golgotha**

III. The Savior's Cross, 22–24
- **A. Atonement**
- **B. Ascension**

Keep in mind these outlines are arbitrary. Their purpose is to give you a little structure and help you know what is ahead when you begin to read these books. These outlines may or may not be original. My purpose is not to be original but to help you understand the different books of the Bible.

Introduction, 1:1-4

The first four verses are introduction. Luke tells why he wrote his Gospel.

I. The Savior's Coming, 1:5–4:13

The first division is the Savior's Coming. It begins in Luke 1:5 and goes through chapter 4:13. The first two chapters include the Birth of the Lord with the remarkable statements about the virgin birth. It also has the Boyhood of Jesus in chapter 2, when He went up to the temple at the age of 12 and astounded the experts, the theologians of that day.

In the third chapter is the Baptism of Jesus and when the Holy Spirit came down upon the Lord Jesus Christ. It includes the Background of the Lord. Right after the baptism of Jesus, Luke gives us an extensive genealogy, the family tree, the family line of Jesus, beginning with verse 23. Now we have encountered something like this already in the Gospel of Matthew. Luke comes along and gives one too.

There is a difference between the genealogies of Matthew and Luke 3. Luke 3:23, "And Jesus himself began to be about thirty years of age [this is why we know when He was baptized], being (as was supposed) the son of Joseph, which was the son of Heli." Luke was saying that people supposed Jesus was the son of Joseph. It really was not the case. Jesus was not the son of Joseph biologically; that is what Luke was trying to say. And then from Joseph Luke traces Jesus' genealogy all the way back to God. Adam and then God.

What was Luke doing? Matthew gives us what we call the legal genealogy of Jesus; it is the royal line. He traces the lineage of Jesus legally through Joseph. Luke, having said he wants the reader to know that Joseph was not really the father of Jesus, traces the genealogy of Jesus biologically through Mary. It is the blood line. Luke traces the blood line all the way back to God. Luke was setting forth the perfect manhood of Jesus. By giving all the background, he was saying Jesus is the Son of God. The fourth chapter is the Battle. It is the temptation narrative telling how Jesus encountered the devil.

II. The Savior's Career, 4:14–21

The second division begins in Luke 4:14 and goes all the way to chapter 21. It is the great body of Luke's Gospel, the Savior's Career. Look at Luke 4:14, "And Jesus returned in the power of the Spirit into Galilee: and there went out a fame of him through all the region round about." Galilee is north of Nazareth, where Jesus was from. From Luke 4:14 through 9:50, you have His work in Galilee. You have His miracles, the different things He did there, and His teachings.

Luke 9:51 begins the Way to Golgotha, and it goes all the way to Luke 21. Luke 9:51, "And it came to pass, when the time was come that he should be received up, he steadfastly set his face to go to Jerusalem." "When he should be received up" is a statement about the ascension. The ascension was when Jesus was received up, but first there had to be the cross, the tomb, the resurrection, and then the ascension, the receiving up. Notice it says He "steadfastly set his face to go to Jerusalem." That is a very important statement in Luke's Gospel. Jesus was going to Jerusalem to die on the cross for the sins of the world. The Son of Man came to seek and to save that which was lost.

All through this section you will have little notations that Jesus was on His way up to Jerusalem (anywhere you went from Israel to Jerusalem, you were going up since it is on a hill). Luke 13:22, "And he went through the cities and villages, teaching, and journeying toward Jerusalem." Luke 17:11, "And it came to pass, as he went to Jerusalem, that he passed through the midst of Samaria and Galilee." Luke 18:31, "Then he took unto him the twelve, and said unto them, Behold, we go up to Jerusalem, and all things that are written by the prophets concerning the Son of man shall be accomplished." Luke 19:11, "And as they heard these things, he added, and spoke a parable, because he was near to Jerusalem, and because they thought that the kingdom of God should immediately appear." Luke 19:28, "And when he had thus spoken, he went ahead, ascending up to Jerusalem."

Look also at Luke 19:37-41, "And when he was come near [he is talking about Jerusalem], even now at the descent of the mount of Olives, the whole multitude of the disciples began to rejoice and praise God with a loud voice for all the mighty works that they had seen, Saying, Blessed be the King that cometh in the name of the Lord: peace in heaven, and glory in the highest. And some of the Pharisees from among the multitude said unto him, Master, rebuke thy disciples. And he answered, and said unto them, I tell you that, if these should hold their peace, the stones would immediately cry out. And when he was come near, he beheld the city, and wept over it." When Jesus saw the city of Jerusalem, He wept over it.

III. The Savior's Cross, 22–24

The final division is the Savior's Cross. There is Atonement in chapters 22–23, the details about the cross: the arrest, the trial, Gethsemane, the betrayal of Judas, and then His death on the cross.

In Luke 24, is the Ascension. We see the Lord Jesus Christ as He is ascended back to the right hand of the Father.

Study #24
Johns Journal

JOHN'S JOURNAL

The Gospel of John could be called the heavenly Gospel. It is a Gospel that was written for believers, but it extends beyond believers; it is a Gospel that has been given for the whole world. A. T. Robertson, who was one of the great Southern Baptist Greek scholars, maybe the greatest Greek scholar of all time, said the Gospel of John is the supreme literary work of the world. I think he is exactly correct.

Its Author

Virtually all are agreed that the human author is John, who was known as the beloved disciple. There are two little phrases or clues inside the Gospel of John itself that give us an indication of the author. John 18:15-16 is the scene of the trial of Jesus the night before the crucifixion. It says, "And Simon Peter followed Jesus, and so did another disciple: that disciple was known unto the high priest, and went in with Jesus into the court of the high priest. But Peter stood at the door outside. Then went out that other disciple, who was known unto the high priest, and spoke unto her that kept the door, and brought in Peter." We believe that this is none other than John, "that other disciple."

This phrase, "that other disciple," occurs several times. Note John 20:2-4, the resurrection scene after the Lord was raised from the dead. Mary Magdalene had gone to the tomb and found it empty. Verse 2, "Then she runneth, and cometh to Simon Peter, and to the other disciple." You see the phrase again, verse 3, "Peter, therefore, went forth, and that other disciple." Verse 4, "So they ran both together; and the other disciple did outrun Peter, and came first to the sepulcher." Sometimes in the Gospel of John, the author is referred to as "that other disciple."

There is another phrase that also occurs in John's Gospel that gives us a clue that John is its writer. It is "whom Jesus loved." John 13 is the night of the Lord's Supper. The disciples were in the upper room, and Jesus said one of them would betray Him. Then the disciples looked at each other, wondering whom Jesus was talking about. John 13:23, "Now there was leaning on Jesus' bosom one of his disciples, whom Jesus loved." That is why John is known as the beloved disciple. It is not that the other disciples did not love Jesus; of course, they did, and Jesus loved all of them.

John 19:26-27 is the scene on the cross when Jesus looked at His mother Mary. "When Jesus, therefore, saw his mother, and the disciple standing by, whom he loved, he saith unto his mother, woman, behold thy son! Then saith he to the disciple, behold thy mother! And from that hour that disciple took her unto his own home." That was John.

There is another phrase in John 21:23. This is after the resurrection and the Lord was on the seashore. "Then went this saying abroad among the brethren, that that disciple should not die." You have the "other disciple," the disciple "whom Jesus loved," and "that disciple." John is talking about himself each time. He is that other disciple. He is the disciple whom Jesus loved.

John 21:24 states, "This is the disciple which testified of these things, and wrote these things: and we know that his testimony is true." He was talking about himself. That is the way they would commonly do it in literature in those days. They would not name themselves specifically but would name themselves in indirect ways.

Evidently John became a disciple of Jesus when he was very young; some think maybe in his teens. Peter, James, John, and the other disciples followed the Lord. John loved Jesus Christ with great intensity. He lived to be an old man; some believe he lived all the way into his nineties.

We know from church history that John became the pastor of the church of Ephesus. He also took Mary, the mother of Jesus, into his home. As the tradition goes, John took her to Ephesus and she died there. That is generally accepted information. John was also exiled to the island of Patmos; he was released later on, went back to Ephesus, and died there.

We need to be aware of the fact that this John, the beloved disciple, wrote at least five books in our New Testament. He wrote the Gospel of John, and he wrote the little Epistles or letters of John: I John, II John, and III John. Then he wrote the last book in the New Testament, the book of the Revelation. We know he wrote it because he identifies himself in the first chapter of Revelation.

You have three categories of books in the New Testament that were written by John. There is the Gospel, which looks to the grandeur of the past. It talks about the person and the work of the Lord Jesus Christ. Then you have the Epistles, I, II, and III John, which lead us to the grace of the present. Then you have the book of the Revelation, which looks forward and lights for us the glory of the future. Those three categories show the whole Christian life given to us.

The Gospel of John deals primarily with salvation. The letters of John, I, II, III John, deal with sanctification. And, of course, the book of the Revelation, looking towards the future, deals with glorification when the Lord returns and we go to be with Him. The Gospel is to convince sinners, the Epistles to confirm the saints, and the Revelation to comfort sufferers.

Its Purpose

The purpose of the Gospel of John is to present Jesus not only as the Son of God but also as God Himself. Look at how the Gospel of John begins. John 1:1, "In the beginning was the Word, and the Word was with God, and Word was God."

When you read John 1:1, you know you are on different ground than you were with the first three Gospels. Matthew and Luke began with the birth of Jesus. Mark began with the ministry of Jesus at the baptism of John the Baptist. The first three Gospels, which are called the Synoptic Gospels, give us the presentation of the Lord Jesus.

John, on the other hand, goes a little deeper and gives the interpretation of Jesus, who Jesus is and what Jesus has come to do. It is not that the others do not do that, but this is the primary emphasis of John's Gospel. It is to present Jesus as the Son of God and to present Him as God the Son in the flesh for a very particular purpose.

John has a way of letting you know why he writes his books. For instance, in the book of the Revelation, he tells at the beginning (v. 19) what the key is to his book: "things which you have seen, things which are, and things which are to come." In his little epistle of I John, he will say several times, "I write this to you because."

In his Gospel, he hangs the key to the book on the back door instead of the front door like he did in Revelation. In the last chapter, John 20:30-31, he tells what his purpose was in presenting Jesus as the Son of God: "And many other signs [notice this word *signs*; it is crucial to understanding how John laid out his Gospel] truly did Jesus in the presence of his disciples, which are not written in this book; but these are written, that ye might believe [notice this word *believe* and connect *signs* to *believe*] that Jesus is the Christ, the Son of God; and that believing ye might have life through his name." John was saying there were others signs Jesus did, but they are not in his book; but he included the signs he did so the readers would believe that Jesus was the Christ, the Son of God. Now connect *believe* to *life*. That is the whole purpose of John's Gospel: signs, believe, and life.

There is not a better book in the entire Bible than the Gospel of John to help win people to Christ. If you are dealing with unsaved people, and they have intellectual difficulties or doubts concerning whether Christ is all we say He is, I would encourage you to refer them to the Gospel of John.

The key verses are John 20:30-31. There are also some key words. I have given you three right here: signs, believe, and life. Life occurs 55 times in this book. It is a book of life. Light occurs 23 times. Darkness occurs nine times; believe occurs 98 times. Witness occurs 50 times. Truth occurs 35 times. Love occurs 55 times.

Remember Isaiah 9:6, "For unto us a child is born, unto us a son is given." You might take those two statements right there and attach them to the Gospels. To the first three Gospels, Matthew, Mark, and Luke, "Unto us a child is born." To John's Gospel, "Unto us a son is given," because John presents Jesus as the Son of God.

Its Miracles

The Bible says Jesus was approved of God by miracles. In other words, the miracles Jesus did not only were beneficial to people in need, but they also attested to the fact that He was God. There are about 35 recorded miracles of Jesus in the four Gospels. He did more miracles than that, but 35 are recorded.

In the Gospel of John, John has already told us specifically that he did not include all the miracles in his Gospel. John selected certain miracles for a specific purpose. What we have to look for are the miracles John included because John uses a special word to apply to those miracles. He uses the word *signs*. He called Jesus' miracles *signs*. He said Jesus did other *signs* besides what he wrote in his Gospel, but he included the *signs* he did so people would believe Jesus was the Son of God.

The first miracle John gives occurred at a wedding. The last miracle, excluding the last chapter [it is like a postscript], was at a funeral. That simply says Jesus Christ is with us in life's gladdest hours and saddest hours. You will find, excluding the miracle in John 21 because that is after His resurrection, that John carefully selected seven of the Lord's miracles as signs. We know that is true because of what John said in John 20, but look also at John 2 and what John said at the end of that miracle. This is talking about the marriage in Cana of Galilee and is the miracle of the water turning into wine (2:1-11). John 2:11, "This beginning of miracles did Jesus in Cana of Galilee, and manifested forth his glory; and his disciples believed on him." The word *miracle* is the same word for *signs*. "This beginning of *signs*"; he was saying this was sign number one. What did that miracle do? It manifested forth His glory.

John 4:46-54 gives us the account of Jesus' second miracle, His healing the son of the nobleman. Look at what John said in verse 54, "This is the second miracle that Jesus did, when he was come out of Judea into Galilee." With the first miracle, John said it was number one, the beginning. Then you read in chapter 4 the next miracle was specifically number two.

He was saying to be alert. He was selecting special miracles that Jesus did in order to teach He was the Son of God. What did John say the purpose of Jesus' signs was? That people might believe and believing might have life. Look at what he said in the second miracle, verse 50, "Jesus saith unto him, Go thy way; thy son liveth. And the man believed the word that Jesus had spoken unto him, and he went his way." He came home and found out that his son was well. Verse 53. "So the father knew that it was at the same hour, in the which Jesus said unto him, Thy son liveth: and himself believed, and his whole house." John was demonstrating that was the purpose of the miracles, that they might believe Jesus was the Christ.

There are seven of these sign miracles, and they are in a specific order; they teach us about salvation. John's Gospel goes down to a deeper level. There is a spiritual message under the things John writes. Now there is a spiritual message in all the Gospels, but John specifically goes beneath the surface. In the first three Gospels you have the presentation of Jesus. In the fourth Gospel, John gives you the interpretation of Jesus. That is why, by the way, there are some passages in John that are so difficult to understand. For instance, in John 1:1, "In the beginning was the Word." Understand that if you can. You will get to certain places in John's Gospel, and John gets absolutely philosophical. It is like you are reading a book of philosophy.

If you want to get lost in the depths of the things of God, read John 6. He shows you the miracle of the feeding of the 5,000, and then he goes deeper and deeper. John's Gospel is the most profound book in the world.

Again, John shares seven of Jesus' miracles, and these miracles show you how salvation comes. For instance, the water turned into wine in John 2 shows the importance of the Word of God in salvation. We are like those old empty water pots, and the water is like the Word. When the water of the Word is poured into our empty water pot lives, Jesus can change the water into wine.

Then the healing of the nobleman's son in John 4 shows the importance of faith. He believed the word of Jesus. The healing of the paralytic in chapter 5 shows the importance of grace.

The fourth miracle, the feeding of the 5,000, shows us how God uses people to get the message of salvation to others. He had everyone sit down, and then the disciples, as the bread was broken, began to pass it out. Jesus does the miracle, but you and I have the opportunity of taking the miracle to the people. It is wonderful to have a part in leading someone to the Lord.

The fifth miracle was when Jesus stilled the storm on the water. That shows some of the results of salvation. One result is salvation brings peace in your life.

Then there is the healing of the blind man in John 9, and it shows Jesus turns the light on in our life. The seventh miracle was the raising of Lazarus from the dead. Of course, that goes right into why John gave us the miracles–that we might believe and in believing we might have eternal life. When a person is saved, it is like the person is raised from the dead. He has a brand-new life.

Its "I Am's"

The "I Am" statements of Jesus are something else you find in the Gospel of John. There are seven of them. Seven times Jesus said, "I Am." What is the point? When Jesus used that terminology, the Jews immediately knew what He was talking about. Remember in the Old Testament the story of Moses when he was at the burning bush. God told him to take off his shoes because he was on holy ground. He told God the people would ask who had sent him, and God said in Exodus 3 to tell them "I Am" had sent him. "I Am" is a title for God. So, when Jesus stood up and said, "I Am," He was claiming to be God.

John records seven times that Jesus said, "I Am." John 6:35, "I am that bread of life." John 8:12, "I am the light of the world." In 10:7, "I am the door of the sheep." John 11:25, "I am the resurrection and the life." John 14:6, "I am the way, the truth, and the light." John 15:1, "I am the true vine." These are the seven "I Am" statements of John. This is a good Bible study to teach.

The Tabernacle

Another interesting thing about the Gospel of John is it is laid out similar to the tabernacle in the Old Testament. The Old Testament tabernacle had three primary locations: the outer court, the holy place, and the holy of holies. As you read through John, you can almost see us moving from the outer court where you have the altar of brass and the laver. In chapter 1 you see the altar, "Behold the Lamb of God, which takes away the sin of the world." In chapter 2, you have the water and the laver. Then you move into the holy place and have the table of showbread. John 6 talks about the bread of life. You have the lamp stands, and Jesus says, "I am the light of the world." Then you have the altar of incense, prayer, in chapter 13. Then you move from these into the holy of holies when Jesus goes to the cross and dies on the cross for our sins. It is an interesting picture to consider when you look at the Gospel of John.

OUTLINE

The Prologue, 1:1-18

I. The Signs of the Son of God, 1:19–12:50
- **A. Deity Declared**
- **B. Deity Disputed**
- **C. Deity Disowned**

II. The Secrets of the Son of God, 13–17
- **A. The Talk in the Upper Room**
- **B. The Walk to the Garden of Gethsemane**

III. The Sorrows of the Son of God, 18:1–20
- **A. Condemnation**
- **B. Crucifixion, 19:16-42**
- **C. Conquest**

Epilogue, 21

I have a prologue and an epilogue in this outline. The prologue is the Introduction. Prologue is just a fancy word for introduction. It is 1:1-18. These verses start off with the eternal nature of the Son of God, "In the beginning was the Word."

I. The Signs of the Son of God, 1:19–12:50

The first division starts in John 1:19 and goes through John 12:50. Jesus' deity is declared in 1:19–4:54 (Deity Declared). Chapter 5 has a series of disputes with the religious leaders. They disputed the claims of Christ and were offended by them (Deity Disputed, 5:1–10:42). Next is His Deity Disowned, 11:1–12:50. They denied Christ; they rejected Jesus Christ.

II. The Secrets of the Son of God, 13–17

These chapters have to be some of the most blessed and most meaningful and moving verses you will ever read in all of the Bible. Look at how John began this, John 13:1, "Now before the feast of the Passover, when Jesus knew that his hour was come that he should depart out of this world unto the Father, having loved his own which were in the world, he loved them unto the end."

Note, as you read along in this Gospel, several times it will say that Jesus' hour had not yet come. For instance, in John 2 when Mary, His mother, had come to Him and said they did not have any wine, Jesus said what was that to Him, His hour had not yet come. You will find that little phrase or some form of that phrase as you move along. But when you get to the cross, Jesus says in John 12:23, "And Jesus answered them, saying, The hour is come, that the Son of man should be glorified." What hour was He talking about? He was talking about the hour for which all eternity had waited. It was the hour He would be on the cross, dying for the sins of the whole world.

Now in John 13:1, when Jesus knew His hour was come that He would depart out of the world to the Father, having loved His own to the end, and that means He loved them all the way, you have that beautiful foot washing. Jesus basically acted out His own incarnation, His whole coming into the world and going back to heaven. He took His garments, laid them aside, got a basin and towel, and got down and washed the disciples' feet. Then when He finished, He put His clothing on and sat down again. He came into this world and laid aside His outward insignia of majesty, so to speak; then He clothed Himself in the garb of a servant and washed us from our sins in the basin of Calvary. Then when it was over, He went from the tomb and ascended back to the right hand of the Father and assumed His role there as the Lord of the universe. That is the sacred setting of John 13.

You have the Talk in the Upper Room, John 13 and 14. Then in chapter 15, they were evidently walking to the garden of Gethsemane, and this is where He gives the talk about the vine and the branches. In John 16 He gives the work of the Holy Spirit. He had already talked about the Holy Spirit in chapter 14. In chapter 16 He talks about Him again, and in John 17 is the Lord's Prayer. We call it the Lord's Prayer when we pray, "O Father, who art in heaven," but that is not really the Lord's Prayer. The Lord's Prayer is really what you find in John 17. He covers the whole Christian life in this prayer. He covers our salvation, our sanctification, and our glorification.

III. The Sorrows of the Son of God, 18:1–20

The third division is when Jesus goes to the cross, John 18–20. John 18:1–19:15 is Condemnation. The Crucifixion is John19:16-42. John 20 is the resurrection chapter, the Conquest, when He conquers death.

John 21 is the Epilogue. That is just a fancy word for conclusion. The way John closes out his Gospel is magnificent. Look at the last verse of John's Gospel. John 21:25, "And there are also many other things which Jesus did, which, if they should be written every one, I suppose that even the world itself could not contain the books that should be written. Amen."

Study #25
Acts Alive

ACTS ALIVE

The Acts of the Apostles is the fifth book in the category of the Historical books of the New Testament. It is one of the most interesting books of the New Testament, and it is a most important book in the New Testament. It is a very graphic book; it is an action-oriented book. You see a great deal of activity and the movement of God in the life of His people in this book.

Remember that the book of Acts is a sequel to the four Gospels, Matthew, Mark, Luke, and John. It is also a bridge from the Gospels to the letters (epistles) of the New Testament. If you did not have the book of Acts, you would be lost in your New Testament when you finished the Gospels.

There is very little mention of the church in the Gospels. There are some references to the church in Matthew. Jesus said upon this rock He would build His church and the gates of hell would not prevail against it, and there is the passage of believers in conflict with one another; but the church is not mentioned a lot. Imagine if you moved from the book of John to the book of Romans. Paul talks about the believers at Rome and the church there. In Romans you would wonder what Paul was talking about. In reading Paul's letters, you would really not know what he was talking about if you did not have the book of Acts.

Acts is absolutely vital to our understanding. It shows us how we get from the period of the Gospels, when our Lord was on the earth (His death, burial and resurrection), to the period of time when the churches were being established, growing, and expanding in the New Testament.

What you have in the book of Acts is the spread of the church of the Lord Jesus Christ from Jerusalem to Rome. It shows you how this takes place.

Its Author

Note Acts 1:1, "The former treatise [that is, previous writings; that is what treatise means; the former book] have I made, O Theophilus, of all that Jesus began both to do and teach." Luke was making a reference to a previous writing to something he had previously written.

In Luke 1, Luke tells us the procedure he followed and the methodology he used in order to put down his Gospel account. In Luke 1:3 he states, "It seemed good to me also, having had perfect understanding of all things from the very first, to write unto thee in order, most excellent Theophilus, That thou mightest know the certainty of those things, wherein thou hast been instructed." Compare Acts 1: "The former treatise [or writing] have I made, O Theophilus." The connection between the two writings is the name *Theophilus*. The name *Theophilus* means "lover of God." Theo is an English transliteration for the Greek word for God. Note the word *theology, theo-ology*; ology means writing, theo means God. Theology is writings about God.

Theophilus' name meant a lover of God. Luke had written a gospel to Theophilus, and now he was writing this book of Acts to him. Notice he said he had written the previous writing of all that Jesus began both to do and teach (Acts 1:1). He was talking about the earthly ministry of the Lord.

Verse 2, "Until the day in which he was taken up." Look back to Luke 24:50-51. Jesus was gathered with His disciples on the mount of Olives, and it says, "And he led them out as far as to Bethany [that was a little village on the slopes of the mount of Olives], and he lifted up his hands, and blessed them, and it came to pass, while he blessed them, he was parted from them, and carried up into heaven." We call that the ascension of Jesus. Jesus lived; He began to do and teach, as recorded in the Gospel of Luke; and He died on the cross. He was buried, and three days later He arose again. Forty days later from the mount of Olives He ascended. That is what he meant in Acts 1:2 when he said until the day in which Jesus was taken up. Luke gave the framework for the Gospel of Luke.

Luke continued in verse 2, "after that he through the Holy Spirit had given commandments [the Great Commission] unto the apostles whom he had chosen." Verse 3, "To whom also he shewed himself alive after his passion by many infallible proofs, being seen of them forty days, and speaking of the things pertaining to the kingdom of God." We know by this that the same author of the Gospel of Luke is the author of Acts.

Luke was from time to time a companion of Paul on some of his missionary journeys. We know this because of some internal evidences in the book of Acts. There are some sections in Acts that are known as the "we" sections. Some sections are about Paul and where he was going. Luke talks about Paul in the third person: Paul went over here, Paul did this, and Paul did that. Then, all of a sudden, it switches over and says "we." This means that Luke had joined Paul, and he was now writing in the first person: "we," Paul and I.

An example is in Acts 16:10-17. This is in Troas when Paul was trying to discern the will of God. Where did God want him to go? What did God want him to do? In the night Paul had a vision and a man spoke to him. A man said to "come over to Macedonia and help us," verse 9. Verse 10 says, "And after he [Paul] had seen the vision, immediately we [Luke and Paul] endeavoured to go into Macedonia." Evidently, Luke was the personal physician of Paul and he journeyed with him.

Another "we" section is in Acts 20. It first talks about Paul in the third person (verses 1-4), and then Acts 20:5, "These going before tarried for us at Troas." Again Luke links himself with Paul. Other examples are Acts 21:1, "And it came to pass, that after we were gotten from them," and Acts 27:1, "And when it was determined that we should sail into Italy." That lets you know Luke was with Paul.

This book was written by Luke the beloved physician, who was also a marvelous historian and who was the companion of the apostle Paul on different occasions. Much of what we have here are eyewitness accounts, eyewitness reports.

Its Theme

The book of Acts resumes history where the Gospels leave off. It traces for us a kind of beginning on the day of Pentecost, historically. We know eternally it began in the heart of God. Acts is a book of the history of the church from the day of Pentecost in Jerusalem until its spread when Paul reaches the city of Rome.

Acts 1:1 has a very important implication made in it. Luke talks about his previous book and says in his previous book he wrote about all that Jesus *began* both to do and teach. Now what is the implication of that word as it applies to the book of Acts? The implication is what you have in Luke is Jesus beginning to do and teach. In Acts Jesus is continuing to do and teach.

When Jesus was on the earth, He did His work or ministry in a physical body. That is what He began to do. Now, ascending back to heaven, He is continuing to do and teach, He is continuing to work, but now not in a physical body but in a spiritual body. The church is the spiritual body of Christ The theme is the work of the church, the growth of the church from Jerusalem through Rome.

The last verses share another important lesson, Acts 28:30-31. Paul was in Rome. He had arrived in Rome, but not the way he thought he was going to get there. He went to Rome as a prisoner, but it says, "And Paul dwelt two whole years in his own hired house, and received all that came in unto him, preaching the kingdom of God, and teaching those things which concern the Lord Jesus Christ, with all confidence, no man forbidding him."

Look at those last four words, "no man forbidding him." They translate one word in the Greek New Testament, and you could translate those four words, "without hindrance." Literally you would translate it, "unhinderedly." The implication is Luke said I wrote my first book of all that Jesus began to do and teach, and now I am writing this book of Acts of what Jesus is continuing to do and teach. When you come to the last words of the book of Acts, the implication is that the work of Jesus continues on. Luke was saying what I started in the book of Acts, I am expecting the churches to continue on until Jesus comes again.

I think God wants us to write a 29th chapter to the book of Acts. You see, we have a history also. We have a ministry, we have a responsibility, until Jesus comes. We are to continue to allow Jesus to do and to teach in and through us until He comes. It is like He leaves the book open, and He tells the church to keep it up, to keep doing what He told the church to do.

God is still working through His church until the end of the ages. God has always been working through His church. In every era of history God is working in His church. God has had His faithful churches. There have been times when the light has not been as bright as at other times. There have been times of spiritual decline when churches have not had the spiritual strength and power they needed to have, but from the day of Pentecost until now the Holy Spirit has been working in and through His churches to carry out the ministry of the Lord Jesus on this earth until Jesus comes again. We should be living out another chapter of the book of Acts.

The keys verse is Acts 1:8, "But ye shall receive power, after the Holy Spirit is come upon you; and ye shall be witnesses unto me both in Jerusalem, and in all Judea, and in Samaria, and unto the uttermost part of the earth." The setting of "But ye shall receive power" is Jesus was getting ready to go back to heaven. The disciples asked the Lord when He was going to come again. Jesus said in verse 7 that it was not for them to know the times or the seasons that the Father has put in His own power. Power is a word we would translate authority. What Jesus was saying was His return, the Second Coming of Jesus, is in the authority of the Father. But note, "But ye shall receive power." Here *power* is a different word. The English versions do not make that apparent. This is the word from which we get our word *dynamite*. Ye shall receive dynamite; ye shall receive inherent power, "after the Holy Spirit is come upon you; and ye shall be witnesses unto me both in Jerusalem, and in all Judea, and in Samaria, and the uttermost part of the earth."

Acts 1:8 is the key verse of Acts and is what Acts is all about, the filling of the Holy Spirit, the power of the Holy Spirit, and then the church moving out from Jerusalem to the ends of the earth.

The key word is found in the key verse. It is the word *witnesses*. This is the witness book. The church is in the world to be a witness, to tell others about Christ. It exists to be a witness for Jesus. That is why we are here. Some people get tired of hearing all the time about witnessing. That is like a surgeon saying he is tired of hearing about surgeries. That is like someone at the grocery store saying all he hears about is groceries, groceries, and groceries. The church is here to be a witness. Of course, there is more to it than that. We win people to Christ, and then we help them grow. That is what Sunday School and church ministry are about. But we can never get away from the fact that the church exists to be a witness for Jesus.

Its Title

In your Bible the title is probably the Acts of the Apostles. It is not a bad title. The titles were not a part of the Greek text though. A better title would be the Acts of the Holy Spirit. That is what you really have in the book of Acts. An even better title would be "The Acts of the Risen Lord by the Holy Spirit through the Churches."

Its Values

We would have a real gap in our understanding if we did not have the book of Acts, so it has a definite historical value. Sir Ramsay, the historian, studied the book of Acts to prove there were geographical and historical errors in it. When he got through he was so convinced of its accuracies that he became a Christian. All through the years people have studied the book of Acts; and what they thought were historical inaccuracies, as time has moved on, have been cleared up. There is just more and more evidence on historical accuracy of the book of Acts.

It also has a doctrinal importance. There is doctrine in the book of Acts. For instance, when you read about the remission of sins, that is doctrine. Doctrine is teaching. There is definitely teaching in the book of Acts, but you have to careful not to make some mistakes in understanding the doctrine you find. That will be discussed later.

There is biographical information in Acts. For instance, we would not know who Paul was if we did not have his biographical story. There are others: Stephen, Philip, Dorcas, Aquila, and Priscilla. There is interesting biographical information in the book of Acts. Studying the different characters in Acts is a good way to study it.

There is missionary value in Acts. It is a great textbook for missions, both missions here and around the world. There are also great principles of missions. Anyone who is called of God into missions should really study the book of Acts because it has a lot of information for missions.

There is dispensational value in Acts. You will find that in certain periods of history, God dealt with mankind in a particular way. You have evidence as you read through your Bible that God dealt with man in a particular way at a particular time. That is what you call dispensation. The Old Scofield Bible has seven dispensations. It is one of the best reference Bibles, but I am a little hard pressed to find all seven of them. Just keep in mind that you use the word *dispensation* as a little handle to help you get at some things that are taught in your Bible. There is no question that two dispensations are taught in the Bible. There is the dispensation of the Law, and there is the dispensation of Grace. God dealt with man in a different way under the dispensation of the Law and under the dispensation of Grace. It is not that people were saved differently; they were not. But they were under a different period, and they were under a different stage of God's dealing with man.

Do not rob yourself of the blessing of Acts because you think something was under a different dispensation. Anywhere in the Bible God has practical truth and application; it is for you and for me. All Bible truth can be taken to extreme. If you are not really careful, you can allow yourself to go to extreme on any area of Bible truth. There is always a balance if you are going to understand the Scriptures. Do not go overboard, but keep yourself balanced scripturally and you will come out ahead.

There is tremendous Personal and Spiritual value in the book of Acts. There are three books I try to read all the time: the book of Psalms to keep me sweet, the book of Proverbs to keep me wise, and the book of Acts to keep me filled with power. Read the book of Acts for your own personal and spiritual welfare.

Its Interpretation

Keep in mind Acts is a transition book. *Transition* is a key word. You are in a transition in the book of Acts. What is going on is a transition between God's dealings with the nation of Israel under Law and God's dealings with New Testament believers under Grace.

When you start off in the book of Acts you have some things that are particularly Jewish. But as you move through the book of Acts, you will see a transition away from those things. An example is in Acts 1 when they were trying to select someone to be the successor of Judas. They cast lots. That was a Jewish method. That was something they did in the Old Testaments. They had two stones, the urim and thummin. They would put them in the high priest's breastplate and shake it up. Whatever came out indicated the will of God. God honored that. He instructed that in the Old Testament. So in Acts 1, they were still using the casting of lots.

Later on when Paul was trying to determine the will of God concerning the direction of his journey, he did not cast lots. Paul had a vision. God gave him a vision and told him what to do. You come to the end of the book of Acts, and you do not even find that. You find prayer and the leading of the Holy Spirit, so there is a transition in determining the will of God, from Jewish territory to church territory. This is why you have to be very careful about building doctrine in the book of Acts. It will get you in all kinds of trouble. You do not make the book of Acts the standard in terms of building doctrine; instead you go to the letters of the New Testament. The letters are where you primarily find your doctrine. It is not that there is not doctrine in the book of Acts; there is. But be careful how you handle it.

Angels is another topic. In the earlier chapters of Acts, you will find angels. In the latter chapters they are not as prominent. Does that mean the angels got out and there are no more angels? No, but they were not as prominent. God's primary method of speaking to man today is not through angels. In fact, in the book of Galatians, Paul warns specifically that you should not let some angel come and bring you another gospel. The Bible teaches the existence of angels, but my source of final authority is not some angel. It is the Word of God.

The matter of the baptism of the Holy Spirit or the baptism by the Holy Spirit is another topic you read about in Acts. You want to see how it happened in Acts, but it is according to which chapter you turn to. I am not saying the book of Acts contradicts itself, not at all. I am saying there is a transition going on. You will read about some believers who had a baptism or filling of the Holy Spirit at one point in Acts and it happens this way. Then you read in another chapter and it happens another way. Then you read a third time, and it happens still another way. What is going on? You have to go to the epistles, the letters, to find out. First Corinthians 12:13 tells you exactly what the baptism of the Holy Spirit is. For we all by one Spirit are baptized into the body, and we know according to the teachings of the epistles that every born again believer is baptized by the Holy Spirit at the moment of salvation. It is not something we seek, but it is something that automatically transpires at the moment of our salvation.

When you are saved, there are several items that go together in the salvation package. When you receive Jesus as your Savior, you are born again, you are baptized by the Holy Spirit, you are sealed by the Spirit, and you are anointed by the Spirit. You are indwelled by the Spirit. There are a number of things that take place at the moment of salvation. But when you read the book of Acts, you will find a different example all the way through. When you interpret the book of Acts, keep in mind you are in a transition book. It is not that you do not find doctrine there, but it is that you do not build your doctrine from Acts. It is an axiom of Bible interpretation that you do not build your doctrine in the book of Acts. If you do, you are going to be confused and you will come up with some bad doctrine.

OUTLINE

I. The Foundation Phase, 1–5
- **A. Preparation**
- **B. Power**
- **C. Persecution**
- **D. Progress**

II. The Forward Phase, 6–12
- **A. New Voices**
- **B. New Victories**
- **C. New Violence**

III. The Foreign Phase, 13–28
- **A. Paul – the Pioneer**
- **B. Paul – the Prisoner**

The book of Acts can be outlined in several different ways. You can outline it geographically. For instance, Jerusalem is chapters 1–7. You read about the church and its activities in Jerusalem in chapters 1–7. Then you read about Judea and Samaria in chapters 8–12. Then chapters 13–28, you have unto the uttermost parts of the earth. The church begins to move out beyond Jerusalem, Judea, and Samaria. This is not a bad way to outline the book of Acts.

Another way to outline the book of Acts, but not quite as good, is biographically around three individuals: Simon Peter, Stephen (and Philip), and then Paul. That is not the best way to outline it, but you can look at it that way.

I. The Foundation Phase, 1–5

I have outlined the book of Acts in three divisions. The first division is what I call the Foundation Phase, chapters 1–5. It is the foundation stage or phase of the church. Chapter 1 is the Preparation of the Church. The Lord Jesus ascends back to heaven and has made the promise about the coming of the Holy Spirit, and the disciples are in the upper room praying and waiting for the Holy Spirit to be given according to Jesus' promise.

Chapter 2 is the Pentecost chapter, the Power of the Holy Spirit coming on the day of Pentecost. Chapter 3, Persecution begins on the church, and the disciples are threatened and told not to preach. Chapters 4–5, the Progress of the Church, the church is beginning to expand and grow. Thousands of people are being saved. Chapters 1–5 are the Foundation Phase, and Simon Peter is prominent in those chapters.

II. The Forward Phase, Chapters 6–12

Chapters 6–12 are called the Forward Phase. The church is beginning to move out. In these chapters you have first some New Voices, and that is where Stephen and Philip come in. You have the first deacons in chapter 6, and we are introduced to Stephen, one of the first deacons. Then in chapters 6–7 you have the sermon Stephen preached and the account of how they stoned him to death. Stephen said he saw Jesus standing at the right hand of the Father. Chapter 8 has Philip and the Ethiopian eunuch. Philips goes down to the desert and preaches the gospel. You have New Voices.

In chapters 9–11, you have New Victories. In chapter 9 is the conversion of the apostle Paul. If you did not have the book of Acts, you would not know who Paul was, whom we read about in much of the rest of the New Testament. Acts 9 is his Damascus Road experience. Also, in chapters 10–11 you have the conversion of Cornelius the Gentile.

In chapter 12, you have New Violence. You have the martyrdom of James, the brother of John, and then they try to kill Peter. The Lord delivers him with an angel. Some ask why did God deliver Peter but did not deliver James? That is one of the mysteries of life. Some get delivered and others do not. Some get healed and others do not get healed. We are dealing with the imponderables of God. You cannot put God in your little box. You cannot dictate to God how He works. God is sovereign.

III. The Foreign Phase, 13–28

Chapters 13–28 are the Foreign Phase. The church begins to move out beyond Jerusalem, Judea, and Samaria. It goes out into the Roman Empire. You have two sections. First you have Paul the Pioneer from Acts 13:1 through Acts 21:26. This is where you get the three missionary journeys of Paul. In the back of most Bibles there are maps that will trace the missionary journeys of Paul. You can see how he founded the churches and how he went to Corinth and other cities. Then when you go to the letters, you will see why he was writing to the different churches. He was writing to churches he had established on his journeys.

Then the last thing you have is Paul the Prisoner, Acts 21:27–28:31. Acts 21 gives the arrest of Paul when he was back in Jerusalem, and that arrest resulted in his being carried into Rome. That is how the book of Acts closes in chapter 28.

The Instructional Books

Study #26
Romans Road

ROMANS ROAD

We are beginning the second main division of the New Testament, the Instructional books. There are three main categories of the Instructional books. Nine are classified Doctrinal because they deal primarily with doctrine. They are called Church Epistles or Church Letters. Romans through II Thessalonians are the Church Epistles. The next category are the Pastoral books. They were written by Paul, the older pastor, to two young pastors, Timothy (I and II Timothy) and Titus (Titus). Philemon is really not pastoral but is included. Paul was writing to an individual in the church there. Then eight letters fall into what we call General Epistles. This starts with Hebrews and goes all the way through the book of Jude. You have there James, I and II Peter, the three letters of John, and the little book of Jude.

The book of Romans may be the most influential book ever written. It has probably had more influence on more people than any one book of the New Testament. There are three remarkable conversions in Christian history that are a direct result of a study or a hearing or a reading of the book of Romans. Two of those conversions are very close to Georgia and Florida. The first is a man named Saint Augustine. Saint Augustine, Florida, south of Jacksonville, is named after him. As a young man, Augustine heard someone say to take and read. He picked up his Bible and was reading the book of Romans. He got to Romans 13:14 where it says, "But put ye on the Lord Jesus Christ, and make not provision for the flesh, to fulfill its lusts." God used this verse to bring Augustine to know Christ as his Savior. He became one of the great theologians and great teachers of the Christian faith.

The second one in church history is a man named Martin Luther. He was the founder of the Great Reformation. He was a Catholic monk; and in his attempt to earn the favor of God as a monk, he began to study the book of Romans. He became convinced that a person could not earn the favor of God and that it was only grace that made it possible for anyone to be saved. As a result of the study of the book of Romans, Martin Luther came to Christ; and he shook the world. The Protestant Reformation was a direct result of his study of the book of Romans.

The third man, John Wesley, is tied into the north Florida area also. He was the founder of the Methodist movement and one of the great Christians in the history of the Christian faith. Epworth by the Sea in Georgia is a popular Methodist encampment and has a plaque there to John Wesley. He came to the new world as a missionary to the colonists and Georgian Indians. On his voyage, he encountered some German Moravian missionaries and became convinced they had something he did not have. Wesley said, "I went to Georgia to convert the Indians, but who will convert me?" He went into a little chapel one night and heard someone reading Martin Luther's introduction to the book of Romans. Wesley said, "I felt my heart strangely warmed." As a result of that experience, John Wesley came to know Christ as his personal Savior.

The book of Romans is still changing lives today. I am convinced that a careful study of the book of Romans will produce a personal revival and many times a church revival.

Its Author

We are told at the very first of Romans that its author was Paul. The letters in the New Testament were put together differently than the way we write letters today. When we write letters today, we say "Dear Mildred," and then we have the body of the letter. Then we say, "Yours truly, Tom." We first tell to whom it is written, then have the body of the letter, and then whom it is from. If I get a letter and I do not recognize it, the first thing I do is go to the end to see who wrote it. Who it is from will have a lot to do with your reaction to the letter.

In the New Testament day, they did their letters in a different way, and I think it is better. They began by telling the author first and then had the body of the letter. We are told specifically in Romans 1:1 that this letter is from Paul. "Paul a servant of Jesus Christ, called to be an apostle, separated unto the gospel of God." Evidently, Paul wrote this letter to the Romans when he was in the city of Corinth during a three-month visit there. We have the record of that visit in Acts 20:1-3.

After he wrote this letter to the Romans, he evidently sent it to Rome by a lady named Phoebe. Romans 16:1-2, "I commend unto you Phoebe, our sister, who is a servant of the church which is at Cenchreae [this was the seacoast town of the city of Corinth], that ye receive her in the Lord, as becometh saints, and that ye assist her in whatever business she hath need of you; for she hath been a helper of many, and of myself also."

Evidently Paul entrusted to this fine Christian lady the responsibility of carrying this letter from Paul to the believers at Rome. At the time Paul wrote this book to the Romans, he had not visited there himself. It is only in the last chapter of the book of Acts that Paul arrived in Rome, so this letter was written before Paul got to Rome.

At the time of this writing, Paul was making his plans. He was anticipating, wanting to go to Rome. Can you imagine the excitement of the Roman believers the first time they opened up this letter? In those days the letters were in scrolls, and the readers would undo the scrolls.

Its Readers

In Romans 1:7 Paul tells to whom the letter is addressed: "To all that be in Rome, beloved of God, called to be saints: grace to you and peace from God our Father, and the Lord Jesus Christ." This is slightly different from how he addresses his other church letters. In First Corinthians 1:2, he writes, "Unto the church of God which is at Corinth." He addresses it to the church of God at Corinth. This verse shows the normal pattern, that is how Paul normally addresses his letters to churches. But to the Romans, he has not been there, he is not familiar with them and so he addresses it to "all that be in Rome, beloved of God, called to be saints." He is writing to the members of the church of Rome, but this indicates to us there may have been a little bit of difference here in his approach to the people of Rome.

In Romans 16, at the end of the letter, Paul lists a number of people who are in Rome and who are personally known to him. He also mentions some folks who are with him who send greetings. He evidently knew some believers in Rome and the folks in Rome knew some folks where Paul was. It is a marvelous list of people who had assisted Paul and had been a blessing to him. Paul always showed appreciation. He was always grateful for those who assisted him and served with him in the things of the Lord.

The big question is who started the church at Rome? Who established the church of Rome? Our Roman Catholic friends say Simon Peter started the church at Rome, but there is no evidence that he did so. In fact, there are indications that he did not do so. Romans 15:20 states, "Yea, so have I strived to preach the gospel, not where Christ was named, lest I should build upon another man's foundation." Evidently there was no one founder of the church in Rome and that may be why Paul did not say "to the church at Rome."

Paul shows in Romans 15:20 that his tendency was to start new works himself and not to go where work had already been started by some other individual. He did not want to build on another man's foundation. That statement indicates to us then that Simon Peter did not found the church in Rome.

How did the church of Rome come about? Notice something in Acts about on the day of Pentecost. This is when the Holy Spirit came and the apostles were given the supernatural gift of languages, not unknown tongues, but *known* tongues, languages and dialects. In Acts 2 the people were amazed when they hear these Galilean fishermen and peasants speaking all of these languages. Notice Acts 2:10: "Phrygia, and Pamphylia, in Egypt, and in the parts of Libya about Cyrene, and strangers of Rome." Evidently there were people who had come to Jerusalem for the feast of Pentecost from Rome and were converted. That verse indicates to us that perhaps these were the people who went back and preached the gospel in Rome, and congregations of believers were founded. We do not know this for sure though.

Its Purpose

The first purpose for this letter is to prepare them for his planned visit. Look at Romans 1:8-15. Paul says in verse 10, "Making request, if by any means now at length I might have a prosperous journey by the will of God to come unto you." He was praying his visit would be in the will of God. He was making his plans to see them. Verse 11, "For I long to see you, that I may impart unto you some spiritual gift, to the end ye may be established." Paul was really looking forward to getting there and being a blessing to them.

Verse 13, "Now I would not have you ignorant, brethren, that oftentimes I purposed to come unto you (but was let hitherto), that I might have some fruit among you also, even as among other Gentiles." What he was saying was he had tried to come before. He was preparing them for his visit. This is seen in Romans 15:23-29 also.

The second purpose is to instruct them in the basic doctrines of Christian faith. The most important thing you can do for young Christians is to instruct them in the faith, to teach them Bible doctrine. There is a trend away from that today. People say doctrine is dull. It is according to who is doing the teaching whether it is dull or not. You are going to tell me that the doctrine of redemption, whereby we were slaves to sin and Christ paid the price for us on Calvary to set us free, is dull? Bible doctrine is not dull; Bible doctrine is exciting.

The book of Romans is the most complete and comprehensive statement of what the Christian faith is all about to be found anywhere in the Bible. Paul just lays out the basic doctrines of the Christian faith. This is why we should be students of the book of Romans. It is where we learn the essential doctrines of the Christian faith, what Christianity is all about.

The third purpose is to explain the relationship between the nation of Israel and the church of the Lord Jesus Christ. That was and still is a big issue. There is a distinction between Israel and the church; they are not the same. People get into trouble when they mix up the nation of Israel and the church. They get into trouble in Bible interpretation. A lot of the incorrect information that is out currently today is because people take promises that were specifically given to the nation of Israel and apply them to the church. Paul explains the relationship between Israel and the church. It is the most comprehensive statement and explanation of it.

The fourth purpose of Romans is to teach Christians their duties to each other and to the state or government. You will find in the letters of Paul, almost without exception, there is a two-fold emphasis in them. Always look for it. Paul will begin giving doctrine, what we believe; then at some point, he will move from doctrine, what we believe, to behavior, what our duty is because of what we believe. He will apply what we believe to daily life.

We are not just reading the Bible for information. We are reading the Bible to help us know how to live life correctly, how to live it positively, and how to live it in such a way that Christ is exalted and our life is what it ought to be. That is the two-fold emphasis of the letters of Paul: doctrine and duty/belief and behavior.

The fifth purpose is to answer any slander against himself (Romans 3:8). Some were saying Paul said to do wrong so good would come from it. Paul said it was a slander. He really answers the critics when he gets to the book of Galatians and also II Corinthians.

Its Position

Habakkuk 2:4 says "The just shall live by faith." There are three books in the New Testament that were written to explain this one verse. The book of Romans explains what it means to be just. The book of Galatians explains what it means to live the Christian faith. The book of Hebrews explains what faith is all about. The just, Romans; shall live, Galatians;

by faith, Hebrews. Romans is written to explain what it means to be just, what it means to be declared righteous.

Its Theme

There is a phrase that explains the theme of Romans for us. The theme is the righteousness of God. We know this because of Romans 1:16-17, "For I am not ashamed of the gospel of Christ; for it [the gospel, the good news] is the power of God unto salvation to everyone that believeth; to the Jew first, and also to the

Greek. For therein it [the gospel] is the righteousness of God revealed from faith to faith; as it is written, the just shall live by faith."

The good news is the good news about the righteousness of God, which is the power of God unto salvation. The technical theme is the righteousness of God.

The simple message of Romans is how sinners can go to heaven when they die. This is one of the reasons why you want to go to Romans when you want to present the gospel of Christ to lead someone to Jesus.

There are four verses in Romans you can use to lead somebody to faith in Jesus Christ. Romans 3:23, "For all have sinned, and come short of the glory of God." That is our condition before God. We are sinners. Romans 6:23, "For the wages of sin is death, but the gift of God is eternal life through Jesus Christ, our Lord." Romans 5:8, "But God commendeth [proves or demonstrates] his love toward us in that, while we were yet sinners, Christ died for us." Romans 10:9, "That if thou shalt confess with thy mouth the Lord Jesus, and shalt believe in thine heart that God hath raised him from the dead, thou shalt be saved." That is why we turn to the book of Romans to give a simple presentation of the gospel.

There are some keys words in the book of Romans. The word *law* occurs 78 times.

The little word *all* occurs 71 times. *Righteousness* occurs 66 times. *Faith* occurs 62 times; *sin*, 60 times. *Death* occurs 42 times. *In Christ*, the little phrase that is so characteristic of Paul, occurs 33 times. It was one of Paul's favorite phrases. *Flesh* occurs 20 times, and *impute*, which means to put down on the record, to count it on your record, to declare, occurs 19 times.

There are more Old Testament quotations in the book of Romans than in all of the other church letters put together. There are 70 Old Testament quotations in the book of Romans alone.

Paul was tying in the New Testament to the Old Testament. Paul was showing that the New Testament has its roots in the Old Testament. The Old Testament was leading us to the good news of Jesus Christ.

OUTLINE

Introduction, 1:1-17

I. Doctrinal: the Principles of Christianity, 1–8
- **A. Sin**
- **B. Salvation**
- **C. Sanctification**

II. Dispensational: the Problem with Christianity, 9–11
- **A. God's Past Dealings with Israel**
- **B. God's Present Dealings with Israel**
- **C. God's Promised Dealings with Israel**

III. Practical: the Practice of Christianity, 12–16
- **A. The Laws of Christian Life**
- **B. The Laws of Christian Love**

Introduction

The Introduction is the first 17 verses, Romans 1:1-17. There are three main divisions for the book of Romans. At the end of each main division there is a doxology, which makes it easy to outline.

I. Doctrinal: the Principles of Christianity, 1–8

The first eight chapters are Doctrinal (Romans 1–8). Paul usually started off with doctrine. But in Romans he does something a little different. Instead of moving directly from doctrine into behavior or how you live, he gives us a second division called Dispensational (Romans 9–11). That is where he takes up the problem of Israel. Then the third division is Practical (Romans 12–16).

The first division is Doctrinal, the Principles of Christianity (Romans 1–8). In those eight chapters you will find the basic teaching principles of what Christianity is all about. When I talk to preachers about analyzing books of the Bible, I compare a book of the Bible to a block of wood. A block of wood has natural grains in it. You look for those natural grains; and if you will take your axe and chop right there on the natural grains, those chunks will fall out easily. Or I compare it sometimes to an exploded diagram in a mechanic shop. A Ford dealership will have exploded diagrams of the motors. They take those parts, explode them, and then label them. That is the way you study the books of the Bible. You look for those main grains, those main divisions. Or if it is a diagram, you look for the main parts.

A. Sin, 1:18–3:20

The first eight chapters have three pieces of wood that explain the whole gospel to you. The first piece of wood is sin, Romans 1:18–3:20. Paul proves the whole world is sinners. We are all sinners. The whole point of this section is how the gospel saves a sinner. People are not going to get saved until they know they are sinners. That is what is so serious about the emphasis we are hearing today away from the gospel. There are some people saying not to tell people they are sinners. There is a total philosophy that says you have to get folks in church and then once you have them in you can give them the hard stuff. That is dishonest. It is false advertising. How are people going to get saved if they do not know they are lost? Paul keeps building the case. In the first chapter he shows that the pagan world is sinners. Then in the second chapter he shows that the religious world is sinners, and he does it by talking specifically about the Jew, the religious Jew. Then in chapter 3 he keeps building the fact that we are all sinners, and finally he hits it in verse 20, "Therefore by the deeds of the law shall no flesh be justified in his sight: for by the law is the knowledge of sin."

B. Salvation, 3:21–5:21

The second thing is Salvation, 3:21–5:21. Romans 3:21, "But now the righteousness of God without the law [not trying to get to heaven by keeping the law, which he proved you cannot do] is manifested, being witnessed by the law, and the prophets." Verse 22, "Even the righteousness of God which is by faith of Jesus Christ unto all and upon all them that believe; for there is no difference." Verse 23, "For all have sinned, and come short of the glory of God." Verse 24, "Being justified freely by his grace through the redemption that is in Christ Jesus." What he has done is moved right into salvation.

Then in chapter 3 through the last verse of chapter 5, he moves into the whole theme of salvation. He shows we are not saved by keeping the law, not by our righteousness, but we are saved by faith in what Jesus did for us when He died on the cross.

C. Sanctification, 6–8

The third section, chapters 6–8, he talks about Sanctification. Sanctification is the progressive growth in righteousness. It is beginning to grow as a Christian believer. He deals with the struggle that goes on in the hearts of believers between their old nature and their new nature. In Romans 7, Paul says he wants to do right but he cannot. He says he does not want to do wrong, but he does. In Romans 8 he shows the solution is the indwelling Holy Spirit. We cannot live the Christian life in and of ourselves any more than we can be saved in and of ourselves. We need God in our lives to help us live right, just as we need God in our lives to save us. That is what sanctification is all about. It is a progressive growth in righteousness as you yield to the indwelling Holy Spirit.

II. Dispensational: the Problem with Christianity, 9–11

Normally Paul would deal next with behavior, the practical part, but in Romans he drops in another section. He drops in the problem of Christianity and how the gospel was related to the nation of Israel. What about the Israelites? How did they fit into God's salvation plan? In Romans 9–11, he talks about God's dealings with Israel, with the Jews: Romans 9, God's past dealings with Israel; Chapter 10, God's present dealings with the Jews. How are Jews saved today? The same way Gentiles are saved. You witness to Jews today the same way you witness to Gentiles. Romans 10:13,"For whosoever shall call upon the name of the Lord shall be saved." That is right in the middle of the section that talks about God's dealing with Jews today.

The third section, chapter 11, is God's promised dealings with Israel. God says that one of these days the Jews, who for the most part have rejected Jesus Christ, will one day as a nation receive Him. The Bible says when Jesus comes again, Israel will look on Him, whom they have pierced.

He explains in chapter 11 the future glorious plan God has for the nation of Israel.

III. Practical: the Practice of Christianity, 12–16

Romans 12:1 begins, "I beseech you therefore." A basic guide of Bible study is every time you see the word *therefore,* ask yourself this question, "What is the therefore there for?" It is normally a signpost that points either backward or forward. In this instance, it points backward. It points back to chapters 1–8. Keep in mind that chapters 9, 10, and 11 are parenthetical chapters that are dropped right in the middle. If you will pull those three chapters out, the first eight chapters are on doctrine and the last five chapters are on Christian behavior. The third division is Practical: the practice of Christianity. Paul is dealing with how the gospel affects conduct. The two main divisions are the Laws of Christian Life, 12:1–13:7, and the Laws of Christian Love, 13:8–16:24.

Study #27
Considering 1 Corinthians

CONSIDERING I CORINTHIANS

The books in the New Testament are not arranged according to chronological order, which means that Romans may not necessarily have been written before I Corinthians. Don't think when you read one book after the other, that it means this book was written and then this book was written next and so on.

The book of I Corinthians is a very interesting book. I find myself constantly going back to it because of the nature of the subject matter. Romans is the great book that sets forth the doctrine of the Christian faith, what the Christian faith is all about. It lays forth the great themes of sin: the fact man is a sinner; God's great plan of salvation; and then God's plan to help us to be sanctified in our lives, to live for the Lord on a daily basis, and then to have the practical application. But when you come to I Corinthians, it takes a different direction. It is most helpful for today. It is Paul's first of his two letters in our New Testament to the Corinthians.

Its City

Corinth was an important city in Greece. It was the capital of the Roman province of Achaia. It was one of the great metropolitan cities of ancient Greece. It had a population of approximately 700,000 people. It was roughly the same size as Jacksonville, Florida, so it was a large metropolitan area.

Corinth had two seaports. One was Cenchreae. It had a huge shopping area. If you ever go to that part of the world, they will take you down the old center street, the shopping district of the city. It had a very large stadium in it. We think in terms of our stadiums today and think they are something brand-new to us.

No, they had stadiums that seated thousands and thousands of people. The Isthmian Games, which were similar to the Olympic Games, were held in Corinth. It was a great trade center because it was located on one of the leading travel routes in the Roman Empire from east to west.

Paul was writing to a church located in a city. You will notice Paul wrote most of his letters to cities. It is not that Paul was not interested in the country, the rural areas, but Paul had a definite strategy. Paul's strategy was to take the gospel to the great population centers, knowing that what happens in the city would have a tendency to move out to the rural areas.

Keep in mind that Corinth was noted for three primary matters: commerce, it was a great commercial center; culture, it was a great cultural center; and corruption, it was a very wicked, godless city. In fact, Corinth was so corrupt that they had coined a phrase. If a person behaved in a very immoral way, that person was said to "corinthianize." It was the terminology used.

Another interesting feature about the city of Corinth, and this is characteristic of Greek cities in general, was a mountain. Greek cities were always somewhere around a mountain. That was true with the city of Corinth. It was located on the *acrocorinthus* or Acrocorinth, that is the hill of Corinth.

That hill, and most Greek cities had those, was where the temples were located. There were two primary purposes for those temples. One, of course, was worship. The other was for protection. When there was an invasion, they would retreat as much as possible up to that *acrocorinthus* or temple area for protection.

The temple at Corinth was dedicated to Venus, the goddess of love. There were a thousand sacred prostitutes, we are told, who were connected with the temple of Venus.

These background matters become very interesting because one of the things that went on in that temple of Venus, along with sexual immorality practiced, was these temple prostitutes would go into ecstasies, speaking different kinds of ecstatic utterances. That comes into play when you read the book of Corinthians because that was characteristic of that area, the temple of Venus, and the sacred prostitutes. For more background on the city of Corinth, read Romans 1 because when Paul wrote the book of Romans, he was in the city of Corinth. As you read down through the last part of Romans 1, where it lays out the depravity of man, you get a pretty good picture of the moral climate of Corinth. This information is important when you read some of the things in this letter to the Corinthians because it gives a little background to understand and know why Paul did what he did and why the church was dealing with the kind of problems they were dealing with.

Its Church

This was a church founded by the apostle Paul on his second missionary journey. In Acts 17, Paul was in the city of Athens and preached at the Acropolis, the hill of the city. *Acro* means the hill; *polis* is the city, the hill of the city. Paul preached there on Mars Hill, which is a little nub right off of the Acropolis. He preached on the creation and the resurrection of the Lord Jesus Christ. When he did, they made fun of him and they laughed at him.

Paul moved from there up to the city of Corinth, which was approximately 50 miles away. Now, it could be he sailed from Athens to Corinth, or it could be that he walked around that body of water, the sea, to Corinth. Regardless, it gave Paul time to think of what kind of message to preach in Corinth. He preached the gospel, the resurrection of Jesus in Athens, and they made fun of it. That's why when you get to I Corinthians 2, it is significant to hear what he said.

First Corinthians 2:1-2, "And I, brethren, when I came to you, came not with excellency of speech or of wisdom, declaring unto you the testimony of God. For I determined not to know any thing among you, except Jesus Christ, and him crucified."

The word *determined* there means "I have come to the settled conclusion." Paul had made up his mind, he had thought about this. You can almost see Paul as he left Athens. After all, no one likes to be laughed at; no one wants to be made fun of. He had preached the gospel and they said that's silly, that's nonsense. Paul, however, said I am going to preach the same message in Corinth, I am going to preach the gospel of the Lord Jesus Christ.

Paul left Athens in Acts 17 and moved to Corinth in Acts 18. In Acts 18, we have the account of Aquila and Priscilla, the people he met there. They had the same trade that he had; they were tent makers. He joined with them there. The Lord appeared to Paul in Corinth and gave him a vision of encouragement and told him to keep on preaching. The Lord told him to not be afraid and said He had many people in this city. This meant that in Corinth God was going to use Paul to win people to Christ.

Acts 18 gives us the historical background of the founding of this church in Corinth.

Paul was there approximately one and a half years. From there he moved to the city of Ephesus (Acts 19).

The people in Corinth, who were converted through the preaching of the apostle Paul, as already indicated, came out of deep sin. They came out of a corrupt culture. That gives us some background to I Corinthians 6:9-11, "Know ye not that the unrighteous shall not inherit the kingdom of God? Be not deceived: neither fornicators [those sexually immoral], nor idolaters, nor adulterers, nor effeminate, nor abusers of themselves with mankind. Nor thieves, nor covetous, nor drunkards, nor revilers, nor extortioners, shall inherit the kingdom of God." How would you like to have a church like that? The truth of the matter is, churches today are made up of people like that today. Churches may not fit all these categories, but that was the group Paul wrote to.

Look at what he said in verse 11, "And such were some of you; but ye are washed, but ye are sanctified, but ye are justified in the name of the Lord Jesus, and by the Spirit of our God." Do you see what Paul was saying? This is the way you were; this was your moral and spiritual condition. But he said you are washed, you are sanctified, and you are justified in the name of the Lord Jesus and by the Spirit of our God. These people had a remarkable conversion.

Now what do you know about people who have been converted out of lifestyles of deep sin? Well, their conversion is a very dramatic thing. When a person who has been a drunkard gets saved, that is pretty dramatic. When a person who has been into sexual immorality gets saved, that is dramatic. You might say any conversion is dramatic, and it is. But I came to Christ as a nine-year-old boy. I did not have that kind of background. My salvation is just as precious to me as to anyone else, but my reaction to it may not be like someone who is a 45-year-old man who came to know Christ. Here were people who had come out of deep sin, and they were very expressive about their conversion experience, as well as they should be.

But another thing to keep in mind is there is a tendency when people are very emotional about their faith for them, in some ways, to become a little unstable about their faith. Unstable may not be the best word, but the emotions are the most dangerous aspect of your personality. They are the most untrustworthy part of your personality. Your emotions must always be guided by your intellect, and your intellect must be informed by the Word of God. You cannot just go by your emotions and lay aside your intellect. That is why it disturbs me when I hear people say to just lay aside your mind and let your emotions take over. That is dangerous advice. Your emotions will get you into all kind of stuff. Again, emotions must be guided by your intellect, and your intellect must be informed by scripture.

Here is something else you need to know about this church. This is very important to an understanding of what was going on in I Corinthians. The Corinthian church was the most carnal church in the New Testament. That's very important for you to have down. In fact, Paul specifically said in the I Corinthians 3:1, "I could not write to you as mature, as spiritual people but carnal." He said they were carnal. As you read and find out what was going on, you understand what he meant. They were very, very carnal. Some would get drunk at the Lord's Supper. They were divided into power groups in the church. They had about four distinct groups in the church trying to run the church.

This is an example of a church allowing the culture around it to change it rather than the church changing its culture. It is the old classic between the thermometer and the thermostat. A thermometer just registers the temperature, and a thermostat changes the temperature. God does not want a church to be a thermometer, just registering the temperature. God wants a church to be a thermostat, changing the spiritual temperature where it is.

Its Correspondence

Paul wrote two letters to the Corinthians. He received a letter from the Corinthian church, in which they asked Paul certain questions about church doctrine and practice. In response, Paul wrote the letter of I Corinthians, evidently while he was in Ephesus. If you remember, he left Corinth and went to Ephesus. He sent that letter by the young man Timothy. Timothy came back and reported things were not doing well, that they were getting worse. So Paul sent Titus to Corinth. During that time there was a riot in Ephesus, and so Paul had to leave. He made the promise that he would come to Corinth. Circumstances delayed him, so he sent Titus up there. Titus came back and gave him the good news that they had responded to his first letter well, but there were still some in the church who were not in line. He then wrote II Corinthians.

Its Purposes

There is a two-fold purpose to the writing of I Corinthians. The first purpose was to answer questions about the Christian life and doctrines. Paul was responding to the questions they had sent to him.

The second thing he did was to rebuke them for the flagrant sin in the church. They were allowing a situation to continue in their church that just could not go without rebuke. Paul specifically addressed that problem in I Corinthians 5.

There is not a book in the New Testament that deals with local church problems to the degree that the Corinthian letter does. It is a church letter that deals with all kinds of problems, and most of the problems that occur in a local church will be reflected in some way in this first letter to the Corinthians.

Now it is especially good for us today to have I Corinthians because of the charismatic issues that are very current. First Corinthians is where you go to really understand the charismatic issues. You need to be well grounded in I Corinthians if you want to understand them. Most of the issues that arise in the Christian church today are not new; they come with a little different wrinkle, and they may come in a different package, but most arose in the first century church age. That is certainly true of charismatic issues.

First Corinthians is the longest of Paul's letters, and it sets forth the importance of decency and order in the local congregation, as we find in I Corinthians 14:40, "Let all things be done decently and in order."

OUTLINE

I. The Carnalities: the Report of Sin, 1–6
- **A. Division in the Church**
- **B. Discipline in the Church**
- **C. Difficulties in the Church**
- **D. Defilement in the Church**

II. The Spiritualities: the Reply to Questions, 7–16
- **A. Marriage**
- **B. Idols**
- **C. Ordinances**
- **D. Spiritual Gifts**
- **E. Resurrection**
- **F. Offering**

We cannot obviously cover everything, but I have divided I Corinthians into two main divisions. The first is "The Carnalities." It was the most carnal church in the New Testament. Paul deals in the first six chapters with "The Carnalities: the Report of Sin." He is responding to the report of sin in the congregation.

The second division is "The Spiritualities." In that section, chapters 7–16, he replies to their questions. There is a key or terminology in I Corinthians 7:1 to let you know this is what is going on. "Now concerning the things whereof ye wrote unto me." He is responding to the questions they had asked. In chapter 7, he responds to questions relating to marriage.

In I Corinthians 8 he says, "Now as touching things offered unto idols." Do you see what he has done? He is giving a little verbal clue. Chapter 7 starts off "Now concerning." Chapter 8 starts off, "Now touching."

Chapter 12 begins, "Now concerning." That is one of the ways you pick up what is going on, the repetition of words or little phrases. "Now concerning spiritual gifts [or spiritualities is literally the rendering]."

Chapter 16:1, "Now concerning the collection." Do you see the little clues he gives? He is responding to their questions. He is answering the questions they had asked.

I. The Carnalities: the Report of Sin, 1–6

A. Division in the Church

The first section in "The Carnalities" is Division in the Church (chapters 1–4). Here was a divided church. He really goes into the problem and cause of that division. Specifically look at what he says in I Corinthians 1:11 after he has given the introduction and prayer, "For it has been declared unto me of you, my brethren, by them which are of the house of Chloe, that there are contentions among you." There were quarrels among them. Then he says, verse 12, "Now this I say, that every one of you saith, I am of Paul; and I of Apollos; and I of Cephas; and I of Christ." Do you see what was happening? You have four distinct parties. You had one group that said Paul was their man. Another group said they liked Apollos; he was their man. Another said Cephas or Peter was their man. But another crowd said they were of Christ.

Paul dives into the matter of division and then begins to really dissect the problem. He goes to the preaching of the cross. In chapter 2, he talks about the wisdom of God versus the wisdom of men. In chapter 3 he tells them the reason they have these divisions is because of their carnality. They are not growing spiritually; they are babes in Christ. He talks about the judgment seat of Christ and the day will come that everyone's work is going to be tested. People will have to stand before the judgment seat of Christ. Everyone's work will be tried. He goes into that issue also in chapter 4.

B. Discipline in the Church

In chapter 5 he goes into Discipline in the Church. He addresses the problem the church is allowing to go undisciplined. It is a problem of fornication in the fellowship. Look at what he says in verse 1, "It is reported commonly that there is fornication among you." And he specifies what kind it is, that a man is having a relationship with his father's wife. We would take that to be his step-mother probably. It was such a flagrant relationship that not even the godless Corinthians went this far. But what really had Paul disturbed was in verse 2, "And ye are puffed up, and have not rather mourned, that he that hath done this deed might be taken away from among you." What he means is they had not even addressed this issue with this person. They had not even spoken to this issue, so he brings up the whole matter of discipline in the fellowship and how to handle sin in the fellowship.

C. Difficulties in the Church

In chapter 6 he deals with Difficulties in the Church (6:1-8). The specific matter he talks about is they had members taking one another to court. Verse 1: "Dare any of you, having a matter against another, go to law before the unjust and not before the saints?" He says don't you know the saints are going to rule the world and the world is going to be judged by you. Are you unworthy to judge the smallest matters? They were running off to courts of law to settle disputes between believers.

D. Defilement in the Church

In verse 9 through the end of the chapter (6:9-20), he deals with Defilement in the Church. He reminds them of what they had come out from, but he points out to them that though they had come out of a life of sin, some of them were still into things they had no business being in. He is deals with church problems.

II. The Spiritualities: the Reply to Questions, Chapters 7–16

The second division is where he begins to reply to their questions, "The Spiritualities: the Reply to Questions" (7–16).

A. Marriage

Chapter 7 is a long and most difficult to understand chapter relative to the whole matter of marriage. It talks about the marriage of a believer with an unbeliever and these kinds of things. It is not an easy chapter to understand, but it does have a lot of very important information about the issue of marriage.

B. Idols

In chapters 8–10, he deals with the matter of things offered to idols, the issue of Christian conscience, and our influence in relationship to other people. The background to that is what went on in these temples with the meat offered to idols. They would take the meat from these animal sacrifices and would put them in the butcher shops. People would come along and buy them. Some Christians were having problems with that because there were some Christians who would buy that meat and go home and have a good meal. But there were other Christians who realized where that meat had come from, and they had a problem with it. They said that meat had been offered up in a pagan temple. It is the whole issue of how a Christian lives in a world that is not Christian. What about my influence on other people?

C. Ordinances

Chapter 11 is the matter of the Lord's Supper, Ordinances. It is a most interesting chapter about dress and the way you appear before God to worship. I do think it is important how a person comes before God to worship. You do not need to have on a tuxedo, but there should be a difference in your appearance when you come into the presence of God to worship. When I went to have dinner with President Ronald Reagan, I did not put on my jogging outfit. I was going to have dinner with the President. It should be important how we come into the presence of the God of this universe. Lost people do not know, and that is why when they get saved it is important for Sunday School teachers and others to tactfully and kindly teach and help them.

D. Spiritual Gifts

Chapters 12–14 cover the matters of Spiritual Gifts. Paul goes into the whole area of spiritual gifts. He points out that every believer has one or more spiritual gifts. He also points out that no believer picks his spiritual gifts. They are given sovereignly by God. He goes into the whole matter of tongues. What you have to keep in mind with Paul's discussion of the tongue issue in the Corinthian church is that it was a problem in the church. Always keep that in mind or you will misunderstand the chapters. It also included the problem of women speaking out in the church in an atmosphere of the sacred prostitutes who were so visible and dominant in their pagan worship. Paul is basically saying if people come into the church and all of this is going on, they will think they are in one of the pagan temples around Corinth. Keep in mind that he writes concerning the tongue issue not to encourage tongues, but he writes to regulate the tongues that were going on in the Corinthian church because it was so similar to what was happening in the pagan temples.

My own personal view is that the tongues in Corinth are very different from what you find on the day of Pentecost in the book of Acts. Paul lays out some guidelines for the Corinthians, knowing that if they went by these guidelines it would eliminate the problem.

E. Resurrection

Chapter 15 is the greatest chapter in the Bible on the Resurrection. It is the classic statement in all the Bible on the matter of the resurrection. He starts off with a clear-cut presentation of the Gospel. Gospel means good news. What is the good news? It has three main points: Christ died, He was buried, and He rose again. The Gospel is the good news about the death, burial, and resurrection of the Lord Jesus. He talks about the resurrection body, he talks about the fact that if there is not a resurrection then we do not have any hope. It is a magnificent chapter. It comes to the climax in verses 57-58, "But thanks be to God who gives us the victory through our Lord Jesus Christ. Therefore, my beloved brethren, be ye stedfast, unmoveable, always abounding in the work of the Lord."

F. Offering

The last subject is in chapter 16, "Now concerning the collection." He talks about the whole matter of how the collection is to be taken. He gives us in verse 2 one of the clearest statements in all the Bible about the matter of our giving and bringing to the Lord a portion of what He has blessed and prospered us with. "Upon the first day of the week let every one of you lay by him in store, as God hath prospered him . . ."

After dealing with the collection, he comes to closing matters, and he gives some personal words and mentions some individuals. Then he closes his letter.

Second Corinthians follows up on this letter. What about that man who was involved in an incestuous relationship with his father's wife? Paul wrote and told them to deal with that issue. What happened? How did they respond? What did this man do? Second Corinthians tells us.

Study #28
Comfort in 2 Corinthians

COMFORT FROM II CORINTHIANS

We are looking at the second letter that Paul the apostle wrote to the believers at Corinth. There is some discussion about how many letters, indeed, Paul wrote to the Corinthians. There are some who view II Corinthians as really two letters that have been put together. I have not spent a lot of time in talking about the manuscripts and texts we have preserved of our New Testament, but there is some indication that II Corinthians is really two letters put together. I personally do not think this is the case, but there is a reason for it, which will later become apparent as we move on through II Corinthians.

Remember Paul founded the church at Corinth. He went there, and God used him in a wonderful way to win people to Christ and to organize people into a local fellowship of believers.

There were some problems in the church of Corinth. It was probably the most carnal and spiritually immature of all the churches of the New Testament. The background to this second letter has its beginning in I Corinthians 5. There was a problem of immorality in the fellowship of the church.

That was bad enough, but Paul was also concerned because the church was tolerating it. They were allowing it to continue and were not dealing with it. Paul wrote to them specifically telling them to deal with this problem. Second Corinthians indicates to us that the problem was dealt with and they did respond to his first letter.

Second Corinthians in some ways is a sad book. Someone once said II Corinthians was written with a quill dipped in tears. That is a pretty good description of what you find. It is the most personal, is the most painful, and has the most pathos of any of the letters of the apostle Paul.

The letter of II Timothy to the young preacher, which was probably Paul's last letter, is a very personal letter, but this is even more personal than II Timothy is. There seems to have been in the church at Corinth a vocal minority. The majority of the people had responded correctly to Paul and had responded in the affirmative. But, evidently, there was still a vocal minority in the church stirring up trouble. Though the majority of the church responded in a proper manner to Paul and carried through on his directions, there still seems to be this hostile minority of people who were really problematic to him.

In once sense of the word, you take a little comfort in that because when you think in terms of the New Testament and the churches and Christians of the New Testament, if you are not careful, you will get the idea that these were perfect individuals and churches, that they never had any problems. But that is not true. So there is a little comfort in that when we encounter problems and difficulties in personal relationships with other believers, we realize this is nothing new. It has been going on since the very inception of the Christian church.

God does not save us and make us perfect saints just like that. We are all having to grow and mature in the Lord.

This minority was coming down hard on Paul. They were making a number of accusations against him. Let's note some of these accusations.

In II Corinthians 1:17, they accused Paul evidently of being fickle. Paul writes, "When I, therefore, was thus minded, did I use lightness [was I fickle]? Or the things that I purpose, do I purpose according to the flesh, that with me there should be yea, yea, and nay, nay?" The background is Paul had told them of his desire to come and visit with them. But because of a series of circumstances which made it impossible for him to do so, then this minority said Paul could not even make up his mind. They said he said he was going to come, and then he did not.

Another thing they accused him of was pride. Second Corinthians 3:1, "Do we begin again to commend ourselves? Or need we, as some others, epistles of commendation to you, or letters of commendation from you?" Paul was asking if they were pushing themselves, if they had their own selfish agendas here. He had been accused of being proud and boastful.

Some even attacked his personal appearance. Look at II Corinthians 10:10, "For his letters, say they [the minority], are weighty and powerful, but his bodily presence is weak, and his speech contemptible." They said he was something when he wrote letters, but he was not much to see when you saw him. They said his speech was contemptible; he was not a good speaker either.

They even questioned his sanity; II Corinthians 5:13, "For whether we be beside ourselves, it is to God; or whether we be of sober mind, it is for your cause." These are King James terms, but "beside ourselves" means to be mentally off and "sober" is not referring to being inebriated but is a reference of being of sound mind. The background to that is some said Paul was off his rocker.

Keep in mind this is the apostle Paul they were talking about. Yet, there were some people who did not like him and who gave him problems.

Its Purpose

There are several reasons why Paul wrote this letter. You might ask why this is important, why not just pick up the book and start reading it? If you know the reasons for Paul writing this, it will help you as you read through it.

The first purpose was to commend the church for disciplining the offender (I Corinthians 5). They evidently did discipline the member, and he showed deep repentance. Now Paul writes back, and he commends them for doing the right thing. He also encourages them to forgive this man and to receive him. The purpose of their discipline was not to drive him away, but it was to draw him back to the Lord and to the fellowship. Look at II Corinthians 2:5-7, "But if any have caused grief, he hath not grieved me, but in part: that I may not overcharge you all. Sufficient to such a man is this punishment, which was inflicted of many. So that contrariwise ye ought rather to forgive him, and comfort him, lest perhaps such a one should be swallowed up with overmuch sorrow."

The purpose of discipline is redemption; it is redemptive in nature, not to drive people down but to bring them closer to the Lord. So Paul says in II Corinthians 2:8-10, "Wherefore, I beseech you that ye would confirm your love toward him. For to this end also did I write, that I might know the proof of you, whether ye be obedient in all things. To whom ye forgive any thing, I forgive also; for if I forgave any thing, to whom I forgave it, for your sakes forgave I it in the person of Christ."

Paul says he had forgiven the person, they had forgiven the person, and so they were to restore him to the fellowship. Paul commends them for handling the problem in the church but urges them to express forgiveness to him.

The second reason was to explain why he had not visited. Look at I Corinthians 16:3-6, and how Paul had told them about this plan. This is why some accused him of being fickle. Verse 3, "And when I come, whomsoever ye shall approve by your letters, them will I send to bring your liberality unto Jerusalem." They were taking up a collection for the saints in Jerusalem who were going through some hard times, so Paul was gathering up this offering. He says in verse 4-6, "And if it be meet that I go also, they shall go with me. Now I will come unto you, when I shall pass through Macedonia; for I do pass through Macedonia. And it may be that I will abide, yea, and winter with you; that ye may bring me on my journey whithersoever I go." That was Paul's plan.

Now look at II Corinthians 1:15-16, and Paul explains the situation. "And in this confidence I was minded to come unto you before, that ye might have a second benefit; And to pass by you into Macedonia, and to come again out of Macedonia unto you, and of you to be brought on my way toward Judea." That is what his intentions were, but circumstances had changed and it was impossible for him to do it.

The third purpose for Paul writing II Corinthians was to answer those who were challenging his authority as an apostle. We see that in chapters 10–12. They were saying Paul was not a real apostle. In this letter, he responds to their charges.

The fourth reason for writing was to answer accusations of wrong motives. Do you see the seriousness of this letter? Do you see the pain underneath this letter? He answers those charges in II Corinthians 4:1-2, "Therefore, seeing we have this ministry, as we have received mercy, we faint not, But have renounced the hidden things of dishonesty, not walking in craftiness, nor handling the word of God deceitfully, but by manifestation of the truth commending ourselves to every man's conscience in the sight of God." Paul says my motives are pure.

The next reason was to encourage them to share in the offering for Jerusalem saints. That is the background of chapters 8 and 9. Look at II Corinthians 8:1, "Moreover, brethren, we do you wit [what he is saying is we want them to know] of the grace of God bestowed on the churches of Macedonia."

He was encouraging them to participate in the offering by pointing out how the churches in Macedonia had participated in it. He was encouraging them by example, so look at what he says in verse 6: "Insomuch that we desired Titus that as he had begun so he would also finish in you the same grace also." Giving here is compared to a grace. Giving is a grace matter. It is something we do out of appreciation for the grace of God. What he is saying is he wants them to share in the offering and be a part of this work of God's grace in their lives just like other people were doing also. Then he talks about it.

Chapters 8 and 9 are very important chapters when it comes to the finances of a church. They lay out the principle of having godly, spiritual people to handle the finances of the church.

The next reason he writes is to prepare them for his planned visit. This is in II Corinthians 13:1-2. He sends a little word of warning to his critics and let's them know they are going to deal with the problems. He says, "This is the third time I am coming to you. In the mouth of two or three witnesses shall every word be established. I told you before, and tell you beforehand, as if I were present, the second time; and being absent now I write to them who heretofore have sinned, and to all others, that, if I come again, I will not spare."

You may think that II Corinthians is a harsh letter, but here is how God worked in the heart of Paul and how God can work in our hearts also. This book has about as many verses that are filled with encouragement, love, grace, and fellowship as any book you will read. Here is a book that deals with problems and difficult people, and yet it is filled with encouragement and comfort.

Its Contrast to I Corinthians

In I Corinthians Paul is dealing primarily with the church in terms of giving us a look at the church. It's like he takes the roof off the church and lets us look in. Second Corinthians is more personal to Paul. You will find him opening up his heart and letting you look in to see him. First Corinthians lets you take a good look at the church; II Corinthians, you are taking a look at the apostle Paul.

Its Messages

There are a lot of references to the sufferings Paul went through. Christians have trouble. When you become a Christian, it does not mean that your troubles are eliminated or that you will not go through the normal problems or difficulties other people have. Everyone is in one of three situations. You are either coming out of a problem, you are in a problem, or you are headed for a problem.

One of the greatest passages on the comfort of God you will find anywhere in the entire Bible is in II Corinthians 1. Paul writes in verse 4, "Who comforteth us in all our tribulation [trouble], that we may be able to comfort them who are in any trouble, by the comfort with which we ourselves are comforted of God."

Look at verse 5, "For as the sufferings of Christ abound in us, so our consolation also aboundeth by Christ." Verse 6, "And whether we be afflicted, it is for your consolation and salvation, which is effectual in the enduring of the same sufferings which we also suffer; or whether we be comforted, it is for your consolation and salvation."

Verse 8, "For we would not, brethren, have you ignorant of our trouble which came to us in Asia, that we were pressed out of measure, above strength, insomuch that we despaired even of life." Paul did not think he was going to make it.

He was not saying all of this to make them feel sorry for him. It was just gushing out of his heart. Second Corinthians 4:8, "We are troubled on every side, yet not distressed; we are perplexed, but not in despair." He did not know which way to turn. Verses 9 and 10, "Persecuted, but not forsaken; cast down, but not destroyed; Always bearing about in the body the dying of the Lord Jesus, that the life also of Jesus might be made manifest in our body." Verse 11, "For we who live are always delivered unto death for Jesus' sake, that the life also of Jesus might be made manifest in our mortal flesh."

You will not find anywhere in the writings of Paul a more comprehensive cataloging of the troubles, heartaches, and difficulties he experienced as you will find in this book. If you are going through a hard time, I would encourage you to read II Corinthians.

That is what is so wonderful about the Bible. No matter where you are in your own Christian experience, there is a word from God for you in that certain circumstance.

Look at what he says in II Corinthians 6:4-10, "But in all things approving ourselves as the ministers of God, in much patience, in afflictions, in necessities, in distresses, In stripes, in imprisonments, in tumults, in labors, in watchings, in fastings; By pureness, by knowledge, by longsuffering, by kindness, by the Holy Spirit, by love unfeigned, By the word of truth, by the power of God, by the armor of righteousness on the right hand and on the left, By honor and dishonor, by evil report and good report; as deceivers, and yet true; As unknown and yet well known; as dying, and, behold, we live; as chastened, and not killed; As sorrowful, yet always rejoicing; as poor, yet making many rich; as having nothing, and yet possessing all things."

Do you see what he was going through? Turn over to II Corinthians 11. Another long list of things Paul went through is in II Corinthians 11: 23-28, "Are they ministers of Christ? (I speak as a fool) I am more; in labors more abundant, in stripes above measure, in prisons more frequently, in deaths oft. Of the Jews five times received I forty stripes, save one. Thrice was I beaten with rods, once was I stoned, thrice I suffered shipwreck, a night and a day I have been in the deep; In journeyings often, in perils of waters, in perils of robbers, in perils by mine own countrymen, in perils by the heathen, in perils in the city, in perils in the wilderness, in perils in the sea, in perils among false brethren; in weariness and painfulness, in watchings often, in hunger and thirst, in fastings often, in cold and nakedness. Beside those things that are without, that which cometh up on me daily, the care of all the churches."

Look at II Corinthians 12:7-10, "And lest I should be exalted above measure through the abundance of the revelations, there was given to me a thorn in the flesh, the messenger of Satan to buffet me, lest I should be exalted above measure. For this thing I besought the Lord thrice, that it might depart from me. And he said unto me, My grace is sufficient for thee; for my strength is made perfect in weakness. Most gladly, therefore, will I rather glory in my infirmities, that the power of Christ may rest upon me. Therefore, I take pleasure in infirmities, in reproaches, in necessities, in persecutions, in distresses for Christ's sake; for when I am weak, then am I strong."

Most people think this infirmity was an eye problem and that Paul had an eye disease to the point that he would have eruptions of pus coming down his face. That is why some would say he was so contemptible looking. We do not know that for sure, but he did have some physical problem, and he said it came from Satan.

He asked God three times to have this problem removed, but God said to him that His grace was sufficient for Paul for God's strength is made perfect in weakness. God does heal people, but sometimes He does not heal people. Paul found out something that is wonderful in those times when God does not heal or deliver. Paul found out that God's grace will carry you through, and sometimes you will have more of God's power and strength in your life in those times of physical weakness than in any other time. This is a wonderful book of the Bible.

The key word in II Corinthians is *comfort.* Some form of the word *comfort* occurs in the verb form 18 times and the noun form 11 times. In spite of the personal attacks he was experiencing from people, in spite of all the physical problems he encountered, and in spite of every difficulty, Paul writes the greatest letter in the New Testament when it comes to the matter of comfort.

The word *comfort* means "encouragement." The verb is to encourage; the noun is encouragement. This is one of the greatest passages in the Bible on comfort.

Look at II Corinthians 1:3-6, "Blessed be God, even the Father of our Lord Jesus Christ, the Father of mercies, and the God of all comfort, Who comforteth us in all our tribulation, that we may be able to comfort them who are in any trouble, by the comfort with which we ourselves are comforted of God. For as the sufferings of Christ abound in us, so our consolation also aboundeth by Christ. And whether we be afflicted, it is for your consolation and salvation, which is effectual in the enduring of the same sufferings which we also suffer; or whether we be comforted, it is for your consolation and salvation."

Keep in mind he is saying this at the very beginning of a book where he is going to have to address his critics, those who were opposing him, and where he is going to have to talk about the physical problems he was enduring. But he begins a book that is going to deal with these problems by praising God for being the Father of mercies and the God of all encouragement. He says God comforts us in all our tribulation or troubles so that we may be able to comfort them who are in any trouble by the comfort or encouragement with which we ourselves are comforted of God. Did you follow the train of what he said? When we have troubles, we experience the comfort of God. God allows us to go through troubles so that when we have the comfort of God in our troubles and we encounter others who have problems or troubles, we can tell them about the same comfort from God we have experienced and can share it with them.

That is real Christianity; that is genuine, the true blue Christianity right there. It is not that you are not going to have any troubles or any problems; but when you do, there is a God in heaven who loves you and who will comfort you and help you in that time. Then that very experience becomes an opportunity for you to help others.

If you have had the experience of losing a loved one and God has comforted you in that, then when others lose a loved one, you can go to them and help comfort them. You can share the comfort of God with them.

Verses 5-6, "For as the sufferings of Christ abound in us, so our consolation also aboundeth by Christ. And whether we be afflicted, it is for your consolation" Whatever we go through we want to use that in order to help other people. When we are going through a time of trouble, we ought to ask the Lord first of all what are the lessons He has for us in this experience, and then how can we use this experience to be a blessing to someone else.

The secret to Paul's joyful victory in everything was the fact that there is a God in heaven who was involved in his life and was working in every situation in his life. Some of the greatest passages in the entire New Testament are right here in II Corinthians.

Look at II Corinthians 1:20, "For all the promises of God in him are yea, and in him Amen, unto the glory of God by us."

The following is one of the greatest passages about Christ in the Bible, II Corinthians 2:14-17: "Now thanks be unto God, who always causeth us to triumph in Christ, and maketh manifest the savor of his knowledge by us in every place. For we are unto God a sweet savor of Christ, in them that are saved, and in them that perish: To the one we are the savor of death unto death; and to the other, the savor of life unto life. And who is sufficient for these things? For we are not as many, who corrupt the word of God; but as of sincerity, but as of God, in the sight of God speak we in Christ."

The following passage is one of the greatest verses in the Bible about the importance of studying your Bible, II Corinthians 3:18: "But we all, with unveiled face beholding as in a mirror the glory of the Lord, are changed into the same image from glory to glory, even as by the Spirit of the Lord."

In the fifth chapter he talks about if our earthly house, this old body, is dissolved, we have a house of God, built eternal in the heavens. In II Corinthians 5:10, he writes we will all appear before the judgment seat of Christ.

Then you get into the suffering passages. Look at II Corinthians 6:9-10, "As unknown, and yet well known; as dying, and, behold, we live; as chastened, and not killed; as sorrowful, yet always rejoicing; as poor, yet making many rich; as having nothing, and yet possessing all things." What a picture this man had in Christ. It is the same picture you and I can have.

OUTLINE

I. Paul's Explanation of His Ministry, 1–5

- **A. Paul Defends His Motives**
- **B. Paul Defends His Message**

II. **Paul's Exhortation to the Church, 6–9**
   A. **Their Faithful Partnership in the Gospel**
   B. **Their Financial Partnership in the Gospel**

III. **Paul's Vindication of His Apostleship, 10–13**
   A. **His Personal Experience**
   B. **His Proven Apostleship**
   C. **His Possible Appeal**

I. Paul's Explanation of His Ministry, 1–5

There are three main divisions. The first one is Paul's Explanation of His Ministry, II Corinthians 1–5. You see Paul the minister in these verses. First Paul Defends His Motives, 1:1–2:17; and then Paul Defends His Message, 3:1–5:21.

II. Paul's Exhortation to the Church, 6–9

In the second division, Paul's Exhortation to the Church, chapters 6–9, Paul is the father. He is like a father exhorting them. He talks about their Faithful Partnership in the Gospel, chapters 6–7. Then he talks about their Financial Partnership in the Gospel, chapters 8–9.

III. Paul's Vindication of His Apostleship, Chapters 10–13

The last division is Paul's Vindication of His Apostleship, chapters 10–13. This is where the tone of the book changes a little because he seems to be dealing directly with this minority. He is now Paul the apostle. In chapter 10, he talks about His Personal Experience. Look at verse 1, "Now I Paul myself beseech you by the meekness and gentleness of Christ." Then he quotes what they had said about him, "who in presence am base among you, but being absent am bold toward you." That is what they were saying. When he was around them, he was not this way; but when he would be off and would write letters, he was really bold.

Then you see His Proven Apostleship, 11:1–12:13, and His Passionate Appeal, 12:14–13:14. Look at II Corinthians 12:14, "Behold, the third time I am ready to come to you; and I will not be burdensome to you; for I seek not yours but you." Paul said he was interested in them. He was coming and he wanted to have a ministry to them.

Study #29
Guidelines from Galatians

GUIDELINES FROM GALATIANS

Galatians ties to the book of Romans. It is the sketch for the finished picture, which is the book of Romans. In other words, in the book of Galatians you find in a smaller degree or a beginning degree the great doctrines of the faith which are expanded in Romans. If you are having trouble understanding the book of Romans, you might go back and read the book of Galatians because the basic doctrinal teaching of Romans is found in the book of Galatians.

Martin Luther, the founder of the Protestant Reformation, was especially partial to the book of Galatians. This was kind of his book. He said: "The epistle to the Galatians is my epistle, I have engaged myself to it, and it is my wife." What he was saying was he had given himself to the study of the book of Galatians. All of us would be wise to study the book of Galatians.

Notice how this book begins, Galatians 1:1-2: "Paul, an apostle, (not of men, neither by man, but by Jesus Christ, and God the Father, who raised him from the dead;) And all the brethren who are with me, unto the churches of Galatia."

There is a totally different feel about this book. Right at the very beginning Paul asserts and declares his apostleship. There is something wrong here; you can tell that there is an agitation of spirit. He is deeply moved and he feels the necessity to declare that he is an apostle; no man made him an apostle, but he was set aside as an apostle by the Lord Jesus Christ.

Paul is moved because he is dealing with a problem. It is the problem of the corruption of the gospel message. There were teachers who had come to the churches of Galatia, and they were polluting the gospel. They were tampering with the message of the gospel. It was a serious situation.

This is very serious business because when you do that, you are tampering with the message that tells people how to get to heaven. It is the most important message on the earth. This life is preparation for the next life. This life is infinitesimally small compared to the eternity which awaits us in the future.

This letter is an attempt on his part to avert a disaster, which he sees coming on the part of these Galatian churches. The Galatian believers had started the Christian life by faith, but now because of the teaching they were receiving from these teachers, they were tempted to try to continue the Christian life by their works. Paul wants to show them that the Christian life is not begun by works, neither is the Christian life continued and lived by works. He points out that we do not live the Christian life in the flesh; we do not live the Christian life on the basis of obeying a series of laws, but we live the Christian life in faith by the Holy Spirit.

Its Background

Galatians 1:2 starts out, "And all the brethren who are with me, unto the churches [plural] of Galatia." This letter was written to the churches in an area known as Galatia.

In ancient days France was known as Gaul. It was peopled by war-like tribes which migrated into what we call Asia Minor or today we would call it Turkey. These war-like tribes came from ancient Gaul or France into Turkey or Asia Minor, and they founded the country Galatia, which means "the country of the Gauls."

Originally Galatia was a country in the northern part of Asia Minor. Twenty-five years before the birth of Christ, the Roman Empire made that whole region, not just the northern part, Galatia. They made it the province of Galatia, so that has brought up what is known as the Galatian problem. This is not a problem to you or me, but we do need to get this background to have a full understanding.

When Paul writes and says to the churches of Galatia, the question is what Galatia is he talking about? Is he talking about the country Galatia up there in the north, or he is talking about the province or area of Galatia. It is the same as if I said I had written to some friends in New York. What would I mean? You may think I was writing to friends in New York City, but it may be I was talking about some friends in Buffalo, New York. We have a city New York, and we also have a state New York. That is the same as Galatia, and it is known as the Galatian problem. Was Paul writing to the north Galatian country, or was he writing to the entire province?

Personally, I believe he was writing to the entire region because we have no account of Paul going up into the northern part, to the country of Galatia, but we do have an account of Paul journeying through the southern portion of the province of Galatia. Note this scripture reference, Acts 13:1–14:28. There you have an account of one of the journeys of Paul, and he goes through that southern portion of the country. He hits the following cities: Iconium, Lystra, and Derbe. So, evidently, when Paul says I am writing this to the churches of Galatia, he is referring to Iconium, Lystra, and Derbe. That is what most people believe, and it is what I believe.

Iconium, Lystra, and Derbe were great population centers down in the southern portion of the province. They were located on great highways of commerce and trade at that particular time, and so they are probably the cities Paul is referring to.

Its Theme

After Paul had come and won these people to Christ and founded these churches, some other teachers had come in and were creating confusion. This is always the way it works. You will always have those who will come in after people have been won to Christ, and they will create confusion. One of the things they were saying was that Paul was not a real apostle. They said this Paul was a Johnny-come-lately; he was not one of the original apostles; therefore, he was not a genuine apostle.

The second way these teachers were causing confusion is they were saying that salvation by grace through faith is okay as far as it goes, but it is not enough. They were saying you just cannot be saved by grace through faith alone, but you had to have more than that. They proceeded to tell you what else you had to have. They said not only are you saved by grace through faith, but you also have to keep the law. They said you have to observe all the Jewish rituals and all of the ceremonies; you have basically got to become a Jew in order to become a Christian.

They were saying Paul was not preaching the right message. They said Paul was all mixed up in his message here, and we have come to straighten the Galatians out; we have come to give you the truth.

They were trying to entice the Gentile believers into the Jewish system. There is a name that has been attached to these teachers, although it is not a Bible name. They were known as the Judaizers.

Evidently, this is a group that started in Jerusalem. They become a thorn in Paul's side; everywhere he went, shortly after he had been there, the Judaizers came also. They would say Paul was all right, but he does not go far enough. They said he did not have the whole message.

We see these people in Acts 15:1, "And certain men which came down from Judea taught the brethren, and said, except ye be circumcised after the manner of Moses, ye cannot be saved." Now circumcision was the rite of initiation on the part of Jewish males into being a full-fledge member of the Jewish faith, so to speak.

Look at Acts 15:2, "When, therefore, Paul and Barnabas had no small dissension and disputation with them, they determined that Paul and Barnabas, and certain other of them, should go up to Jerusalem unto the apostles and elders about this question."

What you have in Acts 15 is what is known as the first Jerusalem council, and it was a very important council because they considered the question of how is a person saved. That is no minor question.

Verse 3 shares as they were on their way to Jerusalem to the council: "And being brought on their way by the church, they passed through Phoenicia and Samaria, declaring the conversion of the Gentiles; and they caused great joy into all the brethren." People were getting saved, but the Judaizers said they had not become Jews yet so they could not be saved.

They go up to Jerusalem and have their council meeting, and Simon Peter stands up and basically affirms what Paul had preached. He affirms that the Gentiles are saved by grace through faith and that Gentiles have to be saved that way and Jews have to be saved the same way. Therefore, look at what Peter says in

Acts 15:11, "But we believe that through the grace of the Lord Jesus Christ we [Jews] shall be saved, even as they [Gentiles].

Look at Acts 15:12, "Then all the multitude kept silence, and listened to Barnabas and Paul, declaring what miracles and wonders of God had wrought among the Gentiles by them."

Starting in verse 13, James speaks. Acts 15:13-14, "And after they had held their peace, James answered, saying, Men and brethren, hearken unto me: Simeon hath declared how God first did visit the nations, to take out of them a people for his name." He makes it very clear that Gentiles do not have to become Jews in order to be saved. Acts 15:22 says, "Then pleased it the apostles and elders, with the whole church, to send chosen men of their own company to Antioch with Paul and Barnabas, namely, Judas, surnamed Barsabas, and Silas, chief men among the brethren."

The Jerusalem council, however, did not solve the problem. As a result of this council, this minority group, this little group of teachers, began to go everywhere and muddle the gospel message. When you read the book of Galatians they pop up all through the book.

Paul addresses this issue with the Galatians in several verses in Galatians. Galatians 1:6-9. "I marvel that ye are so soon removed from him that called you into the grace of Christ unto another gospel, Which is not another; but there are some [the Judaizers] that trouble you, and would pervert the gospel of Christ. But though we, or an angel from heaven, preach any other gospel unto you than that which we have preached unto you, let him be accursed. As we said before, so say I now again, if any man preach any other gospel unto you than that ye have received, let him be accursed." The word *accursed* there is the word *anathema*, which means let him be devoted to destruction. That is what Paul was basically saying, and he says it in verses 8 and 9.

Look at Galatians 3:1, "O foolish Galatians, who hath bewitched you, that ye should not obey the truth, before whose eyes Jesus Christ hath been openly set forth, crucified among you?" What Paul was saying was he had preached the cross of Christ as the only way of salvation. Who has caused you now to be led astray?

Galatians 4:8-11, "Nevertheless then, when ye knew not God, ye did service unto them which by nature are no gods. But now, after ye have known God, or rather are known by God, how turn ye again to the weak and beggarly elements, unto which ye desire again to be in bondage? Ye observe days, months, and times, and years. I am afraid of you, lest I have bestowed upon you labor in vain."

Do you see what was happening to these Galatian believers? They were slipping back into legalism; they were slipping back into works in order to be saved. That is what these teachers had done to them.

Look at Galatians 5:7-9, "Ye did run well; who did hinder you that ye should not obey the truth? This persuasion cometh not of him that calleth you. A little leaven leaveneth the whole lump." What Paul is saying here is just a little false teaching messes up the whole thing.

Galatians 6:12-13, "As many as desire to make a fair show in the flesh, they constrain you to be circumcised; only lest they should suffer persecution for the cross of Christ. For neither they themselves who are circumcised keep the law, but desire to have you circumcised, that they may glory in your flesh." Paul is again talking about the Judaizers.

Judaizers are still around today; we deal with them every now and then. They teach that you have to be saved by Jesus plus something else. Baptism is one thing they say. Well, now you are saved by grace through faith in the Lord Jesus Christ, but you must also be baptized in order to be saved. They also say church membership is required or you must observe certain religious ceremonies or keep certain days or worship on a certain day like the Sabbath day.

By the way we do not observe the Sabbath as taught in the Scriptures. The Sabbath taught in scripture is the Jewish Sabbath. We worship on the first day of the week, the Lord's Day. Now you can call that the Christian Sabbath, that is fine; but the point is we do not believe you have to worship on a certain day and that it is a part of your salvation. Nor do we believe that you have to live a good life in order to be saved. It is not your good works or your good life that saves you or keeps you saved. Jesus saves you and Jesus keeps you saved. You are to do good works not in order to be saved but because you are saved.

Paul summarizes it well in Ephesians 2:8-10, "For by grace are ye saved through faith; and that not of yourselves, it is the gift of God: Not of works, lest any man should boast. For we are his workmanship, created in Christ Jesus unto good works, which God hath before ordained that we should walk in them."

OUTLINE

Introduction, 1:1-2

I. Personal Section: an Explanation, 1–2
- **A. Declaration of the Gospel**
- **B. Distortion of the Gospel**
- **C. Dynamic of the Gospel**
- **D. Defense of the Gospel**

II. Doctrinal Section: an Exposition, 3–4
- **A. Personal**
- **B. Scriptural**
- **C. Logical**
- **D, Dispensational**
- **E. Sentimental**
- **F. Allegorical**

III. Practical Section: an Exhortation, 5–6
- **A. The Law of Liberty in Christ**
- **B. The Law of Likeness to Christ**
- **C. The Law of Love for Christ**
- **D. The Law of Life in Christ**

Conclusion, 6:11-18

I. Introduction, 1:1-2

The first three verses, Galatians 1:1-3, are the Introduction. Paul sets for his apostleship, he addresses the letter to the Galatian churches, and he gives the grace and peace greeting that he normally does.

I. Personal Section: an Explanation, 1–2

A. Declaration of the Gospel, 1:3-5

There are three main divisions. The first division is what I call the Personal Section: an Explanation. Paul gives an explanation of the gospel. He declares the gospel in Galatians 1:3-5. He gives a clear-cut statement of the gospel. He talks about the Lord Jesus Christ who gave Himself for our sins. That is substitution. Jesus became our substitute that He might deliver us from this present evil world according to the will of God, our Father, to whom be glory forever and ever. There is nothing about keeping the law or religious observances. It is Christ who gave Himself for us, and He is the one who delivers us from this present evil world.

B. Distortion of the Gospel, 1:6-10

Paul jumps right into how the gospel is being distorted in Galatians 1:6-10. He marvels that they are so soon removed. Paul is worked up about this, and he should be. We are right at the very inception of the Christian faith, and if people are going to fall for the teaching that they have to earn their salvation, then the whole basic principle of the Christian faith is going to be destroyed at the very beginning. He marvels they are so soon removed. They are in the process of moving away from this. He clearly sets forth the gospel of the Lord Jesus.

C. Dynamic of the Gospel, 1:11-24

Then in Galatians 1:11-24, you have the Dynamic of the Gospel. What I mean by that is Paul shows how the gospel message came to him, how he was given this good news. Look at verse 11, "But I certify you, brethren, that the gospel which was preached of me is not after man." What he is saying is this good news is not something that I just have gotten from someone else. This is not something that was passed on to me from another human being.

Verse 12, "For I neither received it of man, neither was I taught it, but by the revelation of Jesus Christ." Paul says it was revealed to him by Jesus Christ. Then in verse 13, he begins to lay before them his own salvation experience. By the way, Paul never could get over that. Every chance he had, Paul was giving his testimony. We should never get over our testimony.

In verse 13 he states, "For ye have heard of my conversation." Conversation means way of life. He talked about how he persecuted the church, and in verse 14 he talks about where he was in the Jewish religion. Paul was steeped and deeply imbedded in the religious system. He basically is laying the background to say he came out of all that.

Verses 15-16. "But when it pleased God, who separated me from my mother's womb, and called me by his grace, To reveal his Son in me, that I might preach him among the heathen; immediately I conferred not with flesh and blood." We know what he did. He went out into the desert. One writer said Paul went out to the desert with Moses, the Prophets, and the Psalms in his mind, and he came back with Romans, Galatians, Ephesians, and Philippians in his heart. While he was there, God laid before him the truth of the Gospel.

Verse 18, he talks about the fact that he went up to Jerusalem to see Simon Peter and James. He refers to the meetings they had and how they confirmed that the gospel he was preaching was indeed the genuine gospel.

D. Defense of the Gospel, 2:1-21

Galatians 2 is entirely given to the Defense of the Gospel. He talks about how he defended this gospel. He specifically talks about the Jerusalem council and how he went up and conferred with the people. He communicated with them the message he had received and the message he was preaching.

I want to point out one thing in verse 3 because it will come up again when we look at the book of Titus. Verse 3, "But neither Titus, who was with me, being a Greek, was compelled to be circumcised." Titus was one of Paul's converts. He says he took Titus to Jerusalem and they did not compel him to be circumcised. His point was Titus came to Christ by grace through faith. He was not compelled to be circumcised. So he is defending the Gospel in this chapter.

In verse 11, he makes reference to a little encounter he had with Simon Peter in Antioch. This man Paul had courage. This was the great Simon Peter who preached the Pentecostal sermon and 3,000 people got saved. He was one of the original apostles of the Lord. Paul was in Antioch, and the Judaizers also had come to Antioch and were saying to the Gentiles they had to keep all the law and Old Testament rituals. Of course, one of the things they had in the Old Testament was certain dietary restrictions. One was you could not eat pork.

Simon Peter also comes to Antioch to minister to the Gentiles. This is just an imaginary tale of what might have happened, but it may have been one night they invited him over for supper and said they were going to have ham. Simon Peter came in and the Judaizers from Jerusalem came in also. When Peter saw the ham, he walked right over and sat with the Judaizers and would not eat the ham. Again, this is just an imaginary tale of what might have happened.

Let's read about it in verse 11 and following: "But when Peter was come to Antioch, I withstood him to the face, because he was to be blamed. For before that certain came from James, he did eat with the Gentiles: but when they were come, he withdrew and separated himself, fearing them which were of the circumcision. And the other Jews dissembled likewise with him; insomuch that Barnabas also was carried away with their dissimulation." In other words, he separated himself from the Gentile table.

So Paul, right in front of them stands up. Look at verse 14, "But when I saw that they walked not uprightly according to the truth of the gospel, I said unto Peter before them all, If thou, being a Jew, livest after the manner of Gentiles, and not as do the Jews, why compellest thou the Gentiles to live as do the Jews?" A paraphrase would be last night you ate ham with us; why aren't you eating it tonight? In other words, Simon Peter let himself be intimidated by these legalistic Judaizers who were trying to cause the Gentiles to conform to the Jewish law in order to live the Christian life.

They are still around today, and they are difficult to deal with. But you have to stand for the truth of the gospel. We are saved by grace, and we live by grace. We are saved by faith, and we live by faith.

Do you think I go to church to merit God's favor? Do you think I attend the services because I think it will make me a good Christian? That is not the point at all. I go because there is a desire in my heart to go. I go because I want to hear the Word and study the Word and fellowship with God's people. It does not make me better before God. That is not how the Christian life is lived.

The first two chapters are very personal, and Paul is very emotional about it. He is really worked up. There are some things Christians should get worked up about, and one of the things is the purity of the Gospel message.

II. Doctrinal Section, an Exposition, 3–4

The second division is the Doctrinal Section. He gives an Exposition of the whole theme of salvation by grace and not by works. This is a very intense, detailed section. Some points are difficult to understand. He is laying forth the great doctrine of salvation by faith. Look for three words in those two chapters: faith, law, and promise. If I counted correctly, the word *faith* occurs 14 times, the word *law* occurs 14 times, and the word *promise* occurs 11 times.

A. Personal, 3:1-5

Paul uses six arguments to prove that salvation is not by keeping the law. First, Galatians 3:1-5, he uses the Personal argument. In other words, what happened to them personally. He basically asks them how they were saved. Here is what he says in verse 2, "This only would I learn of you, Received ye the Spirit by the works of the law, or by the hearing of faith?" He asks if they were saved because they received the law or did they receive the Spirit, were they saved because of the hearing of faith?

Then he says in verse 3, "Are ye so foolish? having begun in the Spirit, are ye now made perfect by the flesh?" In other words, you started your spiritual life spiritually, but are you now made perfect by the flesh? He gives the personal argument.

B. Scriptural, 3:6-14

Then in chapter 3:6-14, he gives the Bible or Scriptural argument. This is where you find the similarities between Galatians and Romans in particular. He goes back into the Old Testament, and he uses Abraham. He points out that Abraham was not saved by keeping the law either. There are not two ways of salvation; there are not two gospels. There is not an Old Testament gospel and a New Testament gospel.

The same gospel applies to Old Testament believers as it does today. You might ask how that can be since Jesus had not even been born? Jesus had not died on the cross yet. Well, how are we saved? We are saved because by faith we look back to the cross. We look backwards. How were the Old Testament saints saved? They were saved by looking forward to the cross. That is what he is talking about in verse 6 and following, "Even as Abraham believed God, and it was accounted to him for righteousness."

God spoke to Abraham and said He was going to make his seed as numerous as the stars in the sky, and Abraham believed God. He did not have to earn it; he did not have to merit it. By faith he received the promise of God. So in verses 6-14 is the Scriptural argument and he uses Abraham as the great example.

C. Logical, 3:15-29

Then in Galatians 3:15-29 he uses the Logical argument. He appeals to our sense of logic. It is a little complicated section there, but as you study it and listen to it taught, you will understand it.

D. Dispensational, 4:1-11

The fourth chapter, Galatians 4:1-11, is the Dispensational argument. He talks about how in the Old Testament they were in the kindergarten stage so to speak. Now we are made children in the Lord.

E. Sentimental, 4:12-18

Galatians 4:12-18 is the Sentimental argument. Paul appeals to them now on the basis of his having led them to Christ and his personal sentiment. Look at verse 12 and following, "Brethren, I beseech you, be as I am; for I am as ye are; ye have not injured me at all. Ye know how through the infirmity of the flesh I preached the gospel unto you at the first." He reminds them of how they first received him and how he preached.

F. Allegorical, 4:19-31

Galatians 4:19-31 is the Allegorical argument. He gives us an allegory in this section. You have to be careful with the use of allegory in the Bible. Allegory is taking some account in the Old Testament and teaching spiritual lessons from that story. For instance, I do that sometimes when I teach Genesis 24 where Abraham sent his servant out to find a bride for his son Isaac. That is a historical story, but I use it as an allegory of God the Father sending the Holy Spirit to find a bride for His Son, the Lord Jesus Christ.

You have to be careful because you can go overboard with allegory, but there is allegory found in the Bible. Paul uses an allegory here. He talks about the two sons of Abraham. Abraham had two boys. One of those sons was born of his handmaiden, and his name was Ishmael. Hagar was the handmaiden, and Ishmael was the boy that born. But another son was born of his wife Sarah, and his name was Isaac. He shows that Ishmael represents those who try to live the Christian life by the deeds of the flesh. Isaac represents those who come to God by faith. It is really interesting.

III. Practical Section: an Exhortation, 5–6

The third division is the Practical section. He gives us an Exhortation, and he gets very practical. Here he talks about our relationship with Christ and how we live the Christian life not on the basis of keeping rules and obeying laws, but the Christian life is lived by a personal, intimate relationship with Jesus Christ.

A. The Law of Liberty in Christ, 5:1-15

Galatians 5:1-15, he talks about the Law of Liberty in Christ. Look at verse 1, "Stand fast therefore in the liberty wherewith Christ has made us free, and be not entangled again with the yoke of bondage." What he is saying is you are free in Jesus. You do not have to be tied to all the Old Testament ritual and requirements. You are now a brand-new person in Christ. You live not in order to please God, but because you know the Lord you are now free to live in liberty.

B. The Law of Likeness to Christ, 5:16-26

Galatians 5:16-26, he talks about the Law of Likeness to Christ. Look at verse 16, "This I say then, Walk in the Spirit, and ye shall not fulfill the lust of the flesh." He goes right on down, and in verse 19 he gives a contrast between the works of the flesh and in verse 22 the fruit of the Spirit.

C. The Law of Love for Christ, 6:1-6

In Galatians 6:1-6, he talks about the Law of Love for Christ. He talks about restoring people who have been overtaken in a fault. He shows how a beautiful expression of love is seen when believers restore other believers who have wandered away or have been overcome in some sin in their life. Bear one another burdens.

D. The Law of Life in Christ, 6:7-10

Then in Galatians 6:7-10, he talks about the Law of Life in Christ. He talks about the laws of sowing and reaping.

Conclusion, 6:11-18

Then he closes out his letter, his Conclusion, in verses 11-18. I would really encourage you to read and study this book. It will help you understand the book of Romans.

Study #30
Exploring Ephesians

EXPLORING EPHESIANS

Its City

The city of Ephesus was one of the great cities of Asia Minor. It was a large metropolitan city. It was a center of world trade with a large and busy harbor. It was the key city of the entire area of Asia Minor during this time period.

Ephesus was the center of the worship of the goddess Diana, and the temple of Diana was one of the Seven Wonders of the ancient world. The apostle Paul stayed about three years in Ephesus according to Acts 20:31, and from there the gospel was spread throughout Asia Minor.

I had the opportunity of going to Ephesus, and they have done extensive excavations. There are churches throughout America named after these New Testament churches, also like Corinth. I have known several Ephesus Baptist Churches, and there is an Ephesus Baptist Church in my home county in Georgia. If you are not careful, you will read into the New Testament your surroundings today and get the idea that these were little tiny towns. But it was not that way. These churches in the New Testament were in large cities. When you tour the excavations of ancient Ephesus, you become aware of what large cities these were. For instance, they have reconstructed some of the library of Ephesus. It was a library that had 20,000 volumes.

My point is, do not think these cities were little tiny country communities. These were large cities, and it was part of Paul's strategy to go into these cities because he knew what took place in the city would be like ripples in the water extending out to the area all around.

Its Church

Paul did not establish all the churches of the New Testament. He did not establish the church at Rome, but evidently Paul did establish the church of Ephesus. We have evidence of that in the book of Acts.

Acts 18–19 gives the background of how the church came into existence in the city of Ephesus.

In Acts 18 Paul is on his second missionary journey. It was on this journey Paul also had his ministry in Corinth. In verse 19 it tells us Paul came to Ephesus and left Priscilla and Aquila, the couple he had worked with, in Ephesus. Paul went to the synagogue and reasoned with the Jews and stayed evidently for a brief period because he was on his way back to Jerusalem. So it was just a brief visit then in Ephesus. Paul said to them in Acts 18:21, "but I will return again unto you, if God will. And he sailed from Ephesus." He goes on back to Caesarea and Antioch and on down.

In that interval, a man named Apollos came. He was the great orator preacher, the R. G. Lee of his time. That may not mean anything to younger people, but R. G. Lee was the great orator from Bellevue Baptist Church in Memphis years ago. Apollos was the young brilliant orator. He was mighty in the Scriptures. Apollos comes to Ephesus with an imperfect knowledge of the Scriptures, and Priscilla and Aquila, this godly couple, explain to him more fully the truths of the gospel.

In Acts 19, Paul is starting out on his third missionary journey. In Acts 19:1, when Paul arrives in Ephesus and finds certain disciples, he becomes aware of the fact that there was a deficiency in them. He talks to them about the Holy Spirit.

In Acts 19:8, "And he went into the synagogue, and spoke boldly for the space of three months, disputing and persuading the things concerning the kingdom of God." In verse 10, it tells us, "And this continued for the space of two years; so that all they who dwelt in Asia heard the word of the Lord Jesus, both Jews and Greeks." In other words, Paul's ministry in Ephesus reached to the entire region around. All Asia heard the word of the Lord.

Now, the question is how did that happen? How was it that the whole area around there heard Paul preaching in Ephesus? It was not because he got on television or printed a lot of gospel tracts. We find the answer in Acts 20. He is returning again to Jerusalem and goes down to a little place called Miletus, which is near to Ephesus, down the coast from Ephesus. In verse 16 he has decided to go by Ephesus on his way back to Jerusalem, so in verse 17, from Miletus, he sends up to Ephesus and calls the elders or the preachers of the church. The elders come down for a little reunion, so to speak, with Paul; and Paul rehearses his ministry. He goes over what he has done there.

Look at Acts 20:18-20, "And when they were come to him, he said unto them, Ye know, from the first day that I came into Asia, after what manner I have been with you at all seasons, Serving the Lord with all humility of mind, and with many tears, and trials, which befell me by the lying in wait of the Jews; And how I kept back nothing that was profitable unto you, but have shown you, and have taught you publicly, and from house to house."

Notice Paul's strategy. It was to get the gospel from house to house. The gospel was spread by word of mouth. They did not have radio or TV or computer; it was spread by lifestyle witnessing.

Going back to Acts 19, we have the account of the riot that broke out because the people were coming to Christ in Ephesus. When people come to Christ, they come away from idols; they come away from false gods.

There were some silversmiths in Ephesus who got all wrought up. Their businesses were being hurt because people were getting saved. If you really want to get to folks, touch their money. If you dry up the devil's business, that will get to them real quick.

Demetrius, the silversmith, and his craftsmen stirred up folks and they all went to the theater. In the theater they start shouting "Great is Diana of the Ephesians," verse 28. They did it for two whole hours. I have been to that theater. They have dug it out, and you can actually walk in now and see it.

Paul wanted to go into the theater, but his disciples urged him not to do it. So from there in Acts 20, Paul moves on from Ephesus.

I have given you a little of this background so you would understand how the work began in Ephesus. Although there is no biblical record, the strong tradition is that John the disciple of our Lord took the mother of Jesus, Mary, and went to Ephesus where he became the pastor of the church. Remember on the cross Jesus said, "Woman, behold, thy son" and then said to John, "Behold, thy mother"?

They think John lived to be about 100 years of age. He lived to be a very old man. If that be true, here is a church with a remarkable beginning. It has the apostle Paul as its founder, so to speak. Paul writes a letter to the church of Ephesus, and John the beloved disciple was their pastor at one time. In addition to all that, we have another letter sent to the church of Ephesus. The second one was written by our Lord Jesus Christ in the book of Revelation. It is not a pleasant letter; it is a sad letter because Jesus says to the church you have left your first love. This warns us. Here is a church that was started by Paul, had John the beloved apostle as pastor, and yet when the Savior writes them a letter, He says, "I have somewhat against thee, you have left your first love." This says we need to be constantly kindling the fires of love and devotion to the Lord Jesus Christ.

Its Letter

Evidently, Paul wrote this letter about 10 years after he visited Ephesus and had his ministry there. The date is somewhere around A.D. 62. At the time Paul wrote this letter he was a prisoner. Look in the book of Ephesians, and I will show you two statements Paul makes.

Ephesians 3:1, "For this cause I, Paul, the prisoner of Jesus Christ for you Gentiles." He was a prisoner. Then the second reference is in Ephesians 4:1, "I therefore, the prisoner of the Lord." At that time he was a prisoner in Rome.

Paul was writing from a Roman cell. That is why there are certain letters of Paul that are known as the prison epistles or letters. They are Colossians, Ephesians, Philippians, and then the little one page book, Philemon. They were written by Paul when he was in prison, the prison books.

With the exclusion of Hebrews, there are 13 letters in the New Testament authored by Paul. The letters fall into three categories: letters before prison, letters from prison, and letters after prison.

There are six letters Paul wrote before he was in prison: I Thessalonians, II Thessalonians, Galatians, I Corinthians, II Corinthians, and Romans.

The four letters he wrote from prison are Colossians, Ephesians, Philippians, and Philemon. These are the letters written after he was in prison: I Timothy, II Timothy, and Titus, although in II Timothy, he was back in prison again. Technically, Paul was back in prison when writing II Timothy, but it was a different time of imprisonment. Evidently the first time Paul was in prison he was released, and the second time he was in prison, he was not released.

The book of Ephesians is known as the Church Epistle, the church letter. I have said there are others that are church letters, but Ephesians is *the* church letter.

Note "The Church Universal" and "The Church Local." In the New Testament you will find the two-fold emphasis about the church. Who is in the church universal? All born again Christians, all saved people, are in the church universal. The Church Universal is the church invisible. That is, you cannot attend one of the services of the Church Universal. That church does not have local meetings. The Church Universal is the body of Christ, and it will meet when the Lord comes in the air and we are caught up to meet Him in the air.

But also the New Testament teaches about the Church Local. That is the church visible. The Church Local is the church Paul writes these letters to. There was a church in Ephesus, there was a church in Rome, local congregations of believers.

When people were saved in these places, they were baptized and became a part of the fellowship of the church local, wherever that church might be. If you are a born again saved person, a member of a church, you are a member of the church universal, the church invisible; but you are also a member of the church local, the church visible.

The reason the letter to the Ephesians is called *the* Church Epistle is because Paul sets forth in this letter the Church Universal. In fact, there is very little reference to the Church Local. There are some who say there is no reference to the Church Local. You do not have any information about what was going on in the local church of Ephesus.

In the letters to the church in Corinth, he talks about their problems and mentions names. He closes out the book of Romans with a list of names, and Paul says to greet the different ones. But you do not find this in the book of Ephesians. Why not? Because Paul is setting forth in this Ephesian letter the teaching of the Church Universal. That is why it is *the* Church Epistle.

You are a part of the Church Universal, but you should also be a part of the Church Local. When I was starting out as a pastor and was in my second church, there was a man who lived up on Barn Goldmine Hill (there used to be an old goldmine there). He was not a member of a local church. Anytime anybody would talk to him, he would say I am a member of the Church Universal. He said he did not belong to a Church Local, that was all of the devil. I went over to see him one time. I invited him to church, and he said he would not come, it was of the devil. He said he belonged to the Church Universal. I asked him then when they had the Lord's Supper? He looked at me like I was crazy and said they did not have it. I told him in the New Testament, the church observed the Lord's Supper.

The Church Universal never observes the Lord's Supper. The Church Universal never has a baptismal service. The Church Universal has never sent a missionary. So, you see, the Church Universal is to manifest itself in the Church Local, in a local congregation of believers. Always make that distinction in your mind.

Paul gives three beautiful pictures of the church in the letter to the Ephesians. The first picture is in Ephesians 1. Almost without exception, every reference to the church in Ephesians is to the Church Universal.

Ephesians 1:22-23, "And [God] hath put all things under his feet [that is Christ], and gave him [Christ] to be the head over all things to the church, which is his body, the fullness of him that filleth all in all." That is the first picture of the Church Universal. It is the body. The church is the body of Christ. Jesus was here the first time in a physical body; now the Lord Jesus Christ does His work in His spiritual body, the Church Universal.

Look at Ephesians 2:19-22. "Now, therefore, ye are no more strangers and sojourners, but fellow citizens with the saints, and of the household of God; And are built upon the foundation of the apostles and prophets, Jesus Christ himself being the chief corner stone, in whom all the building fitly framed together groweth unto an holy temple in the Lord; in whom ye also are built together for an habitation of God through the Spirit."

There are no more apostles or prophets in the world today. They did the foundational work, they laid the foundation. You do not build a foundation again. He is saying they are a part of the building. The foundation was laid by the apostles and prophets, and Jesus is the chief cornerstone. The church here is compared to a building.

As a body the church points us to the Lord Jesus Christ as the head. As a building the church appoints us and speaks to us concerning Jesus Christ the foundation. The church has to be founded on the Lord Jesus Christ.

The third beautiful picture is in Ephesians 5:25-27: "Husbands, love your wives, even as Christ also loved the church, and gave himself for it, that he might sanctify and cleanse it with the washing of water by the word; That he might present it to himself a glorious church, not having spot, or wrinkle, or any such thing; but that it should be holy and without blemish." He is comparing the church here to a bride; the church is the bride of Christ. So when you hear people talking about Jesus is coming for the bride, that means Jesus is coming for the church.

These pictures are pictures of the Church Universal. The church invisible is like a body, it is like a building, and it is like a bride.

OUTLINE

I. Doctrine: Our Riches in Christ, 1–3
- **A. Our Possessions in Christ**
- **B. Our Position in Christ**

II. Duty: Our Responsibilities in Christ, 4–6
- **A. Walk in Unity**
- **B. Walk in Purity**
- **C. Walk in Love**
- **D. Walk in Light**
- **E. Walk Carefully**
- **F. Walk in Harmony**
- **G. Walk in Victory**

I. Doctrine: Our Riches in Christ, 1–3

There are basically two main divisions in the outline. The first division is what I call Doctrine. Paul customarily in his books began with doctrine. He talks about what we believe, and then he moves into the practical area of our behavior as believers, how we are to conduct ourselves on the basis of what we believe. The first three chapters of Ephesians fall into the division of Doctrine, Our Riches in Christ. Here is the key word for those chapters: blessings. The key verse is Ephesians 1:3, "Blessed be the God and Father of our Lord Jesus Christ, who hath blessed us with all spiritual blessings in heavenly places in Christ." In my King James Version Bible, in the little phrase "heavenly places in Christ," the word *places* is in italics. It means it was added by the translators. The King James is a translation, and this word was added by the translators. It is not especially helpful at this point because the word *heavenly* is plural. Literally what he is saying is God has blessed us with all spiritual blessings in the heavenlies in Christ. That is what it literally says, "in the heavenlies in Christ." That is another key phrase in the book of Ephesians. It occurs several times. It is not always translated the same way; it would have been helpful if they had translated it the same way.

For instance, look at Ephesians 1:20, "Which he wrought in Christ, when he raised him [Christ] from the dead, and set him [Christ] at his own right hand in the heavenly places [heavenlies]." Christ is in the heavenlies. When Jesus rose again from the dead, He ascended back to the right hand of the Father, and He sat down at the right hand of the Father in the heavenlies.

He says in Ephesians 1:3 that God has blessed us with all spiritual blessings in the heavenlies. Our blessings are up there in the heavens.

Ephesians 2:6, "And hath raised us up together, and made us sit together in heavenly places [heavenlies] in Christ Jesus." Do you get the picture? Christ is in the heavenlies, our blessings are in the heavenlies, and now he says we are in the heavenlies. We are sitting right in the middle of Fort Knox in Glory. We are in the heavenlies.

Ephesians 3:10, "To the intent that now unto the principalities and powers in heavenly places [heavenlies] might be known by the church the manifold wisdom of God." He is saying the principalities and powers, talking about the good angels, can behold the manifold wisdom of God in the church. Do you know how the angels learn about the wisdom of God and the salvation of a soul? They see it in the church. Angels, talking about the good angels, have never been saved because they have never been lost. There are some things they can only learn when they see what God does in the lives of believers and in the church. We are a university for the angels. God teaches the angels about the wonder of His salvation in the saints.

Look at Ephesians 6,:12, "For we wrestle not against flesh and blood, but against principalities, against powers, against the rulers of the darkness of this world, against spiritual wickedness in high places [heavenlies]." He is not talking about the good angels now but about the bad angels. He says not only are our blessings in the heavenlies but our battles are also in the heavenlies. The real battle in the universe is behind-the-scenes. The real battle is going on in the heavenlies, and you and I as believers have the opportunity through prayer, the Word of God, and faithfulness to Christ to be involved in the battle.

A. Our Possessions in Christ, 1

Chapter 1:1-14 is Our Possessions in Christ. He says in verse 3 God has blessed us. Then he goes down and shows how God has blessed us. He shows the work of God the Father, what the Father has done. When he gets done with what the Father has done, in verse 6 he says, "To the praise of the glory of his grace, wherein he hath made us accepted in the beloved." The reason we are in the heavenlies is because God has accepted us in the person of His Son, the Lord Jesus. We are seated with Jesus. That is the work of the Father and includes predestination and being founded before the foundation of the world.

In Ephesians 1:7, he talks about the work that Jesus has done for us. He talks about redemption through His blood, the forgiveness of sin, and the riches of His grace. He comes to the climax in verse 12, and he says it again, "That we should be to the praise of his glory, who first trusted in Christ." Our possession is made possible by the work of Jesus.

In verses 13-14, he turns to the work of the Holy Spirit and talks about the fact that we are sealed by the Holy Spirit. The Holy Spirit is our earnest, our down payment, and he closes out verse 14, "unto the praise of his glory." That is our possession in Christ, what we have in Christ. We are forgiven, we are predestinated, and we are sealed.

In verse 15 he gives us a prayer. Some of the greatest prayers of the Bible are the prayers of the apostle Paul. You have two beautiful prayers of Paul in Ephesians. One is right here, verses 15-23. It is a beautiful prayer, and it is a prayer for enlightenment. Look at verse 18, "The eyes of your understanding being enlightened." How do you know that is a prayer? Look at verse 16, "[I] Cease not to give thanks for you, making mention of you in my prayers." Then he tells you what he was praying, and it was a prayer for enlightenment.

B. Our Position in Christ, 2–3

Next is Our Position in Christ," chapter 2. He points out the fact that just as Christ died, was buried, rose again, and is seated at the right hand of the Father, we who were dead in sins have been resurrected by God. We have a spiritual resurrection and we are seated in the heavenlies with Christ. It is the great amazing grace chapter. Ephesians 2 is a great chapter. It talks about how we were dead in sin, but God in His mercy has raised us up together. You have that beautiful passage on grace, Ephesians 2:8-10. In verse 8, note the word *by*, by grace. Note the word *through* in verse 8, through faith. Then drop down to verse 10 and note the word *unto.* Unto good works. I have drawn some lines from those three words to one another. I have drawn a line from *by* to *through* to *unto*. If you will see that sequence right there, you will understand how works fit into the Christian life. We are not saved by works. We are saved by grace through faith unto good works.

The third chapter is another prayer and he goes into detail. Ephesians 3:1, "For this cause I Paul." He is getting ready to pray, but then the Holy Spirit moves him in another direction. In verse 2 and on down he starts talking abut the mystery of the church. In the third chapter he points out that the church until the New Testament day was a mystery hidden in the heart of God. That is why in the Old Testament you do not see a lot about the church except in picture form. He says the mystery of the church was revealed to him, Paul. So he started off to pray but then goes on a little detour talking about the mystery of the church. Then in verse 14 he comes back to it, "For this cause I bow my knees unto the Father of our Lord Jesus Christ." Look at verse 1, "For this cause," and verses 14 and 15 and following, "For this cause I bow my knees unto the Father of our Lord Jesus Christ, Of whom the whole family in heaven and earth is named, That he would grant you, according to the riches of his glory, to be strengthened with might by his Spirit in the inner man." And he continues with the prayer. It is a prayer for enablement, that you might be enabled. Verse 16, "That he would grant you, according to the riches of his glory, to be strengthened with might by his Spirit in the inner man." He was praying for enablement.

II. Duty: Our Responsibilities in Christ, 4–6

The second division or section is Duty, Our Responsibilities in Christ. When you understand your riches, then you must move to an understanding of your responsibilities. The key word in the first section is *blessings*. The key word in the second section is *walk*. You will find in chapters 4 through 6 the word *walk* sprinkled along the way. For instance, Ephesians 4:1, "I therefore the prisoner of the Lord, beseech you that ye walk worthy of the vocation wherewith ye are called." The word *walk* has the idea of lifestyle, the way you live your life. I have broken it down for you in several divisions.

A. Walk in Unity, 4:1-16

Walk in unity, Ephesians 4:1-16.

B. Walk in Purity, 4:17-32

Walk in Purity, Ephesians 4:17-32. Look at verse 17, "henceforth walk not as other Gentiles walk in the vanity of their mind." He is saying do not live your life as lost people live their life. Walk in purity; let your life be different.

C. Walk in Love, 5:1-6

Walk in Love. Look at verse 2, "And walk in love as Christ also hath loved us." Live in love. Live your life in a life of love. Live on the basis of the love principle.

D. Walk in Light, 5:7-14

Then Ephesians 5:7-14, Walk in Light. Look at verse 8, "But ye were sometimes darkness, but now are ye light in the Lord: walk as children of light." Do not walk in the darkness as a Christian, but walk in the light. Jesus is the light. Walk in the light.

E. Walk Carefully, 5:15-17

The next one is Walk Carefully. Verse 15, "See then that ye walk circumspectly, not as fools, but as wise." Do you know what *circumspectly* means? It means when you take a step, look all around you like there was a rattlesnake somewhere. He is saying that is how we ought to live our lives. We should be very careful how we live. There are rattlesnakes out there. There are pot holes out there. Walk circumspectly. Look all the way around you as you walk.

F. Walk in Harmony, 5:18–6:9

Walk in Harmony. He talks about husbands and wives, children, and servants.

G. Walk in Victory, 6:10-24

Walk in Victory. It is the section on spiritual warfare, and it tells us how we win this battle that has its location in the heavenlies. It talks about putting on the whole armour of God, the sword of the Spirit, the Word of God, and prayer.

Study #31
Probing Philippians

PROBING PHILIPPIANS

When you read the heading that many Bibles include, "The Epistle of Paul the Apostle to the Philippians," this has to do with letters inspired by the Holy Spirit and written by Paul to individual believers at these various locations. The letter to the Philippians was addressed to the believers, the saints of God, who were in Philippi.

Philippians is a book that you never tire of reading. I have been studying and reading this book for a long time. It is a brief book, just four chapters. Let me encourage you to read a chapter a day. Look at the verses and just draw out all the blessing you can. It will help your week be a happier, more cheerful week.

Its City

First of all, we want to talk about the city because these letters were sent to Christians at various locations around the Roman Empire. It helps to look at the city and know a little bit about it. The city of Philippi was located in Macedonia. It was named after King Philip and was noted for a number of things. Philippi was noted for the gold in the region and for being a rich farming area.

One of the most important pieces of information, however, about the city of Philippi is to know that it was a colony of Rome. There is a whole historical background behind that statement. In the Roman Empire, from time to time, the Roman government would establish a colony in an area or a city would be known as a colony. They would send to that city retired Roman soldiers and Roman officials. They would then try to reproduce the life of Rome in that particular city. They wanted to have a "Rome" in miniature or a "little Rome." They used the language of the Roman Empire, they observed the laws of the Roman Empire, and they sought to dress like the Romans did.

This background is important because of the statement Paul made in Philippians 3:20, "For our conversation is in heaven . . ." The word *conversation* in the King James Bible is not a helpful reading for us today because when we think in terms of conversation, we think primarily only in terms of speech; but the Greek word used there is where we get our word "colony." He is saying our colony or literally our citizenship is in heaven. People who were members of a colony city of Rome retained their Roman citizenship; and so though they lived in Philippi, they were considered to be citizens of Rome. They were entitled to all of the rights and all of the privileges, and they also had the same responsibilities that people who lived in Rome had.

It is a beautiful picture Paul presents for us with that historical background. Paul is saying our colony or our citizenship is in heaven. He is saying as born again believers, though we live down here in this world, we are actually citizens of heaven. We really belong to heaven. It is where we are going; it is where we are headed. He is saying a church and born-again believers in every way should try to emulate the life of heaven on earth. A church should seek to be a colony of heaven. As individual Christians we should live as heavenly citizens who are strangers and pilgrims just passing through this world.

That is the background. Philippi was a colony, and Paul was writing to Christians who were a colony of heaven.

One of the most personally fulfilling and exciting things I have done is to go on the Journeys of Paul trip. It really helped me fill in the pieces of my New Testament. One of the places, and maybe my favorite place of all the places, I visited was the city of Philippi. There is no city there now as in the days of Paul, but you can see the ruins and the marketplace. They have excavated Philippi and have restored certain pillars and other things. One of the most exciting places to see was down by the riverside. That was where a woman named Lydia was saved. They were having a prayer meeting, and Paul preached the gospel. She was saved and baptized right there in that river. We were able to have a little prayer service by that river and see the river flowing by. It was exciting for me to think I was right there at the location where Paul was when these wonderful events took place in his missionary journey that brought him through Philippi. Then we went from there up to a side of a mountain or hillside overlooking the city of Philippi to find the ruins of the old Roman jail where Paul was. It was really one of the highlights of my Christian life.

Its Church

The second thing I want you to notice in terms of background is the church because Paul founded the church in Philippi. In Acts 16 we have the historical background of how Paul came to the city of Philippi and how the church was established there. In the opening verses of Acts 16 Paul was beginning his second missionary journey. He was trying to determine the leadership of the Holy Spirit and tried to go in several different directions. Notice what it says in Acts 16:6, "Now when they had gone throughout Phrygia and the region of Galatia [probably south Galatia], and were forbidden by the Holy Spirit to preach the word in Asia." For some reason it was not the plan of the Holy Spirit that they stop there. The Holy Spirit had another place for them to be. Verse 7 says, "After they were come to Mysia, they assayed to go into Bithynia [that is to go north]; but the Spirit suffered [or permitted] them not." For some reason the Holy Spirit would not let them go north. The Holy Spirit was leading Paul and his party to move in another direction.

We have wondered how the Holy Spirit did this. How did Paul sense the Holy Spirit was forbidding, or how did he sense that the Holy Spirit was not allowing him to go in certain directions? Maybe it took place like it does with us sometimes. Sometimes the Holy Spirit guides us through the clear teachings of His Word, or at other times the Holy Spirit guides us through the circumstances which surround our life. It is a lot easier for us to look back on a situation and say this is what the Holy Spirit was leading us to do than it is to look forward and know what the Holy Spirit wants us to do. Dr. Luke, as he writes the book of Acts, looks back on the situation and he sees the hand of God in these movements; he sees the leading of the Holy Spirit in these movements.

It says in Acts 16:8, "And they passing by Mysia came down to Troas." This is the jumping off place in Asia Minor. That is as far as they could go. Keep in mind they were constantly moving westward. Then in verse 9, it says, "And a vision appeared to Paul in the night; There stood a man of Macedonia, and prayed him, saying, Come over into Macedonia, and help us." Verse 10, "And after he had seen the vision, immediately we endeavored to go into Macedonia, assuredly gathering that the Lord had called us to preach the gospel unto them." To give you a King Jerry paraphrase, Paul said, "Boys, pack up your bags; we are heading even further west." They asked where they were going, and he said they were going to Macedonia. Maybe he shared with them the vision of the man from Macedonia. He told them this was God's leading, this was what God wanted them to do. They had to set sail. Then they came into Samothracia and then Neapolis, verse 11; and then in verse 12, "And from there to Philippi, which is the chief city of that part of Macedonia, and a colony; and we were in that city abiding certain days."

In verses 13 and following you have the accounts of the conversions of three people. There were three remarkable conversions that took place in Philippi. The first one, as I have already alluded to, was Lydia. Lydia was a career woman and a seller of purple. She was in the business world. In verse 13, it says that on the Sabbath, on the Jewish Sabbath, Paul and his party went out to the city by the riverside where prayer was accustomed to be made, and Paul and his companions "sat down, and spake unto the women which resorted there."

This tells us several other things about Philippi. It tells us there probably was a small Jewish population in Philippi. According to the rules which I have come to understand, there had to be at least ten Jewish men in any location to have a synagogue. If they did not have that many, then they were reduced to having a little prayer meeting somewhere. Evidently, there was not a large Jewish population there, but there were a few individuals and they were gathered together having a riverside prayer meeting. It is a beautiful story to read. As Paul opened up the Word and preached it, the Lord opened up the heart of Lydia and she had a glorious conversion. She and her household were baptized right there in that river. Lydia was the first convert.

Notice back in verse 9 that Paul had a vision, and it was of a man who asked him to come over into Macedonia. When Paul got over there, his first convert was a woman. God was breaking down barriers in the life of Paul. The Lord has a way of doing that, of arranging the circumstances of our lives to remove barriers. Paul was a Pharisee. I am told that strict Pharisees would pray first thing every morning. They would thank God for three things, and two of those things were that they were not a woman and they were not a Gentile.

Notice what happened. The first thing Paul saw was a woman, and she was converted. God was teaching Paul that the gospel is for everyone. It does not matter who you are, where you come from, or what your background is, the gospel of the Lord Jesus Christ is for everyone.

The story of the second convert starts in verse 16. It was the young lady who was demon possessed. Finally Paul got to the man I believe he saw in the vision because he was placed in jail as a result of the conversion of this young slave girl. He was placed in the Philippian jail, and the jailer must have treated him pretty tough because he put him down in the inner part of the prison. He was put in stocks. You can imagine what a situation that was. Yet, the Bible says at the midnight hour Paul and Silas prayed and sang songs (Acts 16:25). I like to say the Lord was enjoying their singing and got so happy He started patting His foot to the music and caused an earthquake and just shook that place. It shook so much that the doors of the prison were opened and the chains that had bound them were broken loose, yet the keeper of the prison had gone to sleep. He had already beaten Paul and Silas black and blue; yet he was so hard and calloused, he was sleeping. He could go home, eat a meal, and forget all about it. But God got a hold of the situation. The jailer rushed in and asked what he needed to do to be saved, and he was saved. He was the third notable conversion.

I have taken time to go into the background of the church because these conversions are evidently the nucleus of the church in Philippi. These are the people who formed the original congregation in Philippi. It seems to have been one of Paul's favorite churches. It is unlike the church of Corinth, for instance. Paul also founded the church at Corinth, but Paul had some real problems with the

Corinthian church. As we saw in our I and II Corinthian studies, he had to write them and at times had to be pretty blunt with them. But there was evidently a deep love between Paul and these people in Philippi.

Sin is not mentioned in the book of Philippians. There is only one glitch in the book: Philippians 4:2-3, "I beseech Euodias, and beseech Syntyche, that they be of the same mind in the Lord. And I entreat thee also, true yoke fellow, help those women which labored with me in the gospel, with Clement also, and with other my fellow workers, whose names are in the book of life." There were two ladies in the congregation who were having a little spat. He beseeched them to be in the same mind in the Lord. That means they were of different minds. Whoever the true yokefellow was, whether the pastor or someone else, Paul asked him to help these ladies. That is the only "fly in the ointment" in this entire book of Philippians.

After Paul started this church in Philippi, he moved on to Thessalonica. When he was in Thessalonica, the Philippian believers sent him some support, a gift. We have a reference to this in Philippians 4:15 and a parallel verse in II Corinthians 11:9. On his return trip, as he concluded this second journey, we have another record of his going by Philippi in Acts 20:1-6.

Its Letter

By the time Paul wrote this particular letter, he was in prison. The Philippians heard of his arrest and sent aid to him. They sent this assistance by a man named Epaphroditus. He is found in Philippians 2:25. Epaphroditus became ill, and in verses 25-30, it talks about his illness. He got well and the Lord spared his life, so Paul evidently sent this letter back to them from this man Epaphroditus.

Its Purpose

There are several purposes in Paul's writing this book. Number one, Paul was writing to explain to them his circumstances at this particular time. Number two, he wrote to explain the ministry of this man Epaphroditus.

Number three, he wrote to thank them for their generous support. That is something we need to learn to do. We need to express our appreciation. Sometimes we just take things for granted. But Paul was never that way. When people sent him gifts, he always responded with appreciation. Another thing you will notice about Paul is at the end of a lot of his letters, he had a list of names of Christians, and he expressed his appreciation to them personally and individually. It is wonderful to express thanks to people for the gifts they give to you, but it is also wonderful to express appreciation for the people themselves.

The fourth thing Paul did was to encourage the Philippians in their Christian life. What a wonderful blessing it is to be an encourager of others. What a blessing it is to have people around you who are encouraging.

Its Theme

What is the theme of the book of Philippians? One of the best ways to find out what a letter or a book of the New Testament is about is to look for repetitions of words. If you see words that are repeated and that occur frequently in a book, it gives you a clue about the theme of the book. The same thing is true about a chapter. If you see a word repeated over and over again in a chapter, it gives you an idea of what that chapter is about. The best example I can think about is I Corinthians 13. You start reading I Corinthians 13, and there is a word that keeps coming up–love. It starts with love, continues with love, and closes the chapter with love. You get the idea he is talking about love before it is over.

When you begin to read through the book of Philippians, there is a word that you cannot miss. It is so prominent. It is the word *joy*. Some form of the word *joy* is used approximately 18 times in this little four-chapter book. In other words, the word *joy* or the word *rejoice,* or some form of this word, is used approximately 18 times in this book. You have to keep in mind the background here. Paul was in a Roman prison. He was writing in the midst of very difficult circumstances. Also, keep in mind that these people knew that Paul had the joy of the Lord in his heart because of what happened in that very Philippian jail. As we saw earlier, at midnight Paul and Silas were praying and singing praises to the Lord. Here was Paul, in prison, writing a letter, and the key note of the letter was joy. It is the joy book.

Warren Wiersbe a number of years ago pointed out something else about Philippians that has blessed and helped me. He pointed out there is another key to Philippians. Joy is pretty easy to see, but he pointed out that some form of the word *mind* or words that refer to the mind are found many times. For instance, the words *remember* and *think* are found. Philippians 1:3, "I thank my God upon every *remembrance* of you." Look at verse 7, "Even as it is meet for me to *think* this of you all, because I have you in my *heart*. . . " Look at Philippians 2:5, "Let this *mind* be in you, which was also in Christ Jesus."

When you take those two keys, joy and the mind, and put them together, what you have is the thrust of the book if Philippians. The whole theme is how a Christian can have a joyful mind.

I have referred to this book as God's book of Christian psychology. The whole point of the book is right thinking leads to right living and right living leads to joy. That is the theme all the way through.

Dr. Wiersbe also points out there are four thieves that rob Christians of our joy. The first thief is Circumstances. Most of the time we either have joy or do not have joy on the basis of what our Circumstances are. For instance, if the car is working right and the air conditioning is running in the hot summer months, you have joy. But if the air conditioner in your car breaks down and your motor starts skipping, you lose your joy. Circumstances rob you of your joy.

The second thief which will rob you of your joy is People. People can bring you joy, or people can cause you to lose your joy. Normally the way that works is if people do what we want them to do, we have joy. If they do not do what we want them to do, we lose our joy.

The third thief is Things. Sometimes things can bring us joy, and sometimes the absence of things can cause us to lose our joy.

The fourth thief is really the combination of the others. It is the thief of Worry. Worry is wrong thinking about circumstances, people, and things. When we worry we think incorrectly about circumstances, people, or things.

OUTLINE

I. The Single Mind, 1
 A. The Fellowship of the Gospel
 B. The Furtherance of the Gospel
 C. The Faith of the Gospel
II. The Submissive Mind, 2
 A. Christ
 B. Paul
 C. Timothy
 D. Epaphroditus
III. The Spiritual Mind, 3
 A. Past: Accountant, "I count"
 B. Present: Athlete, "I press,"
 C. Future, Alien, "I look"
IV. The Secure Mind, 4
 A. God's Presence
 B. God's Peace
 C. God's Power
 D. God's Provision

There are basically four main divisions to the outline. This is not original with me. I have said all along I am not trying to be original. What I am trying to do is get the best information I can into your hands to help you understand and dig into these books of the Bible.

I. The Single Mind, 1

These four chapters gives us the Christian answer to one of these thieves that rob us of our joy. For instance, in chapter 1, Paul is discussing his circumstances. The first division is The Single Mind, chapter 1. How do you get victory over circumstances? The answer is you have a single mind. Your mind is focused on one item. It is focused on Jesus and His gospel.

In chapter 1, Christ is mentioned 18 times if I counted correctly. The gospel is mentioned six times. It is just a constant refrain–Jesus and the gospel. Paul's mind is focused on one thing, and that is the good news about Jesus. His whole purpose in the midst of his circumstances is to use his circumstances as an opportunity to advance Jesus and His gospel. Do you see what that will do for you on a daily basis? Whatever your circumstances may be, look at them as opportunities to advance Jesus and His gospel.

There are three phrases to note about the gospel. Verse 5 is the Fellowship of the Gospel (verses 1-11); verse 12 is the Furtherance of the Gospel (verses 12-26); and verse 27, the Faith of the Gospel (verses 27-30).

Look at verse 12, "But I would ye should understand, brethren, that the things which *happened* unto me have fallen out rather unto the furtherance of the gospel." Paul would never have written what is here. Paul did not write that way. The King James says, ". . . the things which happened. . ." Do you see the word *happened*? In the King James Version, "which happened" are in italics. That means they were added by the translators to make the sentence smoother. Here is an instance when translators added words to make the sentence smoother, and they added something that is contrary to what Paul would have said. Paul would never say things just *happen* to Christians. Things do not just happen to Christians. There is a sovereign God who is in control, and Christians are under the direct guidance of the Lord.

God knows what is going on in your life. You are not a victim of happenstance. You are a beneficiary of providence. But Paul basically said in verse 12 that he wanted the Philippians to know that his circumstances, the fact he was in prison, happened for the furtherance of the gospel. Look at verse 13, "So that my bonds [his chains] in Christ are manifest in all the palace [that is, Caesar's palace] and in all other places."

Paul was joyful because even though he was in prison the gospel had a chance to be furthered. Look at chapter 4:22, "All the saints salute you, chiefly they that are of Caesar's household." Paul was guarded by Roman soldiers. Those Roman soldiers would have shifts of so many hours each. Paul was chained to these soldiers and was also writing these letters. He was winning the soldiers to Christ, and they were returning to the Praetorian Guard as saved men. What Paul was saying was when he was in prison, he was then in contact with some people he could not have won to Christ any other way. It is the same way with your circumstances. God will use your circumstances to put you in situations where you may be able to witness to people you never would have had the opportunity before. That is the victory over circumstances, the Single Mind. How can I use this circumstance to advance Jesus and His gospel?

II. The Submissive Mind, 2

Look at the second division, chapter 2, the Submissive Mind. This chapter deals with the matter of people. How can you keep your joy in dealing with people? Paul sets forth what Dr. Wiersbe calls the Submissive Mind. If you are interested in being served by people, then you are going to lose your joy according to whether or not they serve you according to your desires. But if you adopt the attitude of the servant, the Submissive Mind, then it basically does not matter what people do, you are just a servant. He gives four great examples. The greatest example of the servant mind, the Submissive Mind, is the Lord Jesus Himself, Philippians 2:1-11. "Let this mind be in you, which was also in Christ Jesus," verse 5. By the way, this is one of the four great passages in the New Testament on the deity of Jesus Christ. It is one of the greatest passages in the entire Bible. Though Jesus existed in eternal glory, He was willing to lay aside that outward insignia of His glory to become like a servant and to give Himself on the cross.

The second example is Paul himself, Philippians 2:12-18. He talks about his own service to people. The third example is Timothy, verses 19-24. The fourth example is Epaphroditus, verses 25-30. He gives four examples of the Submissive Mind, and that is how you keep your joy even in dealing with people.

III. The Spiritual Mind, 3

The third division is chapter 3, the Spiritual Mind. It takes care of the thief of things. Things can rob us of our joy unless we look at things with a spiritual mind. This chapter is a remarkable chapter. There are some beautiful pictures here. In verses 1-11, Paul pictured himself as an Accountant. There is a little statement in the first 11 verses which will help you. He says in verse 8, "I count . . ." which means he looked at all the past things as a spiritual accountant. He looked at things from a spiritual mind.

Then in verses 12-16, he pictured himself as an Athlete. The key there is in verse 14, "I press." It is a picture of a runner running a race, pressing towards the finish line. He said in present things, forget the things behind and reach to the things that are before.

The third picture is in verses 17-21. He talked about the Future, and the Christian here is like an Alien, like someone who does not belong here. That is why he said in verse 19 that there are those who mind earthly things, but in verse 20, our citizenship is in heaven. What he was saying is look at everything on this earth from heaven's point of view. Remember, you are a citizen of heaven. Look at everything from heaven's vantage point. One hundred years from now every one of us will be in heaven if we are saved. You will be somewhere in eternity. Ask yourself every day how is this going to look 100 years from now. Is it going to be a big deal? Look at things from a heavenly point of view.

IV. The Secure Mind, Chapter 4

The fourth division is Philippians 4. Paul shows us the solution to worry is the Secure Mind. Your mind is secure and you can maintain your joy when you look to God's Presence, verses 1-5. He was talking about the presence of God. Look at the last part of verse 5, "The Lord is at hand." That could be referring to the second coming, but he may be saying the Lord is right here with us. I wonder how Euodias and Syntyche responded to that? They were having a little spat, and Paul said Jesus was right here. That would change a lot of our behavior and words if we would remember that Jesus is with us. He is with us wherever we are. God's Presence will keep your mind secure.

Then verses 6-9, God's Peace. It is a wonderful passage about the peace of God that keeps you. Notice that passage starts with the peace of God in verse 7 and it ends up with the God of peace in verse 9. It is wonderful to have the peace of God, but it is even better to have the God of peace.

He talks about God's Power in verses 10-13. We can have a secure mind because we have the power of God. We can claim the power of God. That is what he means in verse 13 when he says, "I can do all things through Christ who strengthens me." The word *strengthens* means "puts power down on the inside." He did not say he could do all things, period. That is not the way it reads. He said he could do all things through Christ who puts power down inside of him.

The fourth thing that will bring us a Secure Mind is in verses 14-23, God's Provision. He says basically God will provide. Look at verse 19, one of the great verses of the Bible. "But my God shall supply all your need according to His riches in glory by Christ Jesus." Isn't that a great promise?

Read chapter 1 one day on how to have a joyful Single Mind in the midst of circumstances; the next day read chapter 2, how to have a Submissive Mind in dealing with people. Then on day three, read chapter 3, how to have a Spiritual Mind, dealing with the things and the stuff of life. On the fourth day, read chapter 4, how to have a Secure Mind, and have the peace of God in your life on a daily basis. If you will do that, it will make for a happier week.

Study #32
Considering Colossians

CONSIDERING COLOSSIANS

We are in the section or the division called the Instructional books of the New Testament, and these are primarily letters penned by Paul. The majority of the Instructional books are what we call letters to churches, church letters that the Holy Spirit inspired the apostle Paul to write. Many of these letters were written by Paul to churches he had founded. But in this particular instance, as we are going to see, it is evidently a different story.

Notice Colossians 1:1-2, "Paul, an apostle of Jesus Christ by the will of God, and Timothy, our brother, To the saints and faithful brethren in Christ who are at Colosse: grace be unto you, and peace, from God, our Father, and the Lord Jesus Christ."

Its City

Let's talk about the city of Colosse. This city was in a tri-cities area. It was one of three cities that were close together: Colosse, a city called Hierapolis, and then the third one was Laodicea. Laodicea is one of the famous cities in our Bible because when the Lord Jesus sent the letters to the seven churches in Revelation, the last letter was to the church of Laodicea.

Colossians 4 makes a reference to Laodicea. Colossians 4:15-16, "Salute the brethren who are in Laodicea, and Nymphas [a believer], and the church which is in his house. And when this epistle is read among you [the Colossians], cause that it be read also in the church of the Laodiceans, and that ye also read the epistle from Laodicea." Paul is saying that after the Colossians had read his letter, he wanted them to send it to the church at Laodicea.

Then he says that they likewise are to read the epistle from Laodicea. We do not know what that epistle or letter is; we do not have any record, so there is not much need for us to speculate.

Colosse was about 125 miles southeast of Ephesus. It was a center for philosophers. It was also a center for oriental mysticism, paganism, and Judaism. You had a lot of "isms" around Colosse. They were "isms" that should have become "wasims."

Its Church

Evidently, Paul was not the founder of the church at Colosse, and we have no record that he was ever there. There are some verses that lead us to believe this. In Colossians 1:4, he is giving an introduction like he normally does, and you pick up some clues. "Since we heard of your faith in Christ Jesus, and of the love which ye have to all the saints." Notice that he says we heard about it. In other words, this is something Paul heard. He evidently had no first-hand information.

Colossians 1:9, "For this cause we also, since the day we heard it, do not cease to pray for you, and to desire that ye might be filled with the knowledge of his will in all wisdom and spiritual understanding." He is going on the basis of reports that had been made.

Colossians 2:1 is even more conclusive that Paul had not been involved in the founding of the church directly and had not been there. "For I would that ye knew what great conflict [agony] I have for you, and for them at Laodicea, and for as many as have not seen my face in the flesh." The indication is pretty clear that Paul had never been to Colosse.

Another thing that leads us to believe this is because we find no record of a ministry of Paul in Colosse in the book of Acts. We do find him in other places like Philippi in Acts 16. It tells us about the church and people who were converted there, but we do not have anything in the book of Acts that would indicate Paul was there.

The question arises then, how was it that a church came into existence in Colosse? There are two ideas here that can give us some thought on how a church was started there. One may have been the indirect influence of Paul.

Acts 19:10 tells about Paul when he was in Asia Minor, the area of Ephesus which is just 125 miles from Colosse. "And this continued for the space of two years; so that all they who dwelt in Asia heard the word of the Lord Jesus, both Jews and Greeks." The indirect influence of Paul may have been what brought it about.

Notice Colossians 1:7-8, "As ye also learned of Epaphras, our dear fellow servant, who is for you a faithful minister of Christ, Who also declared unto us your love in the spirit." Focus in on this man Epaphras. Paul says he is a faithful minister of Christ for the Colossians. He is the one who had been giving Paul these reports.

Look at this other reference, Colossians 4:12-13, "Epaphras, who is one of you, a servant of Christ, salutes you [he is evidently with Paul at this time], always laboring fervently for you in prayers, that ye may stand perfect and complete in all the will of God. For I bear him witness that he hath a great zeal for you, and them that are in Laodicea, and them in Hierapolis."

Putting these things together, evidently, he and Paul are friends. Epaphras is on a visit to see Paul, and it is altogether possible that this man, Epaphras, is the one that founded the church and is their pastor.

Another thing we also know is that Philemon is probably there. Look at Colossians 4:9, "With Onesimus, a faithful and beloved brother, who is one of you." If Onesimus was one of them at Colosse, that means Philemon also was one of them. We do have evidence for that in the book of Philemon. The church was evidently started by this man Epaphras.

Its Crisis

What is going on with the Colossians? If you can get the background and know what is going on behind-the-scenes, then you will understand why Paul writes what he does.

In Galatians, right up front Paul said he was an apostle, and that man did not make him an apostle but Jesus made him an apostle. The background of that is there were people who were challenging his apostleship. If you know this background information, it enhances your understanding of the letter.

What is the crisis here? What is the problem? Paul is writing to combat error. There is error that has been brought to the church at Colosse, and he is writing to address this error.

All doctrinal error today has its roots in the New Testament day. There is really nothing new. All these new heresies you run into today are really old heresies that are just brought up-to-date and dressed in contemporary clothing. If you study the New Age movement today, all the mysticism, and all of the cults, you will trace all of it all the way back to the beginning years of the New Testament church. Those errors were beginning to crop up then, and that is certainly true in what you find in Colosse.

There was a new teaching that was causing problems. We do not know if there was just one man who was causing this or not, or if Paul is just using this terminology in a broader term. Notice some statements he makes. Colossians 2:4. "And this I say, lest any man should beguile you with enticing words." Do you see the statement, "lest any man"? Look at Colossians 2:8, "Beware lest any man spoil you through philosophy and vain deceit, after the tradition of men, after the rudiments of the world, and not after Christ." See "lest any man" again?

Colossians 2:16, "Let no man, therefore, judge you in food, or in drink, or in respect of a feast day, or of new moon, or of a Sabbath day." Look at verse 18, "Let no man beguile you of your reward in a voluntary humility and worshiping of angels, intruding into those things which he hath not seen, vainly puffed up by his freshly mind." Again, "let no man."

I do not know if Paul was using that in general terminology to include any man or if there was a specific man. I tend to believe that he was using it in rather general terms because, normally, when Paul had a specific man in mind he did not hesitate to call him by name. Paul had never taken a Carnegie course on how to win friends and influence people to get him what he wanted.

I have a feeling that Paul is talking about teachers in general. It may have been more than one teacher who had come in, so he uses this terminology as a wider term that would include more than one person.

We do know there were two primary sources of the doctrinal crisis occurring in the church of Colosse. The first one was Gnosticism. You need to know about

Gnosticism. There is a Greek word for knowledge called *ginosko*. Take out the "I" and you get *gnosko*. Do see where we are headed? So, the word *Gnosticism* means "to know." If you put an "a" in front of a Greek word, it means just the opposite. If *Gnostic"* means "to know," then *Agnostic* means "not to know."

For instance, take the word *atheist*. The only difference between the word *theist,* someone who believes in God and someone who does not believe in God, is that "a." Instead of *theist,* I believe in God, an *atheist* means I do not believe in God, I do not believe there is a God. A theist is someone who believes there is a God. An atheist says he does not believe there is a God. An agnostic says I do not know if there is a God or not.

We have a lot more agnostic people than we have atheists. It is real hard to be an atheist today. But we do have some agnostics along the way. They just say they do not know.

In the New Testament day, a Gnostic was someone who said I know, I am in the know, and I have some special knowledge. So Gnosticism was a belief which claimed superior knowledge in spiritual things. They claimed they had some knowledge that nobody else had, and you had to get in on their system or you did not get it. In other words, you had to get initiated into their system or you could not know what they knew.

Let me give you a background for this. It is important to understand Colossians. It is also important for you to know where we are today. You will see this cropping up everywhere. The basic root idea of Gnosticism is all matter is evil. All physical things are evil.

Here is how they worked that out. They said all matter is evil; therefore, God could not have created the world. If God had created the world, that means He had created evil. So they developed what they called *emanations*. God was way up there, and below was a series of emanations coming down from God: a little less god and a little less god, and one of those emanations down the ladder created the world.

Another thing that developed from that was they said Jesus had a body; therefore, He could not have been God because God could not have contact with a human body. That went several different directions. They said Jesus had a human body, but it was not a real body, it just appeared to be a body. They said when He stepped, it did not leave a foot print. It just looked like He had a body.

They also said He was the Son of God until He got to the cross, and then the Son of God part of Him was withdrawn, and He died as a mere man on the cross. This was an attack on the deity of Jesus. It is still around today.

It then went into personal behavior and took two opposite directions. The Gnostics were two kinds when it came to personal behavior. They were opposite behaviors: license or legalism.

What I mean by license is if the body is evil, what difference does it make? Just do anything you want to do in your body. That was one extreme. Just live any way you want to live. Anything goes.

You will hear that philosophy today. People will say God made us this way, this is the way we are, and we are just doing what comes naturally. Nothing is necessarily right or wrong, just do what you want to do. Have you heard that today? Some go to the extreme of saying since matter is evil, it doesn't matter. You have a body; just do what you want to do because it is evil anyhow.

The opposite of that extreme is if the body is evil, then you just restrict the body. Put a bunch of rules around the body, and you make life miserable for the body. It drove them into asceticism. Asceticism is the total denial of any of the pleasures of the body. You were not supposed to have any fun at all. If you had any fun, it was evil. You were supposed to keep the body subdued, keep the body under control. That was their legalism.

My friend Warren Wiersbe has said many times "blessed are the balanced." The tendency is to go the extremes.

Gnosticism, basically, just watered the Christian faith down to another philosophy. It was a weak, powerless, and watered-down philosophy. That is the background of what you will read, especially in Colossians 2.

The other thing you will run into though is what I call pharisaical Judaism. There was a strong Jewish element in Colosse. These people taught that the Christian life was to be just a series of rituals and observances. They said for you to be the kind of Christian you ought to be, you had to be a good Jew too. They said you have to observe all the laws and customs of the Jews. That is why they made a big deal of festival days, the Sabbath day. It comes all the way down to today. People get all hung up on these rituals and special ceremonies. That is why Paul says in Colossians 2:16, "Let no man therefore judge you in meal, or in drink, or in respect of an holy day, or of the new moon, or of the Sabbath days."

Much of this has been revived by the cults today. When any group claims that you have to have anything more than Jesus, immediately put up your warning signals. Always be on the watch. Any time someone says it is great to be saved, but you need another step, you need another experience, always watch it. When anybody tries to tell you that you need anything more than Jesus Christ, you are on the borderline of heresy. Some people do not intend to do that, but that is where you are headed.

Its Theme

The best way to combat error is to have a good presentation, a good strong dose of the truth. In Colossians, before Paul addresses these different errors, he sets forth the pre-eminence of Jesus Christ. That is in the first chapter. Colossians 1:15-18 are some of the greatest verses in the Bible on who Jesus is and the absolute sufficiency and the absolute deity of the Lord Jesus Christ.

There are four great passages in the New Testament that set forth the deity of Jesus. If you want to see who Jesus is in terms of His being the Son of God and God in human flesh, look at John 1, Philippians 2:5-11, Colossians 1:15-20, and Hebrews 1. Those are the four great passages that teach the deity of the Lord Jesus Christ, that Jesus Christ is God.

Where do we get the word *preeminence*? Look at Colossians 1:18. "And he is the head of the body, the church; who is the beginning, the first-born from the dead, that in all things he might have the preeminence." The last part says "that in all things he [Christ] might have the pre-eminence." The word *pre-eminence* means "first." In all things he might be first, number 1. Jesus must be first. That is a simple way of saying preeminence.

Paul takes the vocabulary of the Gnostics and uses it against them in Colossians. They had certain words that they were really high on. For instance, the word *all.* This word is used more than 30 times in Colossians. The other words are *fullness, fill, complete,* and *mystery*. Look for the repetition of these words.

The Gnostics, the false teachers, claimed a superior knowledge; and the word *mystery* was used by them to describe a level of knowledge that people could have if they would go through their particular rites and ceremonies. They could be initiated into the mysteries.

Paul picks up that word *mystery* and puts new meaning in it. Paul used their vocabulary but not their dictionary. He took their words but put different meanings to them. When you read the Bible, you have to remove from your mind what you think about when we use certain words today. When we use the word *mystery* today, what do we think about? We think of mystery novels and Sherlock Holmes, Alfred Hitchcock, or John Gresham.

When you read *mystery* in the New Testament, you are talking about a truth. In the New Testament, a mystery is truth, which we could never know unless God revealed it to us. They said you could not find truth except by going through all their ceremonies and rituals and secret deals. Paul said no, mystery is truth that God has revealed.

OUTLINE

Introduction, 1:1-14

I. Doctrine: the Preeminent Supremacy of Christ, 1
- **Creation**
- **Church**
- **Christian Life**

II. Danger: the Proposed Substitutes for Christ, 2
- **Intellectualism**
- **Ritualism**
- **Spiritualism**
- **Legalism**

III. Duty: the Practical Sufficiency of Christ, 3–4
- **Spiritual Life**
- **Social Life**
- **Soulwinning Life**

Conclusion, 4:7-18

Introduction, 1:1-14

The first fourteen verses are what we call Introduction (Colossians1:1-14). That is the hello and the prayer. Then he begins the first of three divisions.

I. Doctrine: the Preeminent Supremacy of Christ, 1

The first division is Doctrine, the Preeminent Supremacy of Christ. In other words, he shows Christ. He presents the truth of Christ. The best way to combat error is a strong presentation of the truth. He shows how Christ is preeminent in Creation (Colossians 1:15-17); He is preeminent in the Church (Colossians 1:18-24). He is the head of the body, the Church. He is preeminent in the Christ Life (Colossians 1:25-29).

II. Danger: the Proposed Substitutes for Christ, 2

The second division is Danger. This is the warning section of Colossians. This is the Proposed Substitutes for Christ, Colossians 2. I have organized them around four "isms." The first one is Intellectualism, Colossians 2:1-10. That is why he says in verse 8, "Beware let any man spoil you through philosophy and vain deceit." Someone has said philosophy is the attempt of a blind man at midnight in a pitch-black dark room to find a black cat that is not there. He is saying do not let people spoil you through intellectualism, trying to approach God by intellect. Some think you can be smart enough to reach God on your own.

The second one is Ritualism, Colossians 2:11-17, and he zeroes in on the ritual of circumcision. To bring this up-to-date, for the word *circumcision* substitute the word *baptism*. Paul says regarding the whole idea that you can make your way to God by a series of rituals, "Which [all these Old Testament rituals] are a shadow of things to come; but the body [or the substance, the reality] is Christ" (verse 17). Do you see the difference? He is saying get out of the shadows and get into the sunshine. Get your reality in Christ.

The third thing is Spiritualism, Colossians 2:18-19. He talks about worshiping angels, the New Age movement. The fourth "ism" is Legalism, 2:20-23. Some do not fall for the first three "isms," but they fall for Legalism. They try to live the Christian life on the basis of a series of rules and regulations, a bunch of dos and don'ts. You are a good Christian if you do this and do this. You are a good Christian if you do not do this and do not do this. There are certain things a Christian should not do, but the whole key is motivation. Why don't you do certain things? Is it to be pleasing to God and for God to say what a wonderful Christian you are, or is it something that stems out of your relationship to the Lord and your love for the Lord? Why is it you don't drink? You do not drink in order to earn points with God, but you do not drink because your body is the temple of the Holy Spirit and you do not want to defile it. You want to be totally committed to the Lord. That changes the whole perspective. You are not abstaining in order to win approval with God; but because you have been approved with God in the Lord Jesus Christ, you abstain from certain things. It is how you go about it.

III. Duty: the Practical Sufficiency of Christ, 3–4

The third main division is Duty. Paul does here what he always does. After having dealt with the heavy issues of doctrine, then he turns right around to duty. In this section he discusses The Practical Sufficiency of Christ, Colossians 3 and 4. He comes right down to practical life. There are three main divisions there. The Spiritual Life, Colossians 3:1-14. He discusses putting off the old man and putting on the new man, putting off the old things of the old unregenerate life and putting on the new things of the new life.

Then, Colossians 3:15–4:1, he talks about the Social Life. He talks here about the family and husband/wife relationships. It is a very similar passage to Ephesians, but there are a few little interesting differences. He talks about the husband/wife relationship, the parent/child relationship, and the servant/master relationship. In Colossians 4:2-6, he talks about the Soulwinning Life or the Witnessing Life.

Conclusion, 4:7-18

He closes it out with the Conclusion in Colossians 4:7-18. He has greetings and personal words for some people.

Study #33
Thrills in 1 Thessalonians and Truths in 2 Thessalonians

THRILLS IN I THESSALONIANS

In I and II Thessalonians we have two of the most helpful books in the Bible for Christians. They are probably as current in terms of what you and I are encountering today as any of the books of the Bible. We are going to look at the city, the church, and the purpose for these two letters by the apostle Paul.

Its City

The city of Thessalonica was one of the largest cities in the New Testament world. It was a very important city in Macedonia, which was really part of the nation of Greece. When I was over there in the 1990s, they did not differentiate between Greece and Macedonia because in some ways they are together and in other ways they are different. If you would think of Athens, Greece, you would go north to find Thessalonica. The original name of this city was Therma. If you think of thermometer or thermostat, it may help you to connect with its name. Thessalonica was named for hot springs that were nearby.

In 315 B.C. it was renamed Thessalonica after the half sister of Alexander the Great. It was a free city and a city of great commerce. It was said that it was located in the lap of the Roman Empire. One of the great things the Romans did was to build a system of roads all over the empire, and one of the most famous of those roads, probably the greatest of them all, was the great Egnatian Way. This highway went right through the city of Thessalonica.

In the New Testament day, Thessalonica had a population of approximately 200,000 people. It is one of the few cities of the New Testament time that continues to thrive. Most of the New Testament cities today are only ruins. You will see where the cities used to be, but Thessalonica is still sitting today. In fact, it is larger. It now has a population of over 300,000 people. It used to be called Salonica, but it is now called Thessaloniki.

Paul had a strategy, as you remember, of going to the strategic cities. He went where the people were and planted the gospel and won people to faith in the Lord Jesus Christ.

Its Church

We do have some background about the church in the book of Acts. Keep in mind that in the book of Acts you get the historical background for many of these churches and the founding of these churches.

You have in the beginning of Acts 17 a kind of the road map that Paul followed that brought him to Thessalonica. In Acts 16 is the account of his miraculous, phenomenal ministry in the city of Philippi. It included the jailer's conversion and other events. Thessalonica was about 100 miles from Philippi.

Acts 17:1 says, "Now when they had passed through Amphipolis and Apollonia [other cities along the way], they came to Thessalonica, where was a synagogue of the Jews. Then we are told about Paul's ministry here. It appears that Paul was in Thessalonica less than a month. We believe this because of verse 2, "And Paul, as his manner was, went in unto them, and three Sabbath days reasoned with them out of the scriptures." Who does that remind you of when it says that about Paul? That is what we also are told about the Lord Jesus.

Paul went to the synagogue, and it says he reasons for three Sabbath days out of the Scriptures. His whole point in verse 3 was proving by the Old Testament Scriptures that Jesus was the predicted Messiah, the Savior of the world.

Verse 4, "And some of them believed, and consorted [they joined] with Paul and Silas; and of the devout Greeks a great multitude, and of the chief women not a few." What that says is Paul had some converts, some people came to know Christ as their Savior. And then a group of Jews were moved with jealousy and incited a riot. You will read about that in verse 5 and following.

Another interesting statement is made here. In verse 6 it says, "These that have turned the world upside down are come here also." That is quite a testimony to what was going on and to the ministry that they had. "These that have turned the world upside down." Of course, you and I know they did not turn the world upside down. The devil had already done that. They were just turning the world right side up. This world has its whole system of values so tipsy-turvy that when people come to Christ and get their lives straightened out, others think they are nuts. That is quite an accolade though for the work of Paul.

Paul had to leave very quickly, and Acts 17:10 says, "And the brethren immediately sent away Paul and Silas by night unto Berea, who, coming there, went into the synagogue of the Jews." Berea was another city nearby.

I have always liked verse 11, "These were more noble than those in Thessalonica, in that they received the word with all readiness of mind, and searched the scriptures daily, whether those things were so." It is a great example for us.

Evidently, Paul was at this city of Thessalonica less than a month. The only thing we have record of is that for three Sabbath days he reasoned in the synagogue about Christ, and some people were saved. Yet, when you read the letters Paul wrote to the believers of Thessalonica, you have evidence of a thriving and growing church. It is one of the miracle stories in the Bible.

Paul goes on to Berea; from there he continues to Athens where he leaves Timothy and Silas. Paul sends Timothy back to inquire of the young church in Thessalonica. We know that because of I Thessalonians 3:1-2: "Wherefore, when we could no longer forbear, we thought it good to be left at Athens alone; And sent Timothy, our brother, and minister of God, and our fellowlabourer in the gospel of Christ, to establish you, and to comfort you concerning your faith." So he sends Timothy back to assist them and help them in their faith.

Timothy returns; I Thessalonians 3:6-7, "But now when Timothy came from you unto us [when he came back], and brought us good tidings of your faith and love, and that ye have good remembrance of us always, desiring greatly to see us, as we also to see you, Therefore, brethren, we were comforted over you in all our affliction and distress by your faith." Do you see the report? Things were going well. The church was growing quite well, and he was happy about this report.

This is the setting, and this is what caused Paul to write this letter to these believers. He sent Timothy to check on them; he gets a good report. Now he sits down and as the Holy Spirit leads him, he writes them this beautiful letter.

We do not know the dates these letters were written, but this could have been the first letter Paul wrote. If so, then it was some time around A.D.50 when it was written. Some feel that Galatians was the first of the letters that Paul wrote. Whether it was the first or not, we do know this was one of the early letters that Paul wrote in our New Testament.

Its Purpose

Why did Paul write these letters? The first purpose was to express his thanks and to encourage the people. He expresses thanksgiving for them, and he encourages the people. We will find that in chapter 1.

The second reason he writes is to defend himself against slander. In chapter 2 you will find a defense of his ministry among them.

The third reason he writes is to warn them against immorality. You will find him dealing with that issue in chapter 4. The fourth reason he writes is to deal with some church problems. One was evidently a lack of respect and a failure to follow their leaders as they should. Keep in mind this was a young church, these were young Christians. In that atmosphere, people who were selected to be leaders were taken right out from among the people themselves. There is a tendency at times for people to say who does he think he is taking leadership? I have been saved as long as he has. I know what kind of guy he was. That is what Jesus meant when He once said a prophet is not without honor save in his own country. Paul was writing to deal with this problem of respect for leaders.

Another reason was to answer questions related to the second coming. There were questions that had arisen about the second coming of our Lord.

You need to remember that these books were written to real people. They were living in a real world. They had real problems, and they were encountering difficulties. These letters were written to help and encourage them to deal with their problems and to handle the difficulties that arose.

Its Theme

What is the theme of this book? The second coming of Christ. There is a lot of excitement and anticipation about the second coming of Christ today. How should the second coming of the Lord affect believers? This is very interesting to me. When I was ordained to preach as an 18-year-old boy, I remember the preachers and pastors on the ordination council. One of the things they said to me was to avoid the book of Revelation. They said no one understands it, so do not get involved in it. It is too complicated. I was a good boy, and I avoided it for a number of years.

Another idea that was going around was don't talk too much about the second coming of the Lord because that is for mature Christians. Keep in mind Paul evidently spent less than a month in Thessalonica starting this church, and yet when he writes back to these young Christians, what is his theme? The second coming of Christ.

The second coming of Christ is one of those truths in the Bible that helps young Christians grow and mature about as much as any other doctrine. Tithing and giving are other truths that help Christians grow and mature. If we can help young Christians get involved in stewardship and being faithful in the matter of their offering, we will help them grow as Christians. But the truth of the second coming is also one of those truths that helps Christians grow and mature in the Lord.

There is a little background needed here. Since Paul had been there, had preached the gospel, and people had been saved, some of those believers had died. The question arose, what about them, what if the Lord comes and these believers have died? Are they going to be left out? This is one of the questions in their minds.

Another question was the day of the Lord. There was confusion about the meaning and the timing of the day of the Lord. Paul was writing about the second coming to clarify this meaning of the day of the Lord.

First Thessalonians has 5 chapters, and at the end of every chapter there is reference to the second coming of Jesus. In chapter 1, the reference is verse 10,

"And to wait for his Son from heaven, whom he raised from the dead, even Jesus, who delivered us from the wrath to come." That is the second coming in relationship to salvation, the saving truth.

Look at I Thessalonians 2:19-20. "For what is our hope, or joy, or crown of rejoicing? Are not even ye in the presence of our Lord Jesus Christ at his coming? For ye are our glory and joy." The truth of the second coming is a stimulating truth; it stimulates us to witness. It stimulates us to soulwinning. If we believe Jesus Christ is coming again, that should stir our hearts and stimulate us to tell others about the Lord Jesus Christ.

Note I Thessalonians 3:13. "To the end he may establish your hearts unblameable in holiness before God, even our Father, at the coming of our Lord Jesus Christ with all his saints." This is a stabilizing truth. He says that you may establish or stabilize your hearts. The second coming of Christ has a stabilizing effect on our hearts. When you look at the world around you and you see all of the problems, difficulties, and seemingly insurmountable obstacles that Christian believers face, it is this truth of the coming of the Lord that has a tendency to stabilize us and to keep us from being unduly alarmed. In fact, in one sense of the word, when you see things rapidly unfolding in the world around you, it becomes an encouragement to you because you read in scripture this is exactly what the Bible says. Jesus said when you see these things come to pass to lift up your heads because your redemption draws night.

The fourth chapter is the great chapter on the second coming of the Lord. It begins in verse 13 and goes down to the rest of the chapter. It is a strengthening truth because at the end of I Thessalonians 4:18, he says, "Wherefore, comfort one another with these words." The word *comfort* means encourage one another. So it is a strengthening truth for us.

Paul closes out with another reference to the second coming of Christ. "And the very God of peace sanctify you wholly; and I pray God your whole spirit and soul and body be preserved blameless unto the coming of our Lord Jesus Christ" (In I Thessalonians 5). The truth of the second coming of the Lord Jesus Christ is a sanctifying truth. It has a way of causing us to set apart our life wholly and totally dedicated to the Lord Jesus Christ.

First and II Thessalonians both deal with the subject of the return of the Lord, but they deal with different aspects of the Lord's return. This will help you understand the Scriptures if you will make this distinction in your thinking about the return of the Lord.

First Thessalonians is the Rapture of Christ; Christ returns in the air for the saints. Second Thessalonians, the Revelation, Christ returns to the earth with the saints. In Revelation 4:1, you have a picture of the rapture; and Revelation 19:11, when we are told about the Lord coming on the white horse, is a picture of the revelation. Keep those two things in mind,

The return of the Lord Jesus Christ has two phases to it. The first phase is the rapture phase. Christ comes in the air for His saints. In the second phase, He comes back to the earth with His saints.

OUTLINE

I. Personal, 1–3
- **A. The Ideal People**
- **B. The Ideal Pastor**
- **C. The Ideal Program**

II. Practical, 4–5
- **A. Concerning Development**
- **B. Concerning the Dead**
- **C. Concerning the Day of the Lord**
- **D. Concerning Duties**

Conclusion, 5:23-28

The first few verses of I Thessalonians are the introduction as Paul introduces the letter. Then I have divided his letter into two main divisions. The first three chapters are Personal in nature. Paul talks to them personally as believers and as a church. Then the second division, chapters 4–5, is Practical. Paul deals with some practical things.

I. Personal, Chapters 1–3

The first three chapters are very interesting and helpful. In chapter 1 Paul just really lets you look into the church and see what the church is all about. Remember when you were little and you used to go to church and Sunday School. They would teach you, "This is the church, this is the steeple. Open the door and see all the people!"

In chapter 1 Paul just opens the door and lets you see the people. He shows what a church ought to be, the Ideal People.

Then in chapter 2, he does something else very interesting. He opens his heart and shows what a pastor ought to be, the Ideal Pastor. He had been accused and slandered of having wrong motives, so he just opens up his heart to them.

In chapter 3, he shows what kind of program the church ought to have for its members, the Ideal Program. He shows what a church program should do. There is a little term that is used several times, "your faith." Look for that term. That is what a church program is intended to do for its members. It is intended to help its members grow in their faith.

A church has two primary purposes; first, to win the lost to Jesus Christ. That is why the church is here. The second purpose is to help the believers to grow in their faith. That is the purpose of the preaching, the purpose of the music, the purpose of the Sunday School, and the purpose of the youth ministry. Everything is to win people to Christ, and then help those we win to grow in their faith. That is what you will read about in this chapter 3.

II. Practical, Chapters 4–5

I have called this last section Practical Matters and divided it into several ways. One is Concerning Developments, 4:1-12, how they are to develop as believers. He goes into sexual immorality in the opening verses and tells them it is the will of God that believers be sexually pure and to keep themselves pure in these areas. He talks to them about loving one another.

The second division is Concerning the Dead, 4:13-18. What about those dead believers? How do they relate to the second coming of the Lord? He goes into that discussion, and it includes the great passage on the rapture and the return of the Lord.

Next is Concerning the Day of the Lord, 5:1-11, and then Concerning Duties, 5:12-22. He talks about different duties. He concludes in verses 23-28.

TRUTH IN II THESSALONIANS

Second Thessalonians is the second letter Paul wrote to the Thessalonians, written within a few months of the first letter, while he was still in Corinth. In this second letter Paul answers some further questions they had about the return of the Lord and the day of the Lord. Evidently someone or some group of people had come to Thessalonica and had shaken the faith. They had unsettled them and created a little confusion. In fact, there seems to have been a spurious letter purporting to be from Paul.

Note II Thessalonians 2:2, "That ye be not soon shaken in mind, or be troubled, neither by spirit, nor by word, nor by letter as from us, as that the day of Christ is at hand." There was a letter circulating that claimed to be from Paul. Paul is denying it. He is saying, don't let that letter shake you up. He is saying, I didn't write the letter. He addresses the false teachings.

There is a lot of false teaching around today. Don't believe every thing you hear just because someone has a Bible in his hands. Do not believe everything I say; check it out. Study for yourself. Every believer is a priest. You have the right and the responsibility as a believer to search the Scriptures yourself and find out if the teaching is consistent with the Scriptures.

Paul explains the day of the Lord. By the way, the day of the Lord is roughly the equivalent of what we call the great tribulation. It is one of the terms used to describe the great tribulation. Some people were saying they were already in the day of the Lord. They were having a tough time. It was difficult to be a believer in that day and in that atmosphere, like it is today. There were difficulties involved in living for Christ, just as there are in our day. Paul writes them and tells them he does not want them to think they are in the great tribulation because of the difficulties they were encountering.

Paul points out two factors necessary before the day of the Lord will begin. The first one is the apostasy has to take place. Where do we get the word *apostasy*? Look at II Thessalonians 2:3. He says, "Let no man deceive you by any means: for that day [the day of the Lord] shall not come, except there come the falling away first [*falling away* translates a word from which we get our word *apostasy*], and that man of sin be revealed, the son of perdition. *Apostasy* means "to stand off from, to stand apart from, to separate from." He says before this day of the Lord comes, there will be a period of time known as the apostasy. In the end of the age, there will be an apostasy. It will be the Laodicean age. That is why I believe we are in the last days. There is no question in my mind that we are experiencing the days of the apostasy, the falling away from the faith.

The second thing that has to happen is also in verse 3. That day will not come until there is a falling away and that man of sin be revealed, the son of perdition. He is talking about the Antichrist. Some people ask me if I think the Antichrist is alive today. I have no way of knowing. But I know this, when the rapture occurs, the Antichrist will then be revealed. He will become the one-world ruler; and the day of the Lord, the great tribulation, will be characterized by the domination of this personality known as the Antichrist or as Paul calls him here, the man of sin, the son of perdition. That is the primary reason he writes II Thessalonians.

There are some other reasons he wrote this letter. There were some believers who were misusing the truth of the second coming. Some were saying Jesus is coming, so there was no reason to work. If Jesus is coming, we do not have to work, we do not have to pay our bills. They thought they could live it up. Some believers had become lazy and irresponsible, so Paul hits them hard. Look at II Thessalonians 3:7-9, "For ye yourselves know how ye ought to follow us: for we behaved not ourselves disorderly among you; Neither did we eat any man's bread for nothing, but wrought with labor and travail night and day, that we might not be chargeable to any of you: Not because we have not power, but to make ourselves an example unto you to follow us." Then verse 10, "For even when we were with you, this we commanded you, that if any would not work, neither should he eat." It sounds hard, but it is not hard. It is just being responsible.

Paul writes to help them in difficult times. Paul writes to deal with the false teachings, and Paul writes to deal with these lazy Christians.

OUTLINE

Introduction, 1:1-2

I. A Word of Admiration, 1:3-12
- **A. Praise**
- **B. Promise**
- **C. Prayer**

II. A Word of Admonition, 2–3
- **A. The Coming Lie**
- **B. The Christian Life**

Conclusion, 3:16-18

I. A Word of Admiration, 1:1-12

After the introduction, verses 1-2, you have a Word of Admiration. He expresses his admiration for them. He has Praises for them in verses 3-4; he shares a Promise of the Lord, that the Lord is going to come and deliver them from the difficulties they are encountering, verses 5-10; and then he has a Prayer in verses 11-12.

II. A Word of Admonition, 2–3

Chapter 2:1-12, is the Coming Lie. He talks about the apostasy and the Antichrist. He talks about the fact that when people will not believe the truth, they will be deceived by the lie of the Antichrist. When you reject God's truth, you are wide open then to the lies of the devil.

Then from chapter 2:13 all the way to chapter 3 and the conclusion of that chapter, he discusses the Christian Life: living for the Lord, being faithful to the Lord, and serving the Lord.

Study #34
Teaching in I Timothy

TEACHING IN I TIMOTHY

Right in between the Church Letters and the General Letters, we have letters that are called the Pastoral Letters. If you take away the last two letters, "al," you get the thrust of what these books are about. These are letters to pastors. The Pastoral Letters are I Timothy, II Timothy, and Titus. The first two are written to a young man named Timothy, and then the third one is written to a young man named Titus. The book of Philemon is sometimes included in this category, and sometimes it is put in another category.

When you look at I Timothy, keep in mind it is a letter written by Paul to a young pastor. He is the young Timothy.

We believe Paul was in the city of Colosse when he writes this letter to the young man Timothy, who at that time was the pastor of the church of Ephesus. We also have a letter in the New Testament to the Ephesians, and we did a little background study of Ephesus. In terms of travel in the Bible world today, the city of Ephesus has about as much excavation completed as any other place. It is a magnificent place to see. Their library has been excavated, and you can see its remains. You can see the main streets and the amphitheater, where they had the riot.

After Paul left Ephesus, the young man Timothy becomes the pastor. Now he has a number of problems. One of the problems is the city itself. Here is a Christian church located in a city that was very, very pagan. It was the center of Diana worship. Diana, of course, was one of the false gods of those days. She was the same as Aphrodite, the goddess of love. It was a city given over to sexual immorality.

Another problem is Timothy was following the apostle Paul who had been there for three years. Keep in mind Timothy was a young man, and he was following the great apostle Paul, who was such a powerful, strong leader. This had to have been a difficult thing for young Timothy. In football, it would be like following Bear Bryant in Alabama. When a person has had a notably successful career, then the next person sometimes has a hard time. So young Timothy was dealing with that.

Paul is writing to a young pastor, but also know there are lessons taught and principles presented which will be helpful not only to pastors but also to church leaders in general. You will find yourself going to the book of I Timothy many times to discover principles of church leadership. You might call this a manual for church leaders. It is a book filled with great encouragement and great leadership principles.

Timothy

Timothy was evidently from the city of Lystra. He came from a mixed family. He was the son of a Gentile father and a Jewish mother. We see this in Acts 16:1, "Then came he [that is Paul, and it is evidently his second missionary journey] to Derbe and Lystra; and, behold, a certain disciple was there, named Timothy, the son of a certain woman, who was a Jewess [she was a Jewish Christian], and believed; but his father was a Greek." That is all it says, but it leads us to believe his father was not a Christian. What you have here is a young man who comes up with a mixed background. More and more in America this is certainly going to be true. More and more people are coming from blended families also. The picture is changing in America in terms of the family and what a family is. This could be an encouragement to many Christians. Here was the young man Timothy, and he came from a home where his mother was a believer, but his father evidently was not a believer.

It says in verse 2 that Timothy was well reported of by the brethren that were at Lystra and Iconium. Verse 3 continues, "Him would Paul have to go forth with him; and took and circumcised him because of the Jews who were in those quarters; for they all knew that his father was a Greek."

Evidently, Paul had won this young man to the Lord. Note I Timothy 1:1-2. We can get the idea that everything in the New Testament times was under optimum circumstances, that everything was just the very best. The more you study, the more you find it was not. Some of the problems we deal with are not really new problems. When you read your New Testament, be encouraged by the fact that a lot of these problems were there also.

Look at what it says in I Timothy 1:2, "Unto Timothy, my own son in the faith." That is the indication that Paul was instrumental in the salvation of this young man. We do know Timothy had been spiritually prepared for his salvation. Look at II Timothy 1:5. This is a good sermon to encourage parents in the bringing up of their children. Verse 5, "When I call to remembrance the unfeigned faith [that is un-hypocritical faith, the genuine faith] that is in thee, which dwelt first in thy grandmother, Lois, and thy mother, Eunice; and I am persuaded that in thee also." Grandmother Lois and mother Eunice and then grandson Timothy is what we see.

Where I came from, basically every church had a "TEL" class. It was always the class for the grandmothers in the churches. It stood for Timothy, Eunice, and Lois. It is a wonderful ministry for grandmothers, and grandfathers by the way. Grandparents can have a real influence on grandchildren.

Look at what Eunice and Lois did for Timothy. This is Paul talking to Timothy, II Timothy 3:14-15, "But continue thou in the things which thou hast learned and hast been assured of, knowing of whom thou hast learned them [evidently referring to his mother and grandmother], and that from a child thou hast known the holy scriptures, which are able to make thee wise unto salvation through faith which is in Christ Jesus." They had taught this boy the Scriptures from the time he was a child.

But now, God evidently has called Timothy into the ministry because when Paul, on his second missionary journey, comes back through there, the brethren are saying to Paul, have you heard about young Timothy. They let Paul know God has His hands on the young boy; God is going to use him.

Paul said he thought he would take Timothy along with him. Paul had a way of getting young preachers around him to mentor them. Let me encourage you to get a young Christian and mentor that young Christian. Teach the young convert the Scriptures. I would encourage all Christian men and women to do that. Lead someone to the Lord and then mentor that young Christian. It is what Paul is doing with the young man Timothy.

Timothy becomes an associate of Paul and Paul writes two letters to him. We know from the letters that Timothy is a committed young man, but we know also he has some physical infirmity or weakness because he seems to have a stomach problem. That is why Paul said to Timothy in I Timothy 5:23, "Drink no longer water, but use a little wine for your stomach's sake." This does not justify in any way social drinking. He is talking about using wine for medicinal purposes only. He is talking about Timothy's infirmity. He evidently had a nervous stomach problem.

Timothy seemed easily discouraged and needed some encouragement. Look at what Paul says to him in I Timothy 1:3, "As I besought thee to abide still at Ephesus." This seems to give a little indication that Timothy was discouraged and was thinking about maybe resigning.

Its Circumstances

What were the circumstances? That is the second thing I want to point out to you. One of the things Timothy is dealing with is he is a younger man, and he is trying to lead older people. He is a young pastor and he has a group of people, a congregation, a little bit older. How do we know that? Look over at I Timothy 4:12, and we draw this conclusion. "Let no man despise thy youth [don't let people look down on you because of your age], but be thou an example of the believers, in word, in conduct, in love, in spirit, in faith, in purity."

Another place is in I Timothy 5:1-2. This lets us know he was a young man pastoring older people also. "Rebuke not an elder, but intreat him as a father; and the younger men, as brethren; The elder women, as mothers; the younger, as sisters, with all purity." Paul is talking to him about how he conducts himself with the older members and younger members of the church.

Another thing is he was missing the apostle Paul. He was close to him. In II Timothy 1:4, Paul says about Timothy, "Greatly desiring to see thee, being mindful of thy tears, that I may be filled with joy." That is a beautiful statement. The old apostle Paul and the young pastor Timothy; he remembers the intensity and the commitment of Timothy. Paul is evidently missing Timothy, and Timothy evidently is missing Paul.

Timothy also faced youth temptations. Look at II Timothy 2:22, "Flee also youthful lusts." There are certain temptations for every age, for every period of life. To this young preacher, God says to him through Paul flee youthful lusts.

Something else is there were false teachers who had come to Ephesus, and they needed to be silenced. Look at I Timothy 1:3, "As I besought thee to abide still at Ephesus, when I went into Macedonia, that thou mightest charge some that they teach no other doctrine." If he was to charge them to teach no other doctrine, it means they were teaching wrong doctrine. He tells Timothy to charge them to teach the right doctrine, to teach the truth. Evidently they were off-base a little bit. Look at verse 6, "From which some having swerved, have turned aside unto vain jangling." That is empty talking, foolish talking. Look at verse 19, "Holding faith, and a good conscience, which some, having put away concerning faith, have made shipwreck." Then Paul calls them by name.

Look at I Timothy 4:1, "Now the Spirit speaketh expressly that, in the latter times, some shall depart from the faith, giving heed to seducing spirits, and doctrines of demons." Notice the repetition of the word *some*. There were some who were deviating from the faith. It started in the New Testament era, departure from the faith, teaching false doctrine. Every heresy we deal with today is nothing more than a revival of heresies that started all the way back in the New Testament day. That is true. So the young man Timothy had to deal with some people who were teaching false doctrine.

Another thing is Timothy needed counsel on managing the affairs of the church. Look at I Timothy 3:1, "This is a true saying, if a man desire the office of a bishop, he desireth a good work." Then Paul proceeds to give the qualifications and the standards for a bishop, and in verse 8 he gives the qualifications and standards for a deacon. There are certain matters of church affairs that needed to be dealt with.

Look at I Timothy 5:3; this was another matter Timothy had to handle. "Honor widows that are widows indeed." Paul gives him some specific guidelines for how the widows of the congregation are to be cared for. It is local church information.

Its Theme

Look at I Timothy 3:15, "But if I tarry long [if I do not get there as soon as I think I will], that thou mayest know how thou oughtest to behave thyself in the house of God, which is the church of the God, the pillar and ground of the truth." The theme of I Timothy is how to behave in the local church, how to conduct the affairs of the local church. Today's standards for deacons are rooted in I Timothy. We try, as best we can, to go to the New Testament and from the New Testament draw the principles and guidelines for how to conduct the activities and affairs of God's church.

The whole matter of the offering, for instance, we try to take from II Corinthians 8 and 9. If you are interested in how finances are to be handled in the church, read II Corinthians 8 and 9.

We do not take the position that if it is not in the New Testament, you cannot do it. Some people say if it is not in the New Testament, then you cannot do it. That is why there are some people who say there can be no musical instruments in the church because we do not have a record of any in the New Testament. That is a dangerous position to take because if you take that position, you cannot have electric lights and air conditioning either. It is not that if it is not in the New Testament, you do not do it; but that in the New Testament you find the guidelines. Then those guidelines are to be inculcated into our contemporary activities so what we do has a Bible basis to it. It has a biblical foundation. That is why I Timothy is so important. It is a book that has to do with how to behave in the local church.

OUTLINE

Introduction, 1:1-2

I. The Church and Its Message, 11
- **A. Teaching Sound Doctrine, 1:3-11**
- **B. Proclaiming the Gospel, 1:12-17**
- **C. Defending the Faith, 1:18-20**

II. The Church and Its Members, 2–3
- **A. Praying Men, 2:1-8**
- **B. Submitting Women, 2:9-15**
- **C. Serving Leaders, 3:1-13**
- **D. Behaving Believers, 3:14-16**

III. The Church and Its Minister, 4
- **A. A Good Minister, Preaching the Word, 4:1-6**
- **B. A Godly Minister, Practicing the Word, 4:7-12**
- **C. A Growing Minister, Progressing in the Word, 4:13-16**

IV. The Church and Its Ministry, 5–6
- **A. The People of God, 5:1-6:2**
- **B. The Peril of Gold, 6:3-19**

Conclusion 6:20-21

Introduction, 1:1-2

The first two verses are an introduction. Paul tells who he is, and he greets young Timothy. Then there are four main divisions.

I. The Church and Its Message, 1

A. Teaching Sound Doctrine, 1:3-11

Chapter 1 I call The Church and Its Message. Paul lays before us the message of the church. First he discusses and shows the church's message involves Teaching Sound Doctrine (1:3-11). Look at the last part of verse 10, "if there be any other thing that is contrary [or opposed] to sound doctrine." The word *sound* is an interesting word. It is where we get our word *hygiene*. We have a dental hygienist, someone who cleans your teeth. We say you are to use good hygiene, wash your hands before and after your meals. These are things that make for good health, healthy things. So when he talks about sound doctrine, he is talking about hygienic doctrine, healthy doctrine, doctrine that will produce strong, healthy, energetic spiritual life.

He comes back to it in I Timothy 6:3, "If any man teach otherwise, and consent not to wholesome words." The translation of wholesome is the same word as hygienic. It is sound words, wholesome or healthy words. The doctrine of the church is to be healthy doctrine. Churches should teach doctrine because that is what makes people spiritually healthy. It concerns me when I hear of churches that do not have solid Bible teaching going on. That is what makes a church strong and healthy.

B. Proclaiming the Gospel, 1:12-17

The next point is Proclaiming the Gospel, I Timothy 1:12-17. Paul gives a little testimony about what the Lord did for him, what he was before Jesus came into his life. Then he gives one of the beautiful "faithful sayings "in verse 15, "This is a faithful saying." There are a number of these in I Timothy, II Timothy, and Titus. A faithful saying–that is, this is true, this is dependable, and worthy of all acceptation. "That Christ Jesus came into the world to save sinners; of whom I am chief."

C. Defending the Faith, 1:18-20

The next point he talks about is Defending the Faith, I Timothy 1:18-20. He encourages young Timothy to defend the faith. Look at verse 18, "This charge I commit unto thee, son Timothy." By the way, that word *charge* is the key word of I Timothy. Sometimes it is translated charge and sometimes it is translated commandment. A charge is a command. "This charge I commit unto thee, son Timothy, according to the prophecies which went before on thee, that thou by them mightest war a good warfare."

II. The Church and Its Members, 2–3

A. Praying Men, 2:1-8

The second main division is The Church and Its Members, chapters 2 and 3. The first eight verses he talks about Praying Men. He talks about the importance of prayer in the fellowship of the church.

B. Submitting Women, 2:9-15

Submitting Women is chapter 2:9-15. People do not understand what submission is all about. They do not understand that submission is not domination. Some people think submission means people are inferior. That is not what it means at all. It just simply means God understands and God has designed for us the principle of leadership, guidance, protection, and care. Submission is a very positive doctrine when it is properly understood.

C. Serving Leaders, 3:1-13

Next is Serving Leaders. Paul lays out the standards for bishops, that is pastors, and their wives, and standards for deacons and their wives.

D. Behaving Believers, 3:14-16

Then verses 14-16 are Behaving Believers.

III. The Church and Its Minister, 4

The third main division is the Church and Its Minister, chapter 4. Paul basically has three emphases here: a Good Minister, Preaching the Word, verses 1-6; a Godly Minister, Practicing the Word, verses 7-12; and a Growing Minister, Progressing in the Word, verses 13-16. I like verse 16, "Take heed unto thyself, and unto the doctrine." Notice the order. Check up on yourself. Be sure that you are where you need to be, and then your teaching. Make sure your teaching is where it ought to be. "continue in them." He is encouraging the young preacher Timothy to continue in his own spiritual growth, to continue in his understanding of scripture and learning how to teach scripture.

IV. The Church and Its Ministry, 5–6

A. The People of God, 5:1–6:2

The fourth division is the Church and Its Ministry, chapters 5 and 6. The first point is the People of God, chapter 5 all the way to I Timothy 6:2. There he talks about the widows and the guidelines and care of them. He talks about the elders of the church, servants and masters, and the people of God.

B. The Peril of Gold, 6:3-19

He closes out this letter with an interesting passage that talks about the peril of material things, the Peril of Gold, I Timothy 6:3-19. This is the passage that talks about the love of money being the root of all evil. If people set that as their goal, they are headed for heartache. The Bible has a whole lot to say about money. It has a lot of warnings. Look at verse 9, "But they that will be rich fall into temptation and a snare, and into many foolish and hurtful lusts, which drown men in destruction and perdition." What he is saying is if that is your goal in life, that is your whole life, you are asking for some heartache. You are asking for difficulty and trouble along the way. He is saying you have to learn to put material things in their proper place.

Conclusion, 6:20-21

Then he closes out the letter with a final appeal in conclusion to the young man Timothy. This is a book for believers. It shows us how to behave in the house of God.

Study #35
Triumphs in II Timothy

TRIUMPHS OF II TIMOTHY

This is the second letter addressed by the great preacher, apostle, and missionary Paul to his young protégé Timothy. He may have written other letters to Timothy, but these are the only two the Holy Spirit has chosen to place in our Bible as a part of inspiration, as a part of revealed truth.

It is interesting to compare I Timothy and II Timothy because immediately when you move into II Timothy and look at Paul's circumstances, you will find they have changed drastically. Paul is in an entirely different atmosphere from what he was in I Timothy.

As best as we can tell, this is Paul's last letter. Remember, the New Testament is not in chronological order. Second Timothy, is believed to be the last of the letters that Paul wrote. It is an intensely personal letter. There are many indications of personal warmth and emotion as Paul writes this letter. He has evidently been arrested again after a brief period of being released from prison.

In Acts 27, Paul goes to the city of Rome as a prisoner, but the best evidence we have is that Paul was released from that imprisonment for a period of time. In II Timothy, we find that he is in prison again.

Its Circumstances

The circumstances are very serious. It is a difficult time for people to be Christians at this point. The persecution, which Jesus had predicted, has now begun. The emperor at this time is a man named Nero, and he is on a rampage against Christians. Nero is the one that fiddled while Rome burned. It is commonly believed that Nero is the one who set Rome on fire, but he blamed the fire on the

Christians. He had to have a scapegoat; he blamed the Christians and this precipitated an even more intense persecution of Christian believers.

Paul is in prison. It is generally believed he is in prison in the Mamertine Prison in Rome. I have visited that prison. It is just a hole in the floor. There was an opening in the ceiling where they could get the food down to the prisoners. There was a river that flowed underneath it, which made it a very damp and cold place of incarceration. It was known as the sepulcher or the tomb because many of the prisoners were eaten alive by rats. Do not get the idea that it was some kind of modern day prison where they had weight rooms and TV rooms. It was indeed a dangerous place to be.

Paul will never be free again as he reflects in his writings. He knows any day now they will come for him; they will walk him across the highway; there he will kneel, his head will be severed from his body, and he will be beheaded. Paul feels in a way abandoned at this point. Notice II Timothy 1:15, "This thou knowest, that all they which are in Asia turned away from me." Paul is talking about believers, Christians. Do you sense the abandonment that he must have felt? Note II Timothy 4:10, "For Demas hath forsaken me, having loved this present world, and is departed unto Thessalonica." Do you see the poignancy of that statement? Do you sense the disappointment? Here is the faithful old man of God. He has been true and faithful to the Lord, and now here are people he has depended upon. Now they are turning away.

Demas is one of the tragedies of the Bible. I do not think this means that Demas went into deep sin. It says he departed and went back into Thessalonica. I think it means he came to the point that Jesus was not first in his life.

Look at II Timothy 4:16. Here is another statement. "At my first answer [that is probably a reference to a series of trials], no man stood with me, but all men forsook me." Do you see his sense of abandonment? "I pray God that it may not be laid to their charge."

As best we can tell, there is only one faithful person still with him. Look back at verse 11, "Only Luke is with me." This was the beloved physician Luke. He was evidently his personal physician. He expresses gratitude that Luke was with him, but he was lonely.

In this letter Paul is asking young Timothy to come as soon as he can. Evidently, Paul is going to send a man named Tychicus to replace Timothy as pastor of the church of Ephesus. Keep in mind that Timothy is the pastor of the church in Ephesus, but he is going to send Tychicus. Look at II Timothy 4:12, "And Tychicus have I sent to Ephesus." Look back in verse 9, "Do thy diligence [talking to young Timothy] to come shortly unto me." He wants this young man Timothy with him.

Paul wants Timothy to come and bring some needed supplies. Look at II Timothy 4:13, "The cloak that I left at Troas with Carpus, when thou comest, bring with thee, and the books, but especially the parchments." Look at the things Paul needed. First of all he says the cloak; it is getting cold, winter is coming, so he says to bring his cloak. He had physical needs. But then he says the books. This is not books like we have today, but he is talking about the scrolls. He does not have long to live, but he wants to keep himself intellectually sharp. You should be a student all of your life. You are never too old to continue to learn. One of the big things in education now is life-long learning. I would encourage you to continue to learn. Do not get to the point where you say you are too old. Continue to stimulate yourself intellectually. Then he says especially the parchments. We believe this is a reference to the Scriptures. He wants the Scriptures in these closing days of his life.

Having said that and having given you the circumstances of Paul's life, as you read II Timothy, you will see he is not concerned primarily for himself. He is concerned for the young preacher Timothy and for the progress and the success of the gospel. That is ever his motivation. He is always concerned about young men of God, young pastors, young preachers, and he is concerned that the gospel of Jesus Christ might continue on.

By the way, this book is a great encouragement and incentive for Christians as they get a little bit older. It bothers me when I hear Christians talk in terms of hanging it up. You may resign or retire from your job, but you do not retire from serving the Lord. Don't do that. You should be more active in service for the Lord than you have ever been. God has given you some time. If you have a camper or a trailer, do not use that as a reason to get off and do nothing. There are times you can get away, but don't come down to the end of your life and spend it riding all over the country. That is not the way you want to end your life. You want to be serving the Lord as you come to the end of your life.

Its Purpose

Paul, as he looks around, sees defeat and apostasy. People are falling away from the faith,

People are giving up; people are quitting. In I Timothy he used the word *some*. Some had done this. When you get to II Timothy, the word changes from some to all. Look at II Timothy 1:15, "all they who are in Asia turned away from me." Look at II Timothy 4:16 again, "At my first defense no man stood with me, but all men forsook me." Do you see the declension and the apostasy that is going on?

Paul is urging young Timothy, in a time when churches are turning from the faith, to be true to the call and to fulfill the ministry which God has given to him. I am personally convinced that we are living in the days of apostasy. I will not belabor the point, but in observing the church world, it is distressing in many ways. Many churches are caving in to the atmosphere of the times. The atmosphere of a lot of churches is what do people want? That is what we will give them. They want to make it as convenient as they can for them. You have to learn how to change the method and not compromise or change the message. What disturbs me today is I see in the church world not only a change of methods, but I also see a change of the message. I see a compromise of the message. We have to be wise and led of the Spirit so we do not fall into the trap of apostasy in the end times.

Though I have pointed out that there is a note of sadness here, that Paul is addressing the matters of apostasy and these kinds of affairs, there is also a note of triumph in this book. This is not a depressing book. This is a book of victory. Paul is not giving a swan song of defeat but an anthem of victory because in the midst of the circumstances and the difficulties which he experiences, Paul faces them with courage. He faces them with a sense of victory and overcoming. Paul has turned this prison of despair into a palace of delight. It is one of the most exciting and interesting books you will ever read.

What is the great value of II Timothy to us today? This book might be called a prophetic photograph. Let's look at II Timothy as a prophetic photograph of 21st century church life. Let's look at our day through the lens of what the Holy Spirit inspired Paul to write the young man Timothy.

OUTLINE

Introduction, 1:1-2

- **I. The Pastoral Appeal, 1:3-18**
  - **A. To Develop His Faith, 1:3-6**
  - **B. To Dispel His Fears, 1:7-18**
- **II. The Practical Appeal, 2:1-26**
  - **A. A Steward, 2:1-2**
  - **B. A Soldier, 2:3-4**
  - **C. A Success, 2:5-7**
  - **D. A Sufferer, 2:8-13**
  - **E. A Student, 2:14-19**
  - **F. A Servant, 2:20-26**
- **III. The Prophetic Appeal, 3:1-17**
  - **A. An Explanation of the Future, 3:1-9**
  - **B. An Example from the Past, 3:10-13**
  - **C. An Exhortation for the Present, 3:14-17**
- **IV. The Personal Appeal, 4:1-22**
  - **A. Preach the Word, 4:1-4**
  - **B. Fulfill Your Ministry, 4:5-8**
  - **C. Be Faithful to the End, 4:9-22**

The first two verses are the introductory verses, 1:1-2. Verse 1, "Paul, an apostle of Jesus Christ by the will of God, according to the promise of life which is in Christ Jesus." Verse 2, "To Timothy." Notice the emotion here. Back in the first letter to Timothy, when Paul addresses the letter to Timothy, he says in I Timothy 1:2, "Unto Timothy, my own son in the faith." This leads us to believe he led Timothy to faith in Christ. Notice the added emotion in II Timothy 1:2, "To Timothy, my dearly beloved son." As you approach the end of your life, people become more precious. They become more dear to you. As you lose them, they become more precious to you. Then he says, "Grace, mercy, and peace, from God the Father and Christ Jesus our Lord."

In most of the letters Paul wrote to the churches, he began with the greeting, grace mercy, and peace. By the way, the two words grace and peace were the two words that were words of greeting in the Greek world and in the Hebrew world. In the Greek world, the greeting word was grace. It is the word *charis;* we get our name Karen from that. In the Hebrews word the greeting was peace, shalom. Do you see what God has done? He has taken the Greek world and the Hebrew world, and in Christ He has put them together. It is always grace and then peace. You cannot have peace until you have experienced grace. It is never peace and then grace; it is always grace and then peace.

When you look at these letters to these young preacher boys, young Timothy and Titus, you will notice that a word has been added. The word added is the word *mercy.* Somebody said the reason Paul added mercy was he knew young preachers would need all the mercy they could get. I do not know about that, but that is the introduction.

There are four appeals Paul gives us in these chapters to encourage young Timothy to be faithful to his ministry in days of apostasy. Each chapter gives us one of those appeals.

I. The Pastoral Appeal, 1:3-18

A. To Develop His Faith, 1:3-6

Chapter 1 is the Pastoral Appeal. Here Paul reminds young Timothy of his call to the ministry and the responsibilities that go along with that call. He urges him to Develop His Faith, verses 3-6. He says in verse 3, "I thank God, whom I serve from my forefathers, with pure conscience, that without ceasing I have remembrance of thee in my prayers night day." He tells Timothy he is praying for him. Verse 4, "Greatly desiring to see thee, being mindful of thy tears, that I may be filled with joy." It is interesting to me that what impressed Paul about Timothy was not his intellect but was his compassion, his tears. Then he says in verse 5, "When I call to remembrance the unfeigned faith [that is un-hypocritical] that is in thee, which dwelt first in thy grandmother Lois, and thy mother Eunice, and I am persuaded that in thee also." He is saying Timothy had a godly heritage.

Verse 6, "Wherefore I put thee in remembrance that thou stir up the gift of God, which is in thee by the putting on of my hands." He is telling Timothy to keep the fire burning. Christian people need to be constantly keeping their hearts stirred. One of the tendencies in the days of apostasy is indifference and coldness. Jesus said because iniquity shall abound, the love of many shall wax cold. It is easy for Christians to get lukewarm, indifferent, and cold in days of apostasy. You have to constantly stir up the flames in your life. Then again he says in verse 6, "which is in thee by the putting on of my hands." That was his ordination.

B. To Dispel His Fears, 1:7-18

In the second division, he urges young Timothy not only to develop his faith but to Dispel His Fears, verses 7-18. Look at verses 7-8, "For God hath not given us the spirit of fear; but of power, and of love, and of a sound mind. Be not thou therefore ashamed of the testimony of our Lord." In other words, in days of apostasy when there is persecution abounding on every hand, there is the temptation for Christians and especially Christian servants and workers, to succumb to fears. Paul tells Timothy not to let that happen to him. God is saying to us through this letter not to let it happen to us. God has not given us the spirit of fear. Paul gives us a little of his own background in verse 11, "Whereunto I am appointed a preacher, and an apostle, and a teacher of the Gentiles." Then he goes on in verse 12 to say he is not ashamed. He knows whom he has believed. That is one of the great verses in the Bible. "For the which cause I also suffer these things: nevertheless I am not ashamed: for I know whom I have believed, and am persuaded that he is able to keep that which I have committed unto him against that day." He is saying to young Timothy to be faithful to the gospel. Do not cave in to the atmosphere of the time.

II. The Practical Appeal, 2

A. A Steward, 2:1-2

The second division is the Practical Appeal, chapter 2. In this chapter he gives a series of word pictures showing young Timothy how to deal with the problems he has. For instance, he is to be like a Steward, verses 1-2. "Thou therefore, my son, be strong in the grace that is in Christ Jesus. And the things that thou hast heard of me among many witnesses, the same commit thou to faithful men, who shall be able to teach others also." Do you notice the order of passing on the truth? The things Timothy had heard of Paul among many witnesses, he was then to commit to faithful men. Paul was saying to pass it on. That is part of the stewardship of the gospel. We are stewards of the message of the gospel. Every generation is just one generation away from paganism. If we fail the next generation, they will not have the gospel. The very fact that we have the gospel is because people who have gone before us have paid the price. We cannot fail succeeding generations. We are entrusted with the gospel, and what we have to do is to find other dependable people and pass it on to them.

B. A Soldier, 2:3

Next he compares a Christian servant to a Soldier, verse 3. "Thou therefore endure hardness, as a good soldier of Jesus Christ." He changes from a steward who is investing in the hearts and lives of people; now we are soldiers fighting the fight. Verse 4, "No man that warreth entangleth himself with the affairs of this life; that he may please him who hath chosen him to be a soldier." Do not get your priorities out of line. Know whose army you are in. If you are going to be a soldier, you cannot get involved in secondary issues or things that really do not count.

C. A Success, 2:5-7

Next is a picture of being a Success, verses 5-7. It is like being a farmer or an athlete. Look at verse 5, "And if a man also strive for masteries, yet is he not crowned, except he strive lawfully." The picture of an athlete is one of Paul's favorite pictures. Paul was a sports fan. Paul took a lot of truth from the field of athletics. There are many lessons and applications, and this is one of them. The player has to go by the rules. He has to stay within the guidelines. In Philippians 2, Paul says he presses toward the mark. It is a picture of an athlete running a race.

Then he uses a picture of the farmer in verse 6. "The husbandman [farmer] that laboureth must be first partaker of the fruits." What he says is you yourself are blessed as you sow the good seed of the Word.

D. A Sufferer, 2:8-13

Chapter 2 is loaded with pictures: a steward, a soldier, a success, and then a sufferer, verses 8-13. In these verses he talks about suffering for Christ.

E. A Student, 2:14-19

Then he uses the picture of a student. Look at verse 15, "Study to shew thyself approved unto God, a workman that needeth not to be ashamed, rightly dividing the word of truth." Study the Bible correctly. Be a student of the Word.

F. A Servant, 2:20-26

In verses 20-26, he compares the Christian life to being like a Servant. Look at verse 24, "And the servant of the Lord must not strive; but be gentle unto all men, apt to teach, patient." Paul makes a practical appeal by using word pictures. I would encourage you to look for the word pictures in the Bible. There are so many of them in the Bible, and the background of them can open up your Bible to you in so many ways.

III. The Prophetic Appeal, 3

The third division is the Prophetic Appeal, chapter 3. In this chapter Paul explains the course of events and the apostasy. He gives an Explanation of the Future in verses 1-9; an Example from the Past, verses 10-13; and then an Exhortation for the Present, verses 14-17.

A. An Explanation of the Future, 3:1-9

First of all he gives an Explanation of the Future. Look at verse 1, "This know also, that in the last days [the end times] perilous times shall come." This means fierce times, dangerous times. Then he goes on and names some of the characteristics of the end times. Verses 2-5, "For men shall be lovers of their own selves, covetous, boasters, proud, blasphemers, disobedient to parents, unthankful, unholy, Without natural affection, trucebreakers, false accusers, incontinent, fierce, despisers of those that are good, Traitors, heady, highminded, lovers of pleasures more than lovers of God; Having a form of godliness, but denying the power thereof: from such turn away."

Read all of those descriptions slowly. What you will find is that it has been characteristic of every age. People in the 1800s read this and said it proved they were in the last times. But I do believe the Bible teaches there will be an intensifying of these characteristics in the end times. Any reasonable person would certainly agree that in looking at our culture today, there is an intensification of this kind of atmosphere that is unlike any thing that has been encountered previously.

B. An Example from the Past, 3:10-13

Then he talks about an Example from the Past, verses 10-13. He talks about himself. Verse 10, "But thou hast fully known my doctrine, manner of life, purpose, faith, longsuffering, charity, patience."

C. An Exhortation for the Present, 3:14-17

In verses 14-17, he gives an Exhortation for the Present. This is one of the great passages of the entire Bible. He says to young Timothy in verse 14, "But continue thou in the things which thou hast learned and hast been assured of, knowing of whom thou hast learned them." I believe he includes in the "whom," not only his mother and grandmother but Paul himself because young Timothy was trained by Paul. He tells Timothy to stay with it.

He continues, verse 15, "And that from a child thou hast known the holy scriptures, which are able to make thee wise unto salvation through faith which is in Christ Jesus." Then he says in verses 16-17, "All scripture is given by inspiration of God, and is profitable for doctrine, for reproof, for correction, for instruction in righteousness. That the man of God may be perfect, thoroughly furnished unto all good works."

IV. The Personal Appeal, 4

A. Preach the Word, 4:1-4

The fourth division is the Personal Appeal, chapter 4. This is where Paul just opens up his heart. Here is the old soldier getting ready to go home. Paul is the old pastor, the old apostle. This is the final appeal, and his first appeal is Preach the Word, verses 1-4. The last words of instruction and encouragement are preach the Word. Verses 1-3, "I charge thee therefore before God, and the Lord Jesus Christ, who shall judge the quick and the dead at his appearing and his kingdom; Preach the word; be instant in season, out of season; reprove, rebuke, exhort with all longsuffering and doctrine. For the time will come when they will not endure sound doctrine; but after their own lusts shall they heap to themselves teachers, having itching ears." That makes me think about today. They will hear what they want to hear. They want you to say what they want to hear. Verse 4, "And they shall turn away their ears from the truth, and shall be turned unto fables." That is the first appeal.

B. Fulfill Your Ministry, 4:5-8

The second appeal is Fulfill Your Ministry, verses 5-8. He says in verse 5, "But watch thou in all things, endure afflictions, do the work of an evangelist, make full proof of thy ministry." Then he gets into that magnificent statement starting in verse 6, "For I am now ready to be offered, and the time of my departure is at hand." He is right on the cusp. He says in verse 7, "I have fought a good fight, I have finished my course, I have kept the faith." If you can say that, that is a testimony. Don't you want to be that way right there? When the time comes for us to cross over, don't you and I want to be able to say that?

Then he gets glory in his soul and he looks up and says in verse 8, "Henceforth there is laid up for me a crown of righteousness, which the Lord, the righteous judge, shall give me at that day: and not to me only, but unto all them also that love his appearing." Paul was not going out whimpering, but he was going out shouting. That is the way to go out. Go out with victory in your heart.

C. Be Faithful to the End, 4:9-22

He finishes with Be Faithful to the End, verses 9-22. He talks about those who had walked out. Verse 16, "all men forsook me." Do not stop at verse 16 though or you will miss what Paul was saying. If you stop there, you think Paul is just feeling sorry for himself. You have to go on into verse 17 because he says, "Notwithstanding the Lord stood with me, and strengthened me." Jesus was there for him. People will let you down. If you are in the ministry for any other reason than Jesus, you will become a bitter person. If you are serving the Lord to get the praise of people and approval of people and the encouragement or faithfulness of people, people will let you down. But Jesus will never let you down. You will never be disappointed in Jesus. He will never leave you or forsake you. When you look at people and they let you down, do not let that discourage you. The truth of the matter is but by the grace of God all of us would be in hell. Any time you see failure in people, just remember that is their old fallen nature. When you see something good in people, rejoice because it is Jesus who has caused them to be that way. Keep your eyes on Jesus all the time, and you will not be discouraged.

It concerns me when I see people who have let the Lord down. It concerns me when I see people who are not faithful to the Lord. All of that is a cause for prayer. But it does not get me down. I do not think a Christian ever has a right to be discouraged. If we get discouraged, we are basically saying there is no hope, that all is lost. Now we can get down in the dumps about it, we can get disappointed, but we ought not get discouraged. The final chapter is Jesus Christ is faithful. You live for Him, and He will never let you down.

Look at verse 17, "I was delivered out of the mouth of the lion." I do not know what that means, but verse 18 says, "And the Lord shall deliver me from every evil work, and will preserve me unto his heavenly kingdom: to whom be glory for ever and ever. Amen." He says I was delivered and the Lord shall deliver. He got me out of one deal back yonder, and He will get me out of everything in the future. We know who wins the game of life. We do through Jesus Christ.

Study #36
Truths from Titus and Postcard to Philemon

TRUTH FROM TITUS

We are looking at the third of the letters which fall in the general category of what we call the Pastoral Letters or Epistles. Titus is not a long book; it is three chapters in length.

Its Man

Titus was a Greek believer. We know this from Galatians 2:1 and 3. He evidently was won to Christ by Paul in his early ministry because of Titus 1:4. Paul says, "To Titus, mine own son after the common faith." This is similar to what he said to Timothy, so the indication by the language here is Paul led this man Titus to faith in the Lord.

Another thing of interest about Titus is he was part of the delegation that was sent to the Jerusalem church to settle a doctrinal issue, the matter of Gentile freedom from the ceremonial law. The Judaizer branch had said Gentiles could not be saved until they first became a Jew. They said they had to go through the Jewish door in order to become a believer. Paul maintained that salvation for the Jew and salvation for the Gentile was exactly the same. Salvation was through faith in Jesus Christ, plus nothing and minus nothing. They went up to the Jerusalem council, and Paul brought this man Titus along as a test case.

Paul was leaving Titus at a church in Crete. Look at Titus 1:5, "For this cause left I thee in Crete, that thou shouldest set in order the things that are wanting." Titus was assigned to do the work of the Lord and to reorganize the church there in Crete. He evidently was young and gifted. He was a helper of the apostle Paul and was very close to Paul.

He seemed to be the kind of man who did well in special assignments. You could give him a difficult job, a special assignment, and he seemed to do quite well in this. In II Corinthians 8, Paul talks about the delegation that was sent to Jerusalem with the special offering that was taken for the Jerusalem believers. Titus was a part of that delegation (II Corinthians 8:6, 16).

Sometimes the Lord honors you by the difficulty of the assignment He gives you. Some parents have handicapped children. They know the difficulty of that assignment. God honors Christians when He gives an assignment like that. Out of all the people in the world that the Lord could have chosen to care for that special child, God picked those parents. It is a great compliment when God gives you a special assignment. How we respond to that assignment and how we carry it out is a great testimony to our devotion and our commitment to the Lord Jesus Christ.

Crete

The second matter is the matter of Crete. Crete is an island of Greece. The Cretians were great sailors. They were famous bowmen, but their reputation for bad morals was also quite well-known. In fact, we have a statement made by the apostle Paul about the Cretians, Titus 1:12-13, "One of themselves [talking about the Cretes], even a prophet of their own, said, the Cretians are always liars, evil beasts, lazy gluttons. This testimony is true. Wherefore, rebuke them sharply, that they may be sound in the faith."

We have no record of the founding of the church at Crete. As Acts 2 lists the names of the people or the countries from which the people gathered on the day of Pentecost, Crete is one of those places mentioned. Acts 2:11, "Cretes, and Arabians, we do hear them speak in our tongues the wonderful works of God." From the island of Crete some people had come, and we naturally tend to believe they came to faith in Christ and then carried the good news of the gospel back to their people.

Its letter

There were two problems, which were confronting the young pastor, that Paul is dealing with in this letter. One of the problems was the Judaizers who were mixing law and grace. The second matter was there were some believers who did not understand the grace of God, and so they tended to abuse it. There is a danger that the grace of God can be abused. We know we are saved by the unmerited favor of God. We do not work or earn our salvation. We do not live a certain way to get our salvation. If Christians are not careful though, they will lean on the grace of God as an excuse for their life. They will say since we are all under grace and not under law, then it is no big deal what we do or do not do. That is an abuse of the teaching of the grace of God in scripture.

Titus had two jobs. Number one was to set in order the things that were lacking. Look at verse 5 again and see the two assignments. "For this cause left I thee in Crete, that thou shouldest set in order the things that are wanting." Wanting is an interesting word. It is a medical word that means to set a broken bone. He is saying to Titus that the church has some things that need to be set back together. One of the beautiful things about the New Testament church is it is compared to a body. It is called the body of Christ. If a bone gets broken in the body, it needs to be set. Sometimes in the work of the Lord, the body of Christ gets out of joint, and it needs to be set back into place. That was one of his assignments.

The next thing he was to do was "to ordain elders in every city, as I had appointed thee." In other words, around the different cities there on the island elders needed to be ordained.

Let me put this little matter before you. I think it will be helpful to you. The office or the role of pastor is described in the New Testament by three different words. They all apply to the same role assignment that we call today pastor. Note these words so you will be able to understand elders in verse 5.

The most familiar word is the word *pastor*. The spiritual leader of a church is called pastor. Literally this means shepherd; it means to shepherd. It is the responsibility of the pastor to lead and to feed the flock. The second word is the word *bishop*. Bishop means "to oversee." A bishop is someone who oversees the work. He is an overseer. Then the word *elder* carries with it the idea of counsel, wisdom, and understanding. So the pastor is to be an elder. It does not mean he is to be necessarily older than people, but he is someone who provides wisdom and spiritual counsel for the people. Those three words are used interchangeably in the New Testament to refer to one and the same office. When you see elder or bishop or pastor, it is talking about the same office.

Its Emphasis

There are several key words you will find in the book of Titus. One of the words is the word *sound*. It is sound as in healthy. It is the same word for hygiene, which was used by Paul in his letters to Timothy (I and II Timothy). He talks about sound doctrine that would produce spiritual health (Titus 1:9, 13; 2:1, 2, 8). A second word that is used is *godliness* (Titus 1:1 and Titus 2:12).

Another word is the word *grace* (Titus 1:4 and Titus 2:11). In Titus 2:11 and following, you have a beautiful statement of the meaning of the grace of God. Look at verse 11, "For the grace of God that bringeth salvation hath appeared to all men." Then it goes on to talk about what grace ought to produce in our lives. We should live godly, and it should also produce a spirit of anticipation, looking for the blessed hope and glorious appearing of our Lord Jesus Christ. Titus 3:7 and 15 are two more references.

The key phrase of Titus is good works. Titus 1:16 talks about those who are spiritual pretenders. They pretend they know the Lord, but they do not. At the end of Titus 1:16, Paul writes, "and unto every good work reprobate," these people are reprobates. When it comes to good works, these people do not pass the test. He says one of the tests of a true believer is his or her works. Jesus said you will know Christians by their works, the life they live, their behavior.

Look at Titus 2:7. Here he is giving requirements for the older men, the younger men, the young men, and the young ladies. Then he says in verse 7, "In all things shewing thyself a pattern of good works." Verse 14, "Who gave himself for us, that he might redeem us from all iniquity, and purify unto himself a peculiar people [this is not odd or strange, but a people of His own possession, a special people], zealous of good works." See that recurrence?

Look at the last part of Titus 3:1, "to be ready to every good work." Verse 8, "This is a faithful saying, and these things I will that thou affirm constantly, that they who have believed in God might be careful to maintain good works. These things are good and profitable unto men." Verse 14, "And let ours also learn to maintain good works." Paul is not saying that good works is the basis of salvation. You are not saved by your works, but he is saying your good works should be an evidence of your salvation. It is not good works in order to obtain salvation, but good works as an indication and evidence that you have salvation.

Ephesians 2:8-10 puts together grace, faith, and good works. When you look at the grace, faith, and works in those verses, you will see how everything fits together. Verse 8, "For by grace are ye saved through faith; and that not of yourselves, it is the gift of God." Verse 9, "Not of works, lest any man should boast." Then he says in verse 10, "For we are his workmanship [not our works, but His works], created in Christ Jesus unto good works, which God hath before ordained that we should walk in them." We see grace, faith, and works. As Paul writes to Titus, he puts the emphasis on this.

OUTLINE

Introduction, 1:1-4

I. Church Organization, 1
- **A. The Naming of Elders in the Local Church, 1:5-9**
- **B. The Nature of Error in the Local Church, 1:10-16**

II. Christian Obligation, 2–3
- **A. Some Personal Matters, 2:1-15**
- **B. Some Practical Matters, 3:1-11**

Conclusion, 3:12-15

Introduction, 1:1-4

The first four verses are verses of introduction.

I. Church Organization, 1

The first division is Church Organization. He discusses two basic areas here. First is the Naming of Elders in the Local Church, verses 5-9. He talks about it in verses 5, and then he gives some standards for elders in verses 6-9. He gives the standards for pastors, what kind of pastors they ought to be. The second matter is the Nature of Error in the Local Church, verses 10-16. He talks about some of the errors that Titus had to correct.

II. Christian Obligation, 2–3

The next section is Christian Obligation, chapters 2 through 3. In chapter 2: 1-15, he deals with Some Personal Matters. He talks about the older men and the older women of the church and how they are to be treated. He talks about the younger men and younger women and how they are to be brought along. Do you see the beautiful mix of a New Testament church? One of the things that has been going on is called target evangelism. What that term means is sometimes a church will say this is our target group. This is who we want to win to Christ. I understand what the terminology means, and I am not being overly critical about it because the fact of the matter is if you are in an area that is a retirement area and everyone is living in retirement centers or rest homes, your target is obviously the elderly. I understand that, but the truth of the matter is in terms of the New Testament assignment, we do not just target one segment of people. Our assignment is everybody, the old and the young. When you look at the New Testament, you will see a beautiful mix. You will find the older and you will find the younger. All of it flows so beautifully to make a wonderful fellowship in a church. The older Christians in a church have a responsibility to be faithful to teach the younger Christians and to also provide them examples.

In chapter 3:1-11, he covers Some Practical Matters. Then verses 12-15, Paul gives the Conclusion of Titus.

POSTCARD TO PHILEMON

This little book of 25 verses has been called a gospel masterpiece. It is the most personal of all of the New Testament letters. As best we can determine it is the only letter in the New Testament addressed to a lay person. It is written from Paul the apostle to a man named Philemon who was a layman in the church of Colosse. It is almost like a postcard.

The Holy Spirit actually lets us read someone else's mail. Evidently this brief letter was written by Paul at the same time he wrote the letter to the Colossians, and evidently this little letter was carried by the same hand that carried the Colossian letter. It is written to a man who is evidently a man in the church who has a wonderful Christian family. Now we don't know this proof positive, but look at the first two verses of Philemon. "Paul, a prisoner of Jesus Christ, and Timothy, our brother, unto Philemon, our dearly beloved, and fellow worker." Philemon is a male name. But then look at verse 2, "And to our beloved Apphia, and Archippus, our fellow soldier, and to the church in thy house."

It is generally believed that Philemon was the man in the house, Apphia was the wife, and Archippus was their son. We do not know that positively, but the indications are that this is true.

Here is evidently a very wonderful Christian family in the church of Colosse. What else did you notice here in verse 2? There was a church in their house.

You know, we are living in a day where we have church auditoriums and meeting centers and these kinds of things, and we just think it has always been that way. But for the first 100 years of the Christian faith, they did not have church buildings; but rather they met in homes and in other places. They had house churches, and that is still true in some parts of the world. It has been tried in American culture in numerous places but has not been overly successful. In those days it was not uncommon to have a church in someone's house.

The spiritual application that I want to make is, is there a church in your house? Your family is a little part of the fellowship of your church. All of us should have churches in our houses.

Its Man

Paul is obviously writing to a dedicated family. Philemon was evidently a wealthy Christian in this church of Colosse. Paul had evidently won him to faith in Christ. Look at Philemon 1:19, "I, Paul, have written it with mine own hand, I will repay it; albeit I do not say to thee how thou owest unto me even thine own self besides." What Paul is basically saying to Philemon is he led him to Christ; he owed his spiritual conversation to Paul.

Its Letter

In Colossians 4:9 and the following verses, there is a reference to Onesimus. This is the background for the epistle to Philemon. Evidently Philemon had a slave named Onesimus, and Onesimus ran away. To expedite his journey, evidently Onesimus stole some money from Philemon. He took off and went to Rome and lost himself in the moral muck of the capital city of the Roman Empire and wound up in jail. But when Onesimus wound up in jail, guess who happened to be in the same jail? A man named Paul. What do you think happened to Onesimus? Paul won Onesimus to faith in Jesus Christ. He then told him he had to return to Philemon and make restitution.

This is a beautiful story. The same man who won the master to the Lord now wins the slave to Christ, and he tells Onesimus he needs to return and make restitution. Did you know that restitution is a part of the salvation package? When we come to Christ, we need to make restitution, not to be saved but to show we are saved. A classic illustration of it in the New Testament is when Paul and Silas were in jail in Philippi. They were beaten and put in stocks. Then that night the earthquake came and the jailer was right on the verge of suicide. Paul told him to do himself no harm because they were all there, the prisoners had not escaped. He asked what he needed to do to be saved, and Paul told him to believe on the Lord Jesus Christ. Then it tells us the jailer took Paul and Silas and washed their stripes. He made restitution. Insofar as it is possible for people when they come to Christ, they need to make restitution of wrongs done. It is not a bad thing for people who have been Christians for a long time to make restitution also if needed.

So Paul is sending this man Onesimus back to his slave master. Let's move on to the lessons then. This has raised some questions.

Its Lessons

This little letter brings the gospel and social issues in tandem for a moment. It raises

the question how does the Christian faith apply to the social issues of the day? The burning social issue of the New Testament time was the issue of slavery. If there has ever been anything on the earth that was wrong, it was the institution of slavery. For one human being to own and control another human being is as bad as it gets. Yet, people have attacked the apostle Paul for not dealing with the social issues including slavery. Well, I beg to differ with that. Paul does deal with the issue of slavery right here in the letter to Philemon. In fact, Paul shows how the whole issue of slavery can be resolved. It is resolved in Jesus Christ. When people come to know Christ as their Savior, then every other person who knows Christ as Savior is their brother or sister in Christ. That is exactly what Paul is saying in this letter to Onesimus. Paul sends Onesimus back to Philemon, not as his slave, but as a brother in Christ. That is the solution. The government cannot solve the racial issue in America. You cannot force people to love one another; you cannot absolutely make people accept one another. But when Christ comes into your heart, He puts love in your heart for everybody regardless of race. The solution to the social issues is Jesus Christ, a personal faith in Jesus Christ.

Look at what Paul says about Onesimus in verse 16; he is sending him back, "Not now as a servant [it is the word slave] but above a servant, a brother beloved." He is no longer a slave, but he is a beloved brother. That is one of the great lessons for us, how the gospel addresses social issues.

Another issue and really the main lesson here is the beautiful picture of what Christ has done for us in salvation. Paul sends Onesimus back and he says to Philemon, if Onesimus owes you anything, put it on my account. Look at that in verse 18, "If he hath wronged thee or oweth thee anything, put that on mine account." Paul is saying whatever Onesimus owes, I'll take his debt. That is exactly what Jesus Christ did for us on the cross. What a beautiful picture this is of salvation. You and I were in debt; we had a debt we could not pay. Christ went to the cross of Calvary and said I'll take all of their sin on My account. That is what reconciliation means; that is what justification means.

We, who were sinners and had no righteousness, were able to have our sins laid on Jesus Christ, who was the perfectly righteousness one. He laid aside His righteousness, so to speak, on the cross of Calvary and took our sins in order that we might be clothed upon with His righteousness. It is a beautiful picture. Not only does it deal with the matter of reconciliation, the distance of sin, it also deals with restitution, the debt of sin. One of the most exciting and thrilling books in your Bible is the book of Philemon.

OUTLINE

Introduction, 1-3

I. Philemon: a Refreshing Saint, 4-7
- **A. His Life Godward "Faith"**
- **B. His Life Manward "Love"**

II. Onesimus: a Reclaimed Slave, 8-16
- **A. His Miserable Condition, 8-11**
- **B. His Marvelous Conversion, 12-17**

III. Paul: A Redemptive Soulwinner, 17-22
- **A. Reconciliation: the Distance of Sin, 17**
- **B. Substitution: the Debt of Sin, 18-22**

Conclusion, 23-25

Introduction, 1-3

The first three verses are introductory in nature. He gives the common introduction.

I. Philemon: a Refreshing Saint, 4-7

In verses 4-7, we build around Philemon, a Refreshing Saint. There are two words that describe his life: his life Godward and his life Manward. His life Godward is described by the word *faith*, verse 5, "Hearing of thy love and *faith*." Verse 6, "That the communication of thy *faith*." The second word, and it describes his life manward, is *love*. Verse 5, "Hearing of thy *love*." Look at verse 9, "Yet for *love's* sake." So it is Philemon, a Refreshing Saint.

II. Onesimus: a Reclaimed Slave, 8-16

Verses 8-17 are wrapped around Onesimus, a Reclaimed Slave. In verses 8-11, you have His Miserable Condition. It talks about what happened. By the way, there is an interesting play on words here with the name Onesimus. Look at verse 10, "I beseech thee for my son Onesimus, whom I have begotten in my bonds." What he says is he won him to the Lord while he was in jail. Verse 11, "Which in time past was to thee unprofitable." Now the word *Onesimus* means "profitable." Paul is doing a little play on words here. He was saying Onesimus indeed had not lived up to his name. He was a no-good. But now he says in verse 11 he is profitable to Philemon and him. His Marvelous Conversion is verses 12-16, and Paul tells about it.

III. Paul: A Redemptive Soulwinner, 17-22

The third section is wrapped around Paul, and we call him a Redemptive Soulwinner, verses 17-22. We see the beautiful two-fold picture here of salvation. Reconciliation: the Distance of Sin, is in verse 17. Then we see Substitution: the Debt of Sin in verses 18-22.

Conclusion, 23-25

The conclusion is verses 23-25.

Study #37
Heeding Hebrews

HEEDING HEBREWS

The book of Hebrews begins like an essay, continues like a sermon, and concludes like a letter.

It is the most unusual of all of the books of the New Testament in terms of where it occurs in the New Testament. It falls into the section known as the Letters of the New Testament.

There are three main divisions of the Letters of the New Testament. There are the Church Letters written by the apostle Paul to the various churches of the New Testament. Then there are some Personal Letters, and then beginning with the book of Hebrews we have what we call the General Letters. If you look at the overall picture of the Letters of the New Testament, you will find that Romans heads up the Church Letters and Hebrews heads up the General Letters.

It is helpful in the study of Hebrews to contrast Romans and Hebrews. Romans has to do primarily with the Christians' relation to the moral law. It shows how we have moved from law to grace. The moral law is dealt with by the book of Romans.

In the Old Testament, we not only have the moral law, but we also have the ceremonial law. The book of Hebrews deals with the ceremonial law and leads us from shadow to substance. In the Old Testament certain moral laws were given. For instance, the Ten Commandments fall into the category of the moral law, the "thou shall not's." But there is also in the Old Testament the ceremonial law, which is a series of directions and instructions for the different sacrifices and offerings that were required under the Old Testament system. All of the sacrifices that they were to make in the tabernacle and the temple fell under the category of the ceremonial law.

The book of Hebrews takes us from the shadow, that is all the Old Testament ceremonies which pointed toward the coming of Christ, into the substance or reality which we have in Jesus. You really cannot even begin to understand the book of Hebrews as you should unless you are familiar with the Old Testament because a lot of the references in the book of Hebrews take you back to the ceremonial law in the Old Testament.

Another thing to note is Hebrews is the only book in the New Testament which has the Divine Name as its opening word. Look at how the book of Hebrews begins, Hebrews 1:1, "God, who at sundry times and in diverse manners spake in time past." We are immediately attracted to this book by the way it begins. Most of the letters in the New Testament begin with some kind of introduction such as "Paul, an apostle to the saints at Rome," but this book right up front says "God." Here is a book which has its very beginning "God."

Its Author

This is one of the books that has no stated author. What do I mean? When you turn to the book of Romans for instance, Paul is the stated author. He tells you he is the author. But there is no author given for us for the book of Hebrews.

There is no destination given. In Paul's letters, for instance, he said, Paul, the apostle to all that be in Rome or to the saints at Philippi or wherever. But in Hebrews no destination is given.

The question comes up who is the author of the book of Hebrews? There have been a number of speculations. Many people believe Paul wrote this book of Hebrews. Other say Apollos, that young charismatic preacher in the early church, wrote this book. Others say Dr. Luke wrote the book of Hebrews. Some say Barnabas did, but the fact is there is no stated author, so no one knows who wrote the book of Hebrews.

However, there are some clues. There is good evidence that whoever the author was he was a Jew because he shows a great deal of familiarity with the Jewish Old Testament, with Jewish ceremonies, and with Jewish rituals. So we are fairly confident he was a Jew. He is also someone who was identified with Timothy; Hebrews 13:22-23, "And I beseech you, brethren, suffer [listen patiently to] the word of exhortation; for I have written a letter unto you in few words. Know ye that our brother, Timothy, is set at liberty; with whom, if he come shortly, I will see you."

There is a difference right there between what Paul normally says about Timothy. Paul usually referred to young Timothy as "my son in the faith." That is one reason why people say Paul did not write the book of Hebrews, that it was someone else.

Another thing to notice is in Hebrews 13:25, "Grace be with you all. Amen." The grace conclusion is fairly consistent of the letters of the New Testament, so we think the author was a Jew and he had some kind of relationship with young Timothy. He closes with the grace benediction.

There are some who say Paul could not have written Hebrews because it has a totally different style of writing. It has a totally different vocabulary from the letters of Paul; therefore, he could not have written this book. It is not a weighty argument against the authorship of Paul because your vocabulary is pretty well determined by your subject matter. And your subject matter, if you are on a different subject, might cause you to use a different vocabulary; so I have never been swayed too much by arguments about different style and vocabulary.

Another argument is the author is anonymous, and that is not Paul's way of doing things. Paul always named himself. He signed all of his other letters. That is not all that powerful either because the author is writing in a different vein altogether. It is evidently in a period of time when the hostility among the Jews towards the Christian faith was rising. Paul was a lightning rod in the whole situation. For that reason, Paul may not have used his name so his letter was not under attack from the outset. Basically you can argue on both sides. You can say Paul wrote it, or you can say Paul did not write it. The fact of the matter is the book itself does not tell us who wrote it.

A young preacher boy of mine who got a Ph.D. from the University of Texas and is now the professor of preaching at the Criswell College wrote his doctoral dissertation on the authorship of the book of Hebrews, and his position is it was written by Luke. He argues pretty persuasively. He does it on the basis of the vocabulary, and he points out that the vocabulary of Hebrews is very similar to the book of Acts and also the Gospel of Luke. He also takes the position that Luke was writing this book to this same man Theophilus to whom the Gospel of Luke and the book of Acts were addressed. His position is very complicated, but basically he says Theophilus was a Jew who became a Christian. He was also a priest. We do know that in the early church a great number of the priests were converted. Acts 6 tells us this. In those days, according to his investigation, they found out that if Jews, especially priests, converted to Christianity, they had deprogramming centers where they would take them and would try to break them down and pull them back into Judaism. His view is Luke was writing Hebrews to Theophilus who had been a priest, was converted, and had been sent to one of these deprogram centers. Basically Luke was saying to him don't turn back, keep on going in your Christian faith. It is an interesting theory, but that is all it is. We do not know.

Its Readers

The readers seem to be the Hebrew Christians. That part does seem to be true, that this book was intended for Hebrew Christians, Jews who had been converted to Christ. They were facing a lot of pressures. For a person who was a Jew to become a Christian was a very traumatic thing in terms of their family, and it is even to this day. It was not uncommon to have a funeral of a Jewish person who converted to Christianity.

The temple was evidently still standing, and all the Jewish ritual and tradition was still very, very strong. The Jews were saying to these Hebrew Christians, come on back. Come back into your Judaism. The book of Hebrews says do not go back, do not be at a spiritual standstill, but go forward, go on in Jesus Christ.

Its Message

Why is this book written? There are several reasons. One is to encourage us. There is probably no book that will give you any more encouragement in your

Christian life like this book of Hebrews will do. Look at the last chapter, Hebrews 13:22, "And I beseech you, brethren, suffer [listen patiently] the word of exhortation; for I have written a letter unto you in few words." It is a book of exhortation, of encouragement. It is written to encourage us.

Number two, it is evidently written to cause us to examine our faith, to see if we are maturing and growing in our faith. This book calls us to examination of our faith.

The third purpose is this book exalts Jesus Christ like few books in the Bible do. If you really want to see Jesus, who He is, what He did, and where He is to be placed in your life, the book of Hebrews will certainly do this.

Its Key Verse

The key to the book of Hebrews is Hebrews 6:1, "Therefore leaving the principles of the doctrine of Christ, let us go on unto perfection; not laying again the foundation of repentance from dead works, and of faith toward God."

What was happening was they were not moving forward, they were not growing in their Christian life. For instance, look at Hebrews 5:11, "Of who we have many things to say, and hard to be uttered, seeing ye are dull of hearing." Verse 12, "For when for the time ye ought to be teachers, ye have need that one teach you again which be the first principles of the oracles of God; and are become such as have need of milk, and not of strong meat." Instead of making progress, they seemed to be going backwards. They needed to hear the ABCs of the faith all over again. They were not making progress, they were not growing, and they were not going forward in their Christian faith.

In that context then is Hebrews 6:1, "Therefore." When you see the word *therefore,* always ask yourself the question what is the *therefore* there for? You are building on what has been previously said in this therefore. He just said to them they were not making progress, they needed to go back to the ABCs again. Instead of the meat of the Word, they needed some milk of the Word again. "Therefore leaving the principles of the doctrine of Christ." That does not mean deserting the principles but basically moving beyond the principles of the doctrine, that is the elementary fundamental basic truths. "Let us go on unto perfection."

Do you see that word *perfection*? You have to keep in mind what is meant by that word. We look at the word *perfection,* and we think in the terms of sinlessness. But when you see it in the New Testament, most of the time it is not talking about sinlessness but it is talking about maturity. He is saying let us go on to spiritual maturity. That is the thrust of the book of Hebrews. Let us move on to spiritual maturity. Move ahead in your spiritual life. It is a good stimulus to use for your own personal Christian life.

Its Key Words

There are some words that appear in Hebrews that are important for us. One of those words is the word *better* (Hebrews 1:4). It is right in the midst of one of the great passages on Christ in the Bible.

There are four great passages about Christ in the New Testament. The first one is John 1:1, "In the beginning was the Word, and the Word was with God, and the Word was God." The second great passage is Philippians 2:5-8, "Let this mind be in you, which was also in Christ Jesus: Who, being in the form of God, thought it not robbery to be equal with God: But made himself of no reputation, and took upon him the form of a servant, and was made in the likeness of men: And being found in fashion as a man, he humbled himself, and became obedient unto death, even the death of the cross." The third great passage is Colossians 1. The Bible says in this chapter Jesus is the creator of all things, He is the first begotten of all creation.

The fourth great passage on the deity of the Lord Jesus Christ is Hebrews 1. In Hebrews 1:4 he is talking about Jesus. How do I know that? Look at Hebrews 1:1, "God spake" and verse 2, "by His Son." The words that are around these words basically say in the past God spoke in a lot of different ways. "But now in the last days." The writer is using these *last days* in the terms of the coming of Christ and His return. In one sense of the word we have been in the last days since the first coming of Christ. God spoke in a lot of different ways in times past, but in these last days, these days of grace, He has spoken to us in His Son, Jesus. That is why it says in verse 4 that Jesus is made so much better than the angels.

Better is one of the key words in the book of Hebrews. Look for that word as you move through the book. He will say Jesus is better than the angels. He will say Jesus is better than the creation. The creation is getting old. It is going to wrap up like an old garment, but Christ will outlast the universe.

He is setting the superiority of Jesus, and he does it by this word *better.* For instance, look at Hebrews 6:9, "But, beloved, we are persuaded better things of you, and things that accompany salvation, though we thus speak." Look at Hebrews 7:7, "And without all contradiction the less is blessed of the better." Look at Hebrews 8:6, "he [Jesus] is the mediator of a better covenant, which was established upon better promises." He is trying to show in Jesus, everything we have today is better than the old covenant, than the old ceremonies.

Today when we come into our church, we do not find an altar with the body of an animal burning on it. We do not have that anymore because we have something better. We have the finished word of Christ on the cross. The book of Hebrews shows the superiority of Christ. He is better. He is better than the prophets and the angels; He is better than Moses and Joshua; He has a better priesthood, better sanctuary, better covenant, and a better resurrection. Everything about Jesus is better.

The second word is the word *perfect.* This word occurs a lot of times in the book of Hebrews. For instance, Hebrews 2:10, "to make the captain of their salvation perfect through sufferings." Look at Hebrews 5:9, "And being made perfect, he became the author of eternal salvation unto all them that obey him."

Another word that occurs a lot in Hebrews is *heavens* or *heavenly.* Hebrews 1:10, "And, thou, Lord, in the beginning hast laid the foundation of the earth; and the heavens are the works of thine hands." Hebrews 3:1, "Wherefore, holy brethren, partakers of the heavenly calling."

Another word that occurs significantly in Hebrews is the word *once.* For instance, look at Hebrews 6:4, "For it is impossible for those who were once enlightened, and have tasted of the heavenly gift, and were made partakers of the Holy Spirit." Look at Hebrews 7:27, "for this he did once, when he offered up himself." The word *once* really means "once for all." Look at Hebrews 9:12, "Neither by the blood of goats and calves, but by his own blood he entered in once [once for all] into the holy place, having obtained eternal redemption for us." Look at Hebrews 10:10, "By which will we are sanctified through the offering of the body of Jesus Christ once for all."

Its Warning Passages

Another introductory matter we want to look at is the warning passages. A better word is probably the encouragement passages. You will find scattered throughout the book of Hebrews a series of passages that encourage us to heed God's Word. They are exhortations or encouragements to us. The word *warning* may be confusing.

These passages are the ones that are difficult to understand. These are the ones that you really have a hard time understanding what he is talking about. How you interpret the overall book of Hebrews will have a lot to do with how you interpret the encouragement or warning passages.

I take the view, and a lot of good people differ on this so I do not think I have the final answer on it, that the book of Hebrews is written to and for the believers of the Lord Jesus Christ. It is not that they are in danger of going back and losing their salvation, but they are in danger of not going on and becoming everything God saved them to become.

Let me share this again. One of the principles of interpretation, which I have found to be helpful to me, is to learn to distinguish between a salvation passage and a fellowship passage. When I am reading a certain passage of Scripture, I will ask what is he talking about. Is he talking about how to be saved? Or he is talking about staying in fellowship with the Lord? Make this distinction in your mind, and it will really help you. This whole matter of eternal security and whether you can lose your salvation boils down to this: there is a difference between being in God's family and being in God's favor. When you are born again, you are born into God's family. You are God's child.

The Bible uses the word son, but it is used generically. It includes daughters. You become God's son, God's child. That relationship is an eternal relationship; nothing can break that relationship. I have two boys. Nothing can take them out of the Vines family. They are my boys. There is a difference between our family relationship and our fellowship relationship. There are some things they can do that will get them out of my favor, out of fellowship with me. The same thing is true in our relationship to the Lord. As members of the family of God, that relationship is eternal, nothing can break it; but in terms of being in fellowship with the Lord, we can have our fellowship with God broken. That helps me a great deal as I come to passages like I find here in the book of Hebrews, these warning passages. What is he talking about here? Is he talking about people losing their salvation? No. He is talking about matters that have to do with fellowship, growth, and maturity in the Christian faith.

Let me list the warning passages, and then we will look at the one in Hebrews 6. The first one is Hebrews 2:1-4. "Therefore, we [believers] ought to give the more earnest heed [attention] to the things which we have heard, lest at any time we should let them slip." What he is literally saying is lest we should let them drift by. He is not talking about slipping back into a lost condition. Then he says, "For if the word spoken by angels was steadfast [reliable], and every transgression and disobedience received a just recompense of reward, how shall we escape, if we neglect so great salvation." What did he not say there? He did not say how shall we escape if we reject. You cannot neglect something you do not have, so he is talking here not about losing your salvation. He is not talking about people who were on the verge of being saved and were getting ready to pull back. He is talking about people who were saved, but who were neglecting their salvation or not growing as they ought to grow as believers.

The second passage is in Hebrews 3:7 through Hebrews 4:13. In the first one he is talking about the danger of drifting from God's Word. The second one he is talking about the danger of doubting God's Word, and he talks about the Old Testament and the children of Israel, how they doubted God's Word and fell in the wilderness and failed to enter into the Promised Land.

The third passage is in Hebrews 5:11 and goes all the way to Hebrews 6:20. It is about the danger of degenerating from God's Word. The fourth one is Hebrews 10:26-29. The danger there is the danger of despising God's Word. The fifth one is Hebrews 12:14-19. It is the danger of departing from God's Word.

Let's go back to Hebrews 6:4, "For it is impossible for those who were once enlightened, and have tasted [this is the key word] of the heavenly gift, and were made partakers of the Holy Spirit."

The word *taste* means to experience. It is used very significantly also in Hebrews 2:9. "But we see Jesus, who was made a little lower than the angels for the suffering of death, crowned with glory and honor, that he, by the grace of God, should taste death for every man." When Jesus died on the cross, He did not just sample death but He experienced death. So the word *taste* means to experience. It is impossible for those who have experienced the heavenly gift and were made partakers of the Holy Spirit–he is talking about saved people.

But then notice, verse 6, "If they shall fall away." Is that talking about salvation? No. Is it talking about losing salvation? No. It is talking about losing their fellowship with God. He says it is impossible to renew them again unto repentance; seeing they crucify to themselves the Son of God afresh, and put him to an open shame."

Let me explain that. I have talked with Christians who got into a backslidden condition. While they are in that condition, while they are in that state of rebellion, you can talk to them until you are blue in the face, and it is impossible to renew them unto repentance. It is only God who can bring them back at that state of time.

What the author is saying to these people is he is expecting something better than this out of them. Look at what he says in verse 7, "For the earth, which drinketh in the rain that cometh often upon it, and bringeth forth herbs fit for them by whom it is tilled, receiveth blessing from God; but that which beareth thorns and briers is rejected, and is near unto cursing, whose end is to be burned." He gives an illustration of a field and a crop in the field. His point is the field is to produce fruit. Do you know what is to be the result of our fellowship with God? Fruit. So that is why he says in verse 9, "But, beloved, we are persuaded better things of you, and things that accompany salvation, though we thus speak." What accompanies salvation? Fruit. Fellowship. If you read these passages in that light, it will make a lot more sense to you.

OUTLINE

I. The Superior Person of Christ, 1:1–8:5
   A. In His Majesty
   B. In His Ministry
II. The Superior Provision of Calvary, 8:6–10:39
   A. A Better Security
   B. A Better Sanctuary
   C. A Better Sacrifice
III. The Superior Principles of Conduct, 11–13
   A. The Powerful Working of Faith
   B. The Patient Waiting of Hope
   C. The Perfect Willingness of Love

Keep in mind Hebrews sets forth the superiority of Jesus. Jesus is better. There are three main divisions in the book of Hebrews.

I. The Superior Person of Christ, 1:1–8:5

Here we see the Superior Person of Christ. In Jesus everything we have is better. He is superior In His Majesty. That is the beautiful picture of the deity of Jesus, chapter 1, all the way through chapter 2, verse 18. It sets forth the glory of Christ.

He is also superior In His Ministry, chapter 3 all the way through Hebrews 8:5. He talks about the ministry of Christ. Look at what it says in Hebrews 3:1, "Jesus is the Apostle and High Priest of our profession." In the Old Testament, they had a high priest. That high priest could go into the holy of holies one time a year with the blood of the lamb. Christ, our High Priest, took His own blood into the holy of holies in heaven, a superior place, and when He put His blood on the altar, it was once and for all. Now the good news is all of us are priests, which means we have the right of access to God through the Lord Jesus Christ our High Priest. You have to tie all this into the Old Testament.

II. The Superior Provision of Calvary, 8:6–10:39

In Hebrews 8:6, the writer starts comparing what happened in the Old Testament economy and what Jesus has done for us under the new covenant of His shed blood. In Hebrews 8:6-13, we have a Better Security. In Christ we have a better security.

Chapter 9:1-10, we have a Better Sanctuary. Look at Hebrews 9:1. He goes back into the Old Testament and talks about that Old Testament tabernacle. He describes the different pieces of furniture, the different articles of furniture. Christ has fulfilled it all, and that is what he is saying. Christ is a better sanctuary. We do not need an Old Testament temple anymore. We do not need the Old Testament tabernacle anymore. What we have in Christ is far superior.

The third point is we have a Better Sacrifice, Hebrews 9:11, all the way through to chapter 10. These are some of the greatest verses in the Bible about the blood of Christ. Look at Hebrews 10:19 and see what Christ has done for us. "Having therefore, brethren, boldness to enter into the holiest [holy of holies] by the blood of Jesus." How do we enter into the holy of holies? By the blood of Jesus Christ. In the Old Testament they had the blood of bulls and goats. All that blood did was look forward to the time when Christ would shed His blood for us.

III. The Superior Principles of Conduct, 11–13

As he closes out the book, what he basically does is show that in the Christian faith we now have a superior lifestyle. We have a lifestyle based on faith, hope, and love. Chapter 11 is the great faith chapter. He talks about the Powerful Working of Faith, and he gives the Old Testament survey. He goes back and names Old Testament characters just one after the other all the way through. He is saying that faith is a superior principle for life. In chapter 12, he talks about hope, the Patient Waiting of Hope, and you will find some wonderful things. He talks about chastisement here, looking unto Jesus, and the hope we have in our Lord Jesus Christ.

The 13th chapter is the Perfect Willingness of Love. It is not all you will find in that chapter though. This book is not an easy book to understand because there are a lot of Old Testament pictures in it, but keep in mind the writer is trying to show that Jesus is better.

Study #38
Journey with James

JOURNEY WITH JAMES

Every book of the Bible has its particular setting and its particular purpose, and the book of James is no exception to this. Of all the books of the New Testament, the book of James is the most practical and the most down to earth.

Its Author

James right up front gives us the author of the book; he tells who he is. James 1:1, "James, a servant of God and of the Lord Jesus Christ." There is one little complicated note because in the New Testament there are three different James mentioned. Which one is this? We are fairly confident that this James was the half-brother of our Lord Jesus. There are several verses of scripture which makes us believe this.

One of the things you want to do, if you are trying to check these kinds of matters out, is get a Bible concordance. A Bible concordance is a book that has the words of the Bible and where they occur, so get a good Bible concordance and look up James. You will find more than one James; but when you find the brother of the Lord, then trace those references.

In Galatians 1:19, it says, "But other of the apostles saw I none, except James, the Lord's brother." That is a pretty clear statement. Paul was talking about going up to Jerusalem and consulting with the early church. One of the people Paul consulted with was James, the Lord's brother.

We know from the Gospels that the Lord Jesus did have a brother named James. For instance, in Mark 6, we learn that the Lord Jesus had brothers and also sisters. Mark 6:3 says, "Is not this the carpenter, the son of Mary, the brother of James, and Joseph, and of Judas, and Simon? And are not his sisters here with us?"

We know Jesus had more than one sister and He also had these brothers. One of them was named James. He was a half-brother of the Lord, brought up in the same family that our Savior, the Lord Jesus Christ, was. That is significant.

Now, we do know that initially the Lord's family did not believe in Him. These kinds of matters may impact what is said in the book sometimes and they assist our understanding. What we are doing here is called background studies, gathering all this evidence because this evidence will have something to do with how we understand these particular books.

In Matthew 13:55, Jesus is teaching at the height of His ministry, and it says, "Is not this the carpenter's son? Is not his mother called Mary? And his brethren, James, and Joseph, and Simon, and Judas?" Verse 57 says, "And they were offended in him." It continues to say, "But Jesus said unto them, a prophet is not without honor, save in his own country, and in his own house." Keep that in mind. He was saying that many times a prophet, a teacher, is not recognized in his own house.

The Gospel of John shows how close that rejection came to the Lord. In John 7 it was time for the feast of the tabernacles, one of feast days, a religious holiday of the Jewish people. In John 7: 3 it says, "His brethren, therefore, said unto him, depart hence, and go into Judea [that is go in before the festival], that thy disciples also may see the works that thou doest." What they were saying to Jesus was for Him to go where the crowds were going to be so they could see all He was doing.

Then they said in verse 4, "For there is no man that doeth anything in secret, and he himself seeketh to be known openly." Notice they made a judgment right there about Jesus. They were suggesting that Jesus was seeking to make a name for Himself. In other words, go show yourself; do all of this. No man is in secret when he is seeking to be known openly. They were judging the heart of the Lord.

Look at verse 5. "For neither did his brethren believe in him." His own household, His own family, Jesus' brothers, did not believe in Him. If James was one of those brothers, evidently he was a part of that unbelief.

Something happened though. When Jesus died on the cross, as best as we can tell, none of His family was there except His mother. We have pretty strong evidence that none of His brothers was there because on the cross when Jesus wanted to care for His mother, He called out to John, the beloved disciple, to take care of His mother. You don't argue from silence all the time, but we have a pretty good idea His brothers were not there. They were humiliated about it all. But something happened. After Jesus died and was buried, three days later He came back from the dead.

First Corinthians 15 is talking about the resurrection. Paul discusses the gospel, which is the death, burial, and resurrection of the Lord Jesus Christ. Then he begins to list the resurrection appearances, the times Jesus was seen after His resurrection. He says in verse 5, "And that he was seen of Cephas, then of the twelve." Who was Cephas? Simon Peter; then of the twelve apostles. Verse 6, "After that, he was seen of above five hundred brethren at once [at one time]. That wipes out the argument that people had hallucinations and just thought Jesus rose from the dead. Five hundred do not have a hallucination at the same time. Verse 6 concludes, "of whom the greater part remain unto this present, but some are fallen asleep."

Then look at verse 7. "After that, he was seen of James." James, the half-brother of the Lord, had not believed that Jesus was the Messiah, the Christ; but after the resurrection Jesus appeared to James. Of course, the clear inference from that is that James became a follower of the Lord.

Not only James but evidently many other family members also became followers of Jesus. This is in Acts 1. In Acts 1, we are told about the ten-day prayer meeting after Jesus went back to heaven and before the Holy Spirit was given on the day of Pentecost. In verse 13 it tells about the upper room and the apostles who were there. It mentions two James, but they are not the James we are talking about. They were part of the twelve disciples: James the brother of John and James the son of Alphaeus. But then it says in verse 14, "These all continued with one accord in prayer and supplication, with the women, and Mary, the mother of Jesus, and with his brethren." Jesus' brothers were in the upper room; they became convinced that their earthly half-brother was indeed the Son of God.

James became a believer, was converted to faith in the Lord Jesus Christ, and became a leader of the church in Jerusalem. In Galatians 2 Paul was talking about going up to Jerusalem to confer with the leaders of the church there on important issues. While Paul discussed these issues with the church at Jerusalem, James is listed as a leader; verse 9: "And when James, Cephas, and John, who seemed to be pillars, perceived the grace that was given unto me, they gave to me and Barnabas the right hands of fellowship." James, evidently, became one of the pillars of the church.

It seems that James may have been the pastor of the church of Jerusalem. It is a little hard to tell whether or not it was James who or it was Peter or if they were co-pastors. In Acts 15 is what is called the first Jerusalem council. Through the history of the Christian church, there have been church councils. When great doctrinal issues arose, when heresies were taught, the church would gather together in councils and they would discuss these doctrinal matters.

Acts 15 tells about the first church council, and the first issue that arose was what was salvation. The first heresy the church had to deal with was the teaching that a person had to work in order to earn or merit salvation and a person had to become a Jew in order to be saved. The Judaizers brought it up. They said except people were circumcised after the Law of Moses they could not be saved, but that was a work. That was not what Paul was preaching, so there became this big issue, how is a person saved? Was it only by faith in Jesus Christ or did a person have to go through the Jewish door in order to get to Christ?

Paul took his stand on salvation by grace through faith, so they had this big church council on it in Acts 15. Paul shared his testimony, what God was doing among the Gentiles and how the Gentiles were being saved. In verse 7, Simon Peter stood up and gave his opinion on the matter, and said in verse 11, "But we believe that through the grace of the Lord Jesus Christ we shall be saved, even as they." What he was saying was that we Jews have to get saved just like the Gentiles do, through faith in Jesus Christ. He was saying there was no advantage to being Jewish because that was not going to get them to heaven a bit quicker than the Gentiles.

Look at what it says in Acts 15:13, "And after they had held their peace, James answered, saying, Men and brethren, hearken unto me." You can almost hear the quietness hit the room. Then he says in verse 14, you know what our brother Simon has just said; then he continues in verse 15, "And to this agree the words of the prophets." This is what the Bible teaches. Then he says in verse 17, "That the residue of men might seek after the Lord"; he is quoting from Amos 9. He continues, "And all the Gentiles, upon whom my name is called, saith the Lord, who doeth all these things." Verses 19 and 20, "Wherefore, my sentence is, that we trouble not them, which from among the Gentiles are turned to God; But we write unto them."

He said we know what salvation is, it is by grace through faith in Jesus Christ. Now let us write our new Gentile brothers this letter of encouragement to encourage them to do these things in verse 20, "abstain from pollutions of idols, and from fornication, and from things strangled, and from blood."

The background of some of that was the Jewish customs. James was saying in order not to bring offense to the Christian Jews who were so strong in some of the errors to encourage the Gentiles Christians to be considerate of their scruples, and to encourage them to apply their new found salvation to their daily life and to their moral and ethical behavior. He was saying something very down-to-earth. He was saying let's be sure that these Gentiles understand that their faith is to be applied to their daily life.

That pleased them all. That solved the issue. The letter was written. Look down at verse 23. The letter was written, and the Holy Spirit preserved the letter for us. Act 15:23, "And they wrote letters by them after this manner: the apostles and elders and brethren send greeting unto the brethren who are of the Gentiles in Antioch and Syria and Cilicia."

There is one other reference to James, Acts 21:18. Paul was going to see James. "And the day following Paul went in with us unto James; and all the elders were present."

That is the background of this man James. He was a believer in the Lord who came to Christ after the resurrection. He was a pillar of the church in Jerusalem, probably its pastor or co-pastor. He was very influential. In addition to what the Bible says, we are told that he was a very godly man and also a great man of prayer. In fact, he had a nickname. They called James "old camel knees" because they said James spent so much time on his knees in prayer that he developed calluses on his knees just like camels have on their knees. Wouldn't that be something if you and I prayed so much we developed calluses on our knees? Tradition is that he was martyred, that he was stoned to death for his faith in the Lord Jesus Christ.

Its Letter

Some say James is the earliest letter of the New Testament. It is debatable; some say I Thessalonians is, and some say Galatians is. Whatever, it was evidently written quite early.

Notice James 1:1, "James, a servant of God and of the Lord Jesus Christ, to the twelve tribes which are scattered abroad, greeting." It is the only letter that is so addressed in the New Testament. When James said let us write letters to the Gentiles, how did the letters start it? Greeting (Acts 15:23). Do you see the connection there?

Notice what he didn't say in describing himself. He didn't say I want you to know I'm brother James here, I'm the half-brother of the Lord. I'm the pillar of the church. He just called himself a servant, a slave of God in the Lord Jesus Christ.

He is writing this letter "to the twelve tribes which are scattered abroad, greeting."

The words *scattered abroad* translate one word, "diaspora." We have a word that comes from that, the word *dispersion*. It is to the twelve tribes who were dispersed, scattered abroad.

Diaspora is made up of two words, *spora,* which means "to sow" and *dia,* which is a preposition, which means "through." It means to sow seed through the field.

There are two things that you have to know about the twelve tribes scattered aboard. The first thing is there was already a group of Jews who had been scattered in other places. There was a group called the dispersion. During the ministry of the Lord Jesus Christ, on one occasion He talked about preaching to another group of people (John 7:32-36). He said you will seek Me, and you won't find Me, and where I am, you can't come. So in John 7:35, "Then said the Jews among themselves, where will he go, that we shall not find him? Will he go unto the dispersed among the Gentiles?" This is the same word, the diaspora.

The Jews had been dispersed among the Gentiles also. There were two groups of Jews. You had the Jews of dispersion and then you had what was known as the Hebrew Jews, the ones who stayed in Palestine. You had the Jews who remained in the homeland, and you had the Jews who were dispersed to other countries.

But this letter is written evidently to Christian Jews. In other words, Jews who had come to Christ, who were scattered out into these areas where other Jews were.

Note Acts 8:1. "And Saul was consenting unto his death. And at that time there was a great persecution against the church which was at Jerusalem; and they were all scattered abroad [dispersion] throughout the regions of Judea and Samaria, except the apostles." The apostles stayed in the center of the flame. Acts 8:4 says, "Therefore, they [the Christian Jews] that were scattered abroad went everywhere preaching the word." These Christians Jews went everywhere preaching the word, the gospel. So, James was writing to the twelve tribes, to Jews, who had been believers in Jesus Christ and were now scattered abroad.

We know that one of the things that happened to the Jews, who were scattered to these other countries, before the spread of Christianity, was they were very tempted to assimilate themselves into the lives and behavior patterns of the land wherever they were. We have archaeological evidence, for instance, that in some of the Jewish synagogues in some of these lands where they were dispersed, they would have drawings of pagan gods on the walls of their synagogues. What happened was the world had spilled in or pagan beliefs had spilled into the synagogues.

These Christians Jews were being scattered. They had the same temptations. The same temptation was to let the culture influence and change them instead of their influencing the culture and changing the culture. Does that sound familiar to you? Is that not where we are today in America? Isn't that the temptation? The danger is that you and I as believers will allow the world around us to cause us to be like it, instead of our changing our world.

The book of James is interesting and important because James is writing a letter to people who were in similar circumstances to you and to me. That is why you will find this book so helpful.

When you read this book of James, you will notice there is a distinct Jewish flavor to it. For instance, James 2:2, "For if there come unto your assembly"; the better word would be synagogue. You see, the early Christians at the beginning continued to go to the synagogue, so he was using a Jewish term here. You will find many Old Testaments figures of speech and references in the book of James.

Here is something else that is interesting. You will find a lot of similarity between what James writes and the Sermon on the Mount given by his half-brother, the Lord Jesus. It reads like the Sermon on the Mount at times.

Its Theme

The theme of the book of James is practical Christian behavior, a belief that behaves. Christians must so live out the principles of their faith that they will impact their culture for good. The theme is practical Christianity, living out your Christianity in a practical goodness.

The fourth thing I want to deal with here is the imagined conflict between what James says and what Paul says about faith and works. Some people have imagined a conflict between Paul's teaching and James' teaching in the areas of faith and works. Paul's basic picture of faith and works is in Ephesians 2:8-9, "For by grace are ye saved through faith; and that not of yourselves, it is the gift of God: Not of works, lest any man should boast." Verse 10 continues, "For we are his workmanship, created in Christ Jesus unto good works, which God hath before ordained that we should walk in them." Paul said we are justified by grace, through faith, plus nothing, minus nothing.

James then says a man is not justified by faith only, he is justified by works. People read that and say Paul and James contradict one another. What resolves the imagined conflict is this, James and Paul are writing about faith, but they are writing on different sides of the issue. Paul is writing on the believing side of faith, and James is writing on the behaving side of faith.

Note these two things and they will help you. Paul is saying that we are justified by faith before God privately. The second statement to note is James says we are justified by works before men publicly. They are talking about faith but on different sides of the matter. Paul says we are justified by faith before God privately, and he illustrates that in the life of Abraham when he believed God and God declared him righteous and God justified him.

James says we are justified by works before men publicly. In other words, James says we prove our faith is the saving kind of faith by our behavior. He is saying if your behavior isn't right, it indicates that something is wrong in your faith.

OUTLINE

Introduction, 1:1

- **I. A Christian and His Battles, 1:2-16**
  - **A. His Testings, 1:2-12**
  - **B. His Temptations, 1:13-16**
- **II. A Christian and His Bible, 1:17-27**
  - **A. A Gift, 1:17-18**
  - **B. A Graft, 1:19-22**
  - **C. A Glass, 1:23-27**
- **III. A Christian and His Brethren, 2:1-13**
  - **A. Partiality and the Lord, 2:1-7**
  - **B. Partiality and the Law, 2:8-13**
- **IV. A Christian and His Beliefs, 2:14-26**
  - **A. Declared, 2:14-17**
  - **B. Debated, 2:18-20**
  - **C. Decided, 2:21-26**
- **V. A Christian and His Behavior, 3:1–4:12**
  - **A. Sin Revealed, 3:1–4:4**
  - **B. Sin Resisted, 4:5-10**
  - **C. Sin Repudiated, 4:11-12**
- **VI. A Christian and His Boasting, 4:13–5:6**
  - **A. Plans, 4:13-17**
  - **B. Prosperity, 5:1-6**
- **VII. A Christian and His Burdens, 5:7-20**
  - **A. Patience, 5:7-12**
  - **B. Prayer, 5:13-18**
  - **C. People, 5:19-20**

The first verse is the introduction, James 1:1. Let's look at the division, which are taken from Dr. John Phillips. It is an elaborate an outline, but it is so good.

I. A Christian and His Battles, 1:2-16

There are two main divisions here; first is the Christian's Testings, verses 2-12. Next is the Christian's Temptations, verses 13-16. He uses a word, but he uses the word in a different way in the two passages. For instance, look at verse 2, "My brethren, count it all joy when ye fall into divers temptations." Divers means many. Count it all joy when you fall into many temptations.

In verse 13 he says, "Let no man say when he is tempted, I am tempted of God: for God cannot be tempted with evil, neither tempteth he any man." Verse 14, "But every man is tempted, when he is drawn away of his own lust, and enticed."

He uses the same word, but he uses it in a different way. There is a difference between testing and temptation. God tests us to bring out the best in us. Satan tempts us to bring out the worst in us. Testings come from God; temptations come from Satan. God allows us to be tested to prove the reality and genuineness of our faith and to help that faith become pure and what it is intended to be. Satan tempts us in order to cause us to sin. That is the first section, a Christian and His Battles. His testings and his temptations.

II. A Christian and His Bible, 1:17-27

The second division is a Christian and His Bible. There are three beautiful pictures of your Bible in these verses. James abounds in beautiful pictures, illustrations. He uses some illustrations to show what the Bible is like. For instance, the Bible is like a Gift; verses 17-18, "Every good gift and every perfect gift is from above." Verse 18, "Of his own will begat he us with the word of truth [the Bible]." The Bible is like a Gift. What a wonderful gift.

Then the Bible is like a Graft, verses 19-22. He talks in verse 21 about receiving the engrafted, the implanted, word into our life. God's Word is engrafted into our life.

Then in verses 23-27, he says the Bible is like a Glass. Verse 23, "For if any be a hearer of the word, and not a doer, he is like unto a man beholding his natural face in a glass." He compares the Bible to a glass. In the morning you look in the mirror, and there you are. We open up the Bible and read it, and it shows us where we are. The good news is it also shows us Jesus. The Bible differs from a mirror glass in that all the physical glass can do is show you the mess you are in; it cannot do anything about it. But the good news about the Bible is it not only shows us ourselves, but it also helps us clean our life and make us more like Christ.

III. A Christian and His Brethren, 2:1-13

The word *brethren* is used generically. It includes sisters too. It talks about partiality, showing respect of persons and favoritism, and being partial to people. James basically says not to do that. Verses 1-7 are Partiality and the Lord. The Lord has no respect of persons. Verses 8-13 cover Partiality and the Law.

IV. A Christian and His Beliefs, 2:14-26

This division is the faith and works section. Here is the key. There is a statement that is made pretty much the same way three times. Look at verses 17, 20, and 26. It says in verse 17, "faith, if it hath not works, is dead, being alone." Verse 20, "But wilt thou know, O vain man, that faith without works is dead?" Verse 26, "For as the body without the spirit is dead, so faith without works is dead also." Three times he says faith without works is dead. He is not saying that you are saved by your works. He is saying that your works prove the reality and genuineness of your faith. In verses 14-17, he Declares that truth, and he uses an illustration. It is not enough to tell a man who is cold and hungry be warm and be fed. He says you have to do something about it. Then he Debates it in verses 18-20 with an imaginary objector. In verse 18, "Yea, a man may say." He puts in an imaginary objector. Then he responds. Then he Decides the whole issue in verses 21-26 by using the Bible illustration of Abraham. He shows Abraham was justified by faith before God in Genesis 15. That is when Abraham got outside that night and the stars were up in the sky. God asked him if he saw all those stars. He said, "Yes, Lord." God then said his offspring would be as numerous as those stars. The Bible says Abraham believed God, and God declared him righteous. God justified him. God saved him. That was private, just Abraham and God.

Then James goes to Genesis 22 where Abraham was told to take his son Isaac and sacrifice him. Abraham proved that his faith in God was real by what he did, by laying his son on the altar. Publicly the whole world could see Abraham had faith.

V. A Christian and His Behavior, 3:1–4:12

He talks about Sin Revealed, James 3:1–4:4. It is an interesting illustration. If you were going to give an illustration on sin and how detrimental, dangerous, and destructive it is, what would you use? There are a lot of different things, but do you know what James does? James picks the illustration of the sin of the tongue and how destructive the tongue is. He uses a series of illustrations. Sin revealed, James 3:1–4:4. The he gives Sin Resisted, 4:5-10, and he shows how to resist sin and the temptation to sin. He talks about resisting the devil, submitting yourself to God, and drawing near to God. Then James 4:11-12, he shares Sin Repudiated.

VI. A Christian and His Boasting, 4:13–5:6

In these verses he uses two fascinating illustrations. One is of the business man in verse 13. He makes all these plans, but the Bible says you do not even know what tomorrow may bring. Your life is like a vapor of smoke. You ought to be saying if the Lord wills, I will do these things. It is not good to boast.

Then in James 5:1-6, he talks about Prosperity and the danger of riches, boasting about material things. He says you heap together treasures for the last days, you rich man. It is not an across-the-board condemnation of rich men. The Bible does not forbid a person from becoming rich, but the Bible warns of riches becoming the center of your life, that your material possessions become the main thing in your life. We need to keep things in the right perspective.

VII. A Christian and His Burdens, 5:7-20

He talks about being patient and the burdens of life sometimes call for patience. Then verses 13-18 is the beautiful section on Prayer. Then verses 19-20, he talks about People and recovering damaged goods. You need to be interested in people and in reaching out to people.

Study #39
Promises in 1 Peter

PROMISES IN I PETER

First Peter is the first of two letters in our New Testament written by Simon Peter. As we consider the introductory matters, we do come to the matter of the author.

Its Author

There seems to be little question that the author of this book and the second book which bears his name is indeed Simon Peter who was one of the disciples of the Lord. In fact, he specifically says this in I Peter 1:1, "Peter, an apostle of Jesus Christ." The integrity of the letter is on the line because if Peter did not write it, then someone forged the letter and it is a forgery.

When I was involved in issues relative to the Southern Baptist Convention and some of the liberal teaching that was going on, one area of concern was that some were ascribing Bible books to authors rather than the ones that bear their names. When you come to the book of Hebrews, we don't have an author ascribed to it, and so that is open for a difference of opinion. But when you come to a book which specifically says someone wrote it, like I Peter, and people go in another direction and say Peter did not write it, but it was actually written by someone else who used his name, then the integrity of the document is called into question. We believe the stated authors of the books of the Bible are indeed the authors, as is Simon Peter.

It is interesting to think about the different authors of the books of the New Testament, who they were and how God used them in spite of their failure. For instance, Matthew was the tax collector who, according to what we understand about that profession in Israel at that time, was certainly a man of less than stellar character; yet because of what Christ did in his life, God used him to write the book of Matthew.

Then there was young John Mark, who appeared to have failed at the outset. He had a rocky start in his service for the Lord, so much so that he was a catalyst for a disagreement between Paul and Barnabas. They split up over the fact that John Mark did not stay with them, and yet God gave Mark a second chance so he wrote the second Gospel. Of course, there is John, the beloved disciple. Paul, who wrote half or more of the books of the New Testament, was a blasphemer. He consented to the death of Christians in the early church, and yet God saved him and used him to be a writer of the books of the Bible.

Then we come to Simon Peter. He is the one who the night before the crucifixion denied he even knew the Lord. Yet God forgave Simon Peter, and now he is the author of I and II Peter.

There are two things that the Lord Jesus said to Simon Peter which bear on his letters. One is found in Luke 22:32. The Lord told Simon Peter the night before the cross that he was going to deny that he knew Him and Simon Peter vehemently said, Lord, not me, You can count on me; everybody else may forsake You but not me. The Lord said to him that before the rooster would crow three times, Peter would deny Him. But then Jesus said this to him: "Simon, Simon, behold, Satan hath desired to have you, that he may sift you as wheat; But I have prayed for thee, that thy faith fail not. And when thou art converted, strengthen thy brethren." The Lord Jesus said to Simon Peter, Simon I'm going to give you a ministry of strengthening the brethren.

The second thing is in John 21:15-17. This is after the resurrection and the disciples were on the sea of Galilee. Simon Peter was probably down in the dumps having denied his Lord and certainly feeling like you and I feel when we don't measure up to what we should be with the Lord. The Lord prepared breakfast for them, and then the Lord gave Simon a little test. He asked, Simon, do you love Me? Peter replied, Lord, You know I love You. In the setting of that passage Jesus said to Simon Peter, feed My sheep.

Simon Peter had basically a twofold assignment from the Lord: strengthen the brethren and feed His sheep. We see Simon uniquely obeying this assignment from the Lord in the writing of I Peter and also in the writing of II Peter.

The first book of Peter is a very strengthening book for Christians. It will strengthen your faith, it will encourage you, and it will feed you. For instance, look at I Peter 5:10, "But the God of all grace, who hath called us unto his eternal glory by Christ Jesus, after ye have suffered awhile, make you perfect, establish, strengthen, settle you." He is talking about the strength which comes from the Lord.

Notice he addresses this letter in chapter 1:1, to the strangers who are scattered throughout Pontus, Galatia, Cappadocia, Asia and Bithynia, five locations. He is writing to five particular areas; he lets us know in I Peter 5:13 from where he is writing, "The church that is at Babylon, elected together with you, greeteth you; and so doth Mark, my son."

He is evidently where the church of Babylon was located. The question is where is that? Someone will say Babylon is in Iraq, but there was no Babylon at that time. There was no inhabitable place where they were living at that point. It is pretty well believed that Simon Peter is referring to Rome, that the church at Babylon is a reference to the church at Rome and he was in Rome.

This is an area where we differ with our Catholic friends; we do not believe that Simon Peter founded the church of Rome. One of the reasons we don't believe he did is because Paul specifically says in Romans 15:20 that his strategy was to go places where there was no established work, not to build on somebody else's foundation. That being true, we don't believe Simon Peter established the church of Rome, but evidently Simon Peter did visit Rome and had a ministry there.

Why does Peter call it the church at Babylon if he was in Rome? There is pretty good evidence that Babylon is a symbol for Rome. Look at Revelation 17:3 and 9. In this chapter it is talking about the judgment of the great whore that sits upon the waters and the kings that had committed fornication with her. Then verse 3 says, "So he carried me away in the spirit into the wilderness and I saw a woman sit upon a scarlet colored beast, full of names of blasphemy, having seven heads and ten horns." Notice the seven heads.

Note Revelation 17:9, "And here is the mind which hath wisdom. The seven heads are seven mountains, on which the woman sitteth." It is generally agreed this is a reference to the city of Rome, the city of seven hills.

Verse 3 describes the beast and the seven heads, and then verse 5 says, "And upon her forehead was a name written, mystery, Babylon the great, the mother of harlots and an abominations of the earth."

Simon Peter was writing at a time when persecution was breaking out. In times of great persecution, when it was not popular to be a Christian and when people were having to, so to speak, be undercover with their faith, it was common to use code language, to speak in code language. It is believed that the church at Babylon was code terminology for the church at Rome.

I am really not much into the matter of the hidden codes found in the text of the Bible. It does not appeal to me because you can find just about anything you want to find. The skip codes that are used to come up with those kinds of things are rather arbitrary. It is not the best way to study the Bible. You do not need to be looking for hidden numerical codes. There is truth in the fact that numbers in certain parts of the Bible have significance. There is no question that the number 666 has symbolic significance because six is the number of human failure. It is one short of coming up to perfection, seven. So 666 is the epitome of human failure. The Antichrist is going to be the best that man can produce, but he will fall short. You need to be very careful about finding hidden meanings and being dogmatic about them. Do not misunderstand when I talk about codes and think I am endorsing the numerical codes and those kinds of things. I am not. If that be true, if that is the only way you can get the true message of the Bible, then no one before the days of the computer could ever have gotten the true message of the Bible.

I am saying certain words were used, and one of the reasons you have the book of the Revelation written in code language is because great persecution had burst upon the Christian church and they wrote in coded language for the protection of certain individuals.

Peter was probably in Rome and was writing to Christians who were in the area where Paul went on one of his missionary journeys. These were five different parts of the Roman Empire in the northern part of Asia Minor, known today as modern Turkey.

The letter of Peter is associated with two other individuals. One was Silas or Silvanus, a faithful brother (I Peter 5:12). He was evidently with Peter at this time. It is also associated with Marcus (I Peter 5:13), "so doth Marcus my son." I do not think he was talking about a physical son here. I think he was talking about John Mark. It is commonly believed Simon Peter won John Mark to the Lord. That being true, when you read the Gospel of Mark there is pretty good indication that Mark took the sermons of Simon Peter and, using those sermons as his basic reference material and under the inspiration of the Holy Spirit, composed the Gospel of Mark.

Its Readers

Evidently the readers were people in regions associated with the ministry of the apostle Paul.

Notice he says, "Peter, an apostle of Jesus Christ, to the strangers scattered throughout." He used the term strangers. That means those who were scattered, the scattered ones, the sojourners. This is a terminology that Peter picks up again in I Peter 2:11. Connect this verse with I Peter 1:1. One of the things you want to do when studying the books of the Bible is to look for words that are repeated. They can give you the substance or subject matter of that particular book.

Note I Peter 2:11, "Dearly beloved, I beseech you as sojourners and pilgrims, abstain from freshly lusts which war against the soul." That is a beautiful picture of Christians. Christians are strangers and pilgrims. What that means is as Christians this is not our home; we are strangers here, we don't belong here.

When you come to Christ and receive Him as your personal Savior, then Philippians 2 teaches that you now have a new citizenship; you are no longer a citizen of this world but a citizen of Heaven. Our citizenship is in Heaven, and that makes us strangers down here.

The word *sojourner* means we are just passing through, but we are on our way somewhere. I do not know about you, but that is encouraging to me. When I was a boy and used to get ready for church on Sunday morning, I would hear the "Old-Fashioned Revival Hour" with Dr. Charles E. Fuller. The Old-Fashioned Revival Hour choir with Rudy Atwood at the piano would come on that program with "This world is not my home, I'm just a-passing through. My treasures are laid up somewhere beyond the blue. The angels beckon me from heaven's open door, and I can't feel at home in this world anymore." I will never forget it. Well, that is taken right here from this passage of scripture. Peter wanted these believers in the day in which he wrote to know they did not belong here, but they were passing through and headed to a better world because things were getting pretty tough down here for them. Always keep in mind too that we get the benefit of Peter's letter, but his first readers were people living at that time. They were glad to hear their citizenship was in Heaven.

Its Situation

First Peter was written probably in the mid 60s. In July A.D. 64, Nero the emperor burned the city of Rome. The word was that Nero wanted to build new buildings and in order to make way for new buildings, he burned the old ones. But this caused an upheaval in Rome; the people became upset about this. Nero had to have a scapegoat for his acts so he blamed the burning of Rome on the Christians.

Nero would burn Christians alive to illuminate his gardens at night, and it became a time of great persecution. That is significant because in I Peter 4:12, Peter was saying, evidently writing from Rome: "Beloved, think it not strange concerning the fiery trial which is to try you, as though some strange thing happened unto you." What he is saying is don't be surprised by this persecution.

He is writing in the context of the persecution that was breaking out as the result of Nero. He is also writing to get them ready for even more serious persecution and trouble that were coming. What he was saying is we live in a hostile world, and we are going to face many temptations, trials, and tribulations. It is going to get even worse.

That brings us to today because in our day it is becoming more and more unpopular to be a Christian. When the tide finally changes, and it is moving in that direction in our society, I believe before the Lord comes a complete turn will happen. It will no longer be the popular thing to be a Christian or to be a member of a Christian church. It has been a popular thing for politicians to be a member of a church somewhere. But when the culture comes to the point that being a Christian is going to be a liability instead of an asset, then you will see a total change. Christians need to be ready for it and not be surprised when we suffer for our faith in the Lord.

Persecution, trouble, or tribulation can do one of two things for people. It can cause you to grow or it can cause you to become a bitter, resentful Christian. Simon Peter has written this beautiful little letter to encourage us to let it cause us to grow.

Its Theme

The theme of Simon Peter's first letter is built around three words. Remember that one way you can understand a book is to look for repetition of words. There are three words in I Peter that recur quite a bit.

The first word is Suffering. It occurs about 15 times, and he uses about eight different Greek words to talk about suffering. The great example for suffering he uses is none other than the Lord Jesus Christ.

The second word is Glory. It is used a number of times. The third word is Grace. It is used in every chapter.

Consider suffering and glory. There are certain words in the Bible that go together. For instance, these three words go together in the Bible: faith, hope, and love.

Two words that also are connected in the Bible are suffering and glory. Suffering in the Bible is presented as the pathway to glory. No suffering, no glory. If you want to experience God's glory, then the road to that glory is suffering. Note I Peter 1:11, "Searching what, or what manner of time the Spirit of Christ which was in them did signify, when he testified beforehand the sufferings of Christ, and the glory that should follow." Note it was suffering, then glory.

Note I Peter 4:13, "But rejoice, inasmuch as ye are partakers of Christ's sufferings, that when his glory shall be revealed, ye may be glad also with exceeding joy." Suffering and then glory.

Note I Peter 4:16, "Yet, if any man suffer as a Christian, let him not be ashamed, but let him glorify God on this behalf." This is one of the great promises in the Bible.

Note I Peter 5:1, "The elders which are among you I exhort, who am also an elder, and a witness of the sufferings of Christ, and also a partaker of the glory that shall be revealed." There they are again. Suffering and then glory.

God takes the sufferings of our life and uses those sufferings to bring us to a point of a deeper understanding and experience of His glory in our life.

The third word is grace. It is the word that helps us put the suffering together with the glory. In other words, when we suffer, we turn to God's grace. Suffering causes us to rely or to fall on the grace of God; so when we suffer, if we turn to God's grace and ask God to work through that suffering, then we see His glory in our life.

Suffering does not automatically bring glory in our life. If a Christian becomes bitter because of his suffering or his persecution, if a Christian allows that suffering to drive him away from the Lord, then there is no glory in that. But when a Christian has heartache, difficulty, trial and trouble in his life, and he lets that draw him to the Lord, then God will bring great glory out of that experience.

There is a verse that puts all of this together, I Peter 5:10, "But the God of all grace, who hath called us unto his eternal glory by Christ Jesus, after ye have suffered awhile, make you perfect, establish, strengthen, settle you." That is the route to mature Christianity. Christ went to Glory by way of the cross. Christians come to the point where God gets glory in their life by way of the cross of death to self. It is a beautiful theme. When you read I Peter, look for the interweaving of suffering, glory, and grace.

OUTLINE

I. The Question of Salvation, 1:3-9
  A. An Expectant Hope, 1:3-4
  B. An Experiential Faith, 1:5-7
  C. An Expressive Love, 1:8-9
II. The Question of Scripture, 1:10-12
III. The Question Sanctification, 1:13-25
IV. The Question of Separation, 2:1-12
  A. The Birth (newborns), 2:1-3
  B. The Belief (living stones), 2:4-10
  C. The Behavior (strangers/pilgrims), 2:11-12
V. The Question of Submission, 2:13–3:13
VI. The Question of Suffering, 3:14–4:19
  A. Experienced, 3:14-17
  B. Exemplified, 3:18-22
  C. Expected, 4:1-19
VII. The Question of Shepherding, 5:1-7
VIII. The Question of Satan, 5:8-11
Conclusion, 5:12-14

Introduction, 1:1-2

The Introduction is in the first two verses. Then he moves into the first division.

I. The Question of Salvation, 1:3-9

The first division is the Question of Salvation. He discusses salvation around these three words: faith, hope, and love. Verse 3, he has "begotten us again unto a lively hope." Verse 7, "That the trial of your faith." Verse 8, "Whom having not seen, ye love." So verses 3-4, an Expectant Hope. That is a part of our salvation. Verses 5-7, an Experimental Faith; and then verses 8-9, an Expressive Love.

II. The Question of Scripture, 1:10-12

In this short section, we see the Question of Scripture. Verse 10 begins, "Of which salvation the prophets have enquired and searched diligently, who prophesied of the grace that should come unto you." He goes back to the Old Testament writers. The only scripture they had in the New Testament was the Old Testament, so he was referring to the Old Testament Scriptures and the writing of the prophets. Verse 10 continues with verse 11, "Who prophesied of the grace that should come unto you; Searching what, or what manner of time the Spirit of Christ which was in them did signify when it testified beforehand the sufferings of Christ, and the glory that should follow." What he was saying was the Old Testament prophets were given prophecies and predictions from God concerning the sufferings of Christ and the glory.

The Jews understood the glory passages about Christ in the Old Testament, but they did not understand the suffering passages in the Old Testament. They did what we do sometimes. They read what they wanted to read. The things they were not too keen on they let pass by. For instance, Isaiah 53 is one of the clearest passages in the whole Bible on the suffering of Christ, but many of our Jewish friends have never read Isaiah 53. Because it is so clear cut, they are not encouraged to read it.

Now notice what he says in verse 12, "Unto whom it was revealed [that is these Old Testament writers], that not unto themselves, but unto us they did minister the things, which are now reported unto you by them that have preached the gospel unto you with the Holy Spirit sent down from heaven; which things the angels desire to look into." He was saying the Old Testament prophets wrote about these things; they had the testimony of the Scriptures.

III. The Question Sanctification, 1:13-25

In the rest of chapter 1 is the Question of Sanctification. Right in the heart of these verses is "But as he which hath called you is holy, so be ye holy in all manner of conversation; Because it is written, Be ye holy; for I am holy" (verses 15-16). Here is a section of sanctification, being set apart to the Lord in your daily lifestyle.

IV. The Question of Separation, 2:1-12

In this section, he gives three pictures of the Christian life, which teach the fact that we have been separated unto the Lord, that we belong to the Lord. He uses the picture of Birth in the first three verses. We are like newborn babies. Note verse 2, "As newborn babes, desire the sincere milk of the word." A Christian is like a newborn babe, and we should desire milk.

Believe is another picture, verses 4-10. He uses the picture of living stones. Verse 5, "Ye also, as lively [living] stones." Verse 4, Jesus is a living stone, singular; we are living stones, plural.

Behavior is verses 11-12, and he uses the picture of strangers and pilgrims.

V. The Question of Submission, 2:13–3:13

In the fifth division, he talks about submission in several different relationships here. Notice different statements about submission. For instance in 2:13, "Submit yourselves to every ordinance of men for the Lord's sake: whether it be to the king, as supreme; Or unto governors." Now he was saying a Christian should be a good citizen. We should obey the laws of the land. We should submit to the laws of the land and to the powers that be. Of course, a good parallel passage to that is Romans 13.

Note verse 18, "Servants [this is really slaves], be subject to your masters with all fear." We have already seen in I Timothy submission on the part of Christian slaves. Then in chapter 3:1, it says, "Likewise, ye wives, be in subjection to your own husbands." He talks about submission in the matter of role assignments in the family. In terms of the family, God has assigned the husband as the leader of the family. The wife is really the heart of the family. Submission is not a degrading position at all because Christ submitted Himself to the heavenly Father. Jesus set the example of submission Himself. He submitted to the will of the heavenly Father, "not My will but Thine be done."

He deals with the matter of relationships here. Verse 7, "Likewise, ye husbands, dwell with them [wives] according to knowledge."

VI. The Question of Suffering, 3:14–4:19

In the sixth division he zeroes in on the Question of Suffering. He goes from chapter 3:14 all the way through to chapter 4:19. He talks about the Experience of suffering itself, verses 14-17. He talks about what is involved in the experience of suffering. Then he gives an example in verse 18, the example of Christ. It is suffering Exemplified, verses 18-22. It includes the interesting passage about Jesus going and preaching to the spirits in prison. Then in I Peter

4:1-19, the fourth chapter, he talks about we can expect suffering to come, suffering Expected.

VII. The Question of Shepherding, 5:1-7

This passage is directed towards the pastors specifically. It is where you get the statement in verse 2, "Feed the flock of God." Remember what Jesus said to Peter, "feed My sheep." The word *pastor* means a shepherd. The shepherd means one who feeds the flock. A pastor is to be a shepherd who feeds his flock. That is why you should always have a high priority on Bible teaching. God has assigned pastors to feed the sheep, to feed the flock of God.

VIII. The Question of Satan, 5:8-11

In this division Peter makes a statement about Satan and his action.

Conclusion, 5:12-14

Peter concludes with his closing remarks and greetings.

Study #40
Progressing with II Peter

PROGRESSING WITH II PETER

Its Author

We know that Simon Peter, the apostle and the disciple of the Lord Jesus Christ, is the author of I Peter and II Peter. It is not a controversy with you or with me, but in some academic circles there has been denial that II Peter was composed by Simon Peter.

One of the reasons for the controversy is the subject matter in II Peter is different from I Peter, so some believe there had to have been a different person write it. Another thing is there are many similarities between II Peter and the book of Jude, so some people in the liberal community believe that someone just took the name of Simon Peter and attached it to this letter.

We reject this, and the only reason I am noting it is because you or college students in your family may hear this kind of thing. I do not want you to be unprepared when and if that happens. It is good to be aware of what is going on.

There are strong compelling internal reasons in the letter to believe that the author is none other than Simon Peter. First of all, in the first verse, II Peter 1:1, it specifically says that Simon Peter is the author. "Simon Peter, a servant and an apostle of Jesus Christ." There is the direct claim that he is the author.

A second internal evidence is that in II Peter 1 reference is made to the transfiguration experience of Jesus. When Jesus was on the mount of transfiguration, He was transfigured before Peter, James, and John. Moses and Elijah were there as well. Notice II Peter 1:16: "For we have not followed cunningly devised fables when we made known unto you the power and coming of our Lord Jesus Christ, but were eyewitnesses of his majesty." Simon Peter is saying we saw the transfiguration of Jesus, and the only three who saw the transfiguration were Peter, James and John. There is internal evidence.

Another thing to note is that in John 21 the Lord Jesus basically told Simon Peter that he would die and He told him how he was going to die. John 21:18-19, "Verily, verily, I say unto thee, when thou wast young, thou girdedst thyself, and walkedst where thou wouldest; but when thou shalt be old, thou shalt stretch forth thy hands, and another shall gird thee, and carry thee where thou wouldest not. This spake he, signifying by what death he should glorify God." Jesus made reference to his death, and in this letter Simon Peter also makes reference to his death. Note II Peter 1:13. "Yea, I think it meet, as long as I am in this tabernacle [talking about his physical body], to stir you up by putting you in remembrance." Then he says in verse 14, "Knowing that shortly I must put off this my tabernacle [I must die], even as our Lord Jesus Christ hath shown me." That seems to be a direct reference to what Jesus had told him in John 21.

I think the final nail that drives down the issue is the reference in II Peter 3:1, where he says specifically, "This second epistle, beloved, I now write unto you." He was saying I have written you a previous letter. What was that letter? I Peter. So the evidences are all there.

Peter was aware that his death was near. He was writing a letter fulfilling what the Lord told him to do, to feed the sheep.

Its Theme

There is some very practical teaching in II Peter. It is in many ways one of the most unique books in the entire Bible and in the New Testament. Some of its information is really mind boggling when you consider it and look at the setting in which it was written.

There is a reoccurring theme in II Peter. The theme is the word *knowledge* or some form of the word such as knowing or know. Those words occur about 13 times in three chapters. For instance, II Peter 1:3, "According as his divine power hath given unto us all things that pertain unto life and godliness, through the knowledge of him that hath called us to glory and virtue." Verse 2,

"Grace and peace be multiplied unto you through the knowledge of God, and of Jesus, our Lord."

Verses 5 and 6, "And beside this, giving all diligence, add to your faith virtue; and to virtue, knowledge; and to knowledge, temperance." The word *knowledge* occurs throughout the letter.

There are three main reasons why Simon Peter was led by the Holy Spirit to write this particular letter. Number one was to encourage them. Simon Peter was writing to encourage believers and, of course, now he is encouraging us. The encouragement was you have started the Christian life well; now finish the Christian life well. Simon Peter was saying I want you to go all the way to the end in your Christian life. That is my prayer, that the Lord will help me to finish well, that the Lord will help me to keep going all the way and not stop.

What Simon Peter says in II Peter 1:11 should be the desire of all Christians. "For so an entrance shall be ministered unto you abundantly." He is saying, I want you to have an abundant entrance when you go into the gates of glory.

In I Corinthians 3 Paul talked about believers who lived carnal lives and the day when their works would be tested and examined. He said they would be saved but so as by fire; they were saved by grace but were just barely getting in. I don't know about you, but that is not the way I want to go in. I want an abundant entrance. Peter has written us a book to show us how to have an abundant entrance, how to finish the race of the Christian life well.

Toward that end, he shares in chapter 1 some things that we need to add to our Christian life to help us have this abundant entrance. Again, reason number one was to encourage his readers of his day and also us today.

Number two, he writes to expose heresy. Paul and John also wrote about heresy. You need to be aware here that Simon Peter was writing in the first century. It is the beginning stages of the Christian faith, but heresies were already beginning. Heresy is not something that appears on the scene in the end times. Heresy is something that has been going on all along the way.

Heresy means a departure from the teachings of the Scriptures. It is a denial of the basic doctrines of the faith. To deny the virgin birth of Jesus is heresy. To deny the shed blood of Christ as the atonement of our sins is heresy. To teach that there are errors in the Bible is heresy.

There are no new heresies. Anytime you run into a heresy today, it is just an old heresy that may be wearing a new garment. So he writes to expose these heresies. For instance, in II Peter 2:1, he says, "But there were false prophets also among the people [that is talking about the Old Testament], even as there shall be false teachers among you, who privily shall bring in damnable heresies, even denying the Lord that bought them, and bring upon themselves swift destruction."

There were two perils Simon Peter addressed which the church faces. In his first letter he addressed the peril of persecution, that is the danger on the outside. Satan comes as the roaring lion seeking whom he may devour. But the more serious danger is what he addressed in this letter. It is the danger of the trouble on the inside, the heresy that originates on the inside, the false doctrine.

In I Peter, Satan comes as the roaring lion to persecute. Now, in II Peter we see Satan, not as a roaring lion, but as a serpent coming to deceive, coming to beguile, coming to sow seeds of false doctrine. So Simon Peter addresses the problem on the outside, persecution; he addresses the problem on the inside, false doctrine. God uses Simon Peter to answer heresy, and Peter does it in a unique way.

One of the best ways to understand what heresy is is to have a good thorough understanding of what the real thing is. I read some time ago about FBI agents who were trained to recognize counterfeit money. I was told that the way they are trained to recognize counterfeit money is to make them totally familiar with the real thing. They become so familiar with the genuine item that whenever they encounter a counterfeit, they recognize it immediately. That is exactly what Simon Peter does in II Peter.

In the first chapter Peter sets before us the genuine article, he sets before us the real faith. Look at verse 1, "Simon Peter, a servant and an apostle of Jesus Christ, to them that have obtained like precious faith with us through the righteousness of God and our Savior, Jesus Christ." Then he talks about that faith in chapter 1.

Having given us the genuine article, the real thing, in chapter 2, Peter discusses the counterfeit, the false. When you get a good foundation, you know what the real is, then you can more easily recognize the other.

So he writes to encourage them, and he writes to expose heresy. Number three, he writes to set forth the last days and the coming of the Lord.

There are some fascinating statements that are made in II Peter about the last days. Simon Peter was a Galilean fisherman and was not trained in the schools of the day. In fact, in the book of Acts, when he and the other disciples started preaching, folks were astounded and asked where they got this knowledge, they were ignorant and unlettered men. That did not mean they were ignoramuses, but it meant they were not trained in the official schools of the day.

Here is a Galilean fisherman who is going to write some things in his letter that are absolutely astonishing. The question is where in the world did a fisherman get information like this? He got it from the Holy Spirit; the Holy Spirit inspired him to write. This, by the way, just does away with the argument that somebody else had to have written this letter because Simon Peter was not capable of doing it. When a person has the help of the Holy Spirit, it is amazing what he or she can do.

OUTLINE

I. The Convictions of the Faith, 1
- **A. The Walk with God, 1:1-15**
- **B. The Word of God, 1:16-21**

II. The Contention for the Faith, 2
- **A. Heretical Doctrine, 2:1-3a**
- **B. Heretical Doom, 2:3b-9**
- **C. Heretical Deeds, 2:10-22**

III. The Consummation of the Faith, 3
- **A. Scoffers Exposed, 3:1-13**
- **B. Saints Exhorted, 3:14-18**

There are three main divisions in II Peter. Keep in mind that outlines are something that people develop and impose on the scripture. This is not a part of the book itself. These outlines are meant to help you see what you are dealing with when you come to the chapters and verses. I do not make any claim for originality. Whatever I thought would be the best outline and would be helpful is what I have used. I have drawn from many sources, but there are three basic divisions here, and they are by the chapters.

I. The Convictions of the Faith, 1

Simon Peter talks about the faith. There are two main sections: Walk with God (verses 1-15) and the Word of God (verses 16-21).

A. The Walk with God, 1:1-15

In verse 1, he is talking about we have obtained like precious faith. Then in verse 4 he says God has given us exceeding great and precious promises. In verse 5 he begins talking about the ingredients that need to be added to our faith. Our faith can grow in and of itself, but there can also be some additives. This is what I call your spiritual STP. He says in verses 5-7, "add to your faith virtue; and to virtue knowledge; And to knowledge temperance; and to temperance patience; and to patience godliness; And to godliness brotherly kindness; and to brotherly kindness charity." He says then in verse 8, "For if these things be in you, and abound, they make you that ye shall neither be barren nor unfruitful in the knowledge of our Lord Jesus Christ." He keeps coming back to knowing, growing in our knowledge of the Lord and growing in our knowledge of the faith. So in the first 15 verses he is primarily talking about our walk with God, adding these things to our Christian life.

B. The Word of God, 1:16-21

In verse 16 he does something rather interesting. You remember Simon Peter was on the mountain of transfiguration. He saw the Lord transfigured. The word *transfiguration* or transfigured is a word that is taken from science. It is our word *metamorphosis*. When Jesus was transfigured, the word used there is He was metamorphosed. It is a scientific term, which means what is on the inside is manifested on the outside. A beetle wraps a cocoon around itself and goes through a process called chrysalis, and when that process is over, out comes a beautiful butterfly. Jesus was metamorphosed. That is, everything He was on the inside was manifested on the outside. That is why the Bible says they saw His face above the brightness of the sun and His garments glistened. Peter talks about it. In verse 16, he says they were not making this up. He says in verse 16: "For we have not followed cunningly devised fables." What he is saying is we are giving you historical truth, factual information. The verse continues, "when we made known unto you the power and coming of our Lord Jesus Christ, but were eyewitnesses of his majesty." In verse 17 he talks about how heaven opened and the Father spoke out of heaven. Then he says in verse 18, "And this voice which came from heaven we heard, when we were with him in the holy mount." It is pretty spectacular. Then he says in verse 19, "We have also a more sure word of prophecy." Do you get what he just said? He has been talking about one of the most spectacular events that occurred in the life of the Lord Jesus Christ, the transfiguration experience. And yet he comes along in the next verse and says we have something better than that. He is saying his readers had and today we have something better than witnessing the transfiguration of Jesus on the mount. He continues verse 19, "whereunto ye do well that ye take heed, as unto a light that shineth in a dark place, until the day dawn, and the day star arise in your hearts."

Verse 20 continues, "Knowing this first, that no prophecy of the scripture is of any private interpretation." He is talking about the Scriptures, the Bible. He is saying you and I have something that is more sure than to have been an eye witness of the transfiguration of Jesus. Always keep this in mind that we must always judge our experience by scripture. We are never to judge the Scriptures by our experience. Someone may say I had a vision and I saw this and I was told this. That is fine, but what does the Bible say about it? Does the Scripture contradict it? Does the Scripture lend support to it? There is something far more stable and secure than any experience, and it is the written Word of God.

He lays out a beautiful statement of inspiration. It is one of the great statements in the Bible about inspiration. Verse 21, "For the prophecy [talking about the Scriptures, God's Word] came not in old time by the will of man [folks did not just make this stuff up]: but holy [set apart] men of God spake as they were moved by the Holy Spirit." That is a great statement about the inspiration of the

Bible. That is why Simon Peter could write what he wrote here. He was specially set apart to speak and to write, moved by the Holy Spirit.

The word *moved* there is a beautiful word. It is a word that was used of a breeze that blew a vessel along in the water. He is saying God's Holy Spirit, the Breath of heaven, moved on the hearts and minds of these men so that what they wrote under the inspiration of the Holy Spirit of God is a more sure word of prophecy.

The first chapter is on the Convictions of the Faith. He closes the section talking about the stability and surety of the Scriptures. That is why it is so important to get into the Scriptures. It is important to have a daily time to read and study the Bible. There is nothing like God's Word for your daily life. I am talking about not just looking for a sermon or a Bible lesson to teach, but I am talking about studying it to feed your own heart, to direct your own life, and to grow in the knowledge of the Lord.

When I talk to Christians who are away from the Lord, who have things in their lives that ought not to be, one of the things I ask them is about their quiet time. Ninety-nine times out of 100, they will say to me they have not been reading God's Word the way they should. God's Word is not a guarantee you will never fall along the way, I am not saying that. But the reading of God's Word will help you grow, mature, and become strong in your faith.

II. The Contention for the Faith, 2

The second division is the Contention for the Faith. Having laid out for us the genuine and true faith, he shows how to handle these heresies that come. There are three main divisions.

A. Heretical Doctrine, 2:1-3a

Verse 1 through the first part of verse 3 talk about Heretical Doctrine. He gives an example. "But there were false prophets also among the people, even as there shall be false teachers among you, who privily shall bring in damnable heresies." Privily means to bring in alongside. Heresy is always kind of slipped in on the side. It will be privily brought in on the side. The shepherd or pastor of the church has to always be watching for it. Peter continues, "even denying the

Lord that bought them, and bring upon themselves swift destruction." There you see the denial of the shed blood of Christ. He has bought us with His precious blood, but he says they will deny these kinds of things.

In verses 2-3 he says, "And many shall follow their pernicious [evil] ways; by reason of whom the way of truth shall be evil spoken of. And through covetousness shall they with feigned words make merchandise of you." It is good to check to see where the money is. Check and see what teachers and preachers are getting out of the deal. Do not believe everything you see on TV.

B. Heretical Doom, 2:3b-9

In verses 3b through 9, he talks about Heretical Doom. He gives some Old Testament illustrations about how God judged heretics, and he talks about the angels that sinned in verse 4. He talks about the days of Noah in verse 5, and he talks about Sodom and Gomorrah in verse 6. He talks about Lot in verses 7 and 8. He talks about how God dealt with heresy.

C. Heretical Deeds, 2:10-22

In verses 10 through 22, he talks about Heretical Deeds. That is a description of the lifestyle of heretics. There are a lot of parallels between II Peter and the book of Jude. They are fascinating scriptures.

III. The Consummation of the Faith, 3

A. Scoffers Exposed, 3:1-13

The third division of the book we are calling the Consummation of the Faith, chapter 3. In the first 13 verses he talks about the Scoffers Exposed. Note what he says in chapter 3:1, "This second epistle, beloved, I now write unto you; in both which I stir up your pure minds by way of remembrance." Verses 2-4, "That ye may be mindful of the words which were spoken before by the holy prophets, and of the commandment of us the apostles of the Lord and Savior: Knowing this first, that there shall come in the last days scoffers, walking after their own lusts, And saying, Where is the promise of his coming?" In other words, people will say they have heard about the second coming talk all through the years, but Jesus has not shown up yet. Where is the promise of His coming? Every time you hear someone say that, it is another sign of the coming of the Lord. When people start making fun, scoffing, and laughing at the whole matter of the second coming of Jesus Christ, you have just seen another sign that the coming of the Lord draws nigh.

I do not know when Jesus is going to come, but I do know it is one day closer than it was yesterday. It is getting closer every day. Peter is talking about the scoffers, and then in verse 5 he says they are willingly ignorant. Some people are willingly ignorant. Some people are not willingly ignorant.

Next he moves into a discussion that is astonishing. Keep in mind that this was written 2,000 years ago. He talks in verse 6 about the world that was back during the flood. Then in verse 7 he talks about the earth that is now, the heavens and the earth now. Then in verse 13 he talks about the earth that will be, the new heaven and the new earth. You have three worlds here: the world that was, the world that is now, and the world that is to come. He uses some combinations of words that are mind boggling. For instance, verse 10, "But the day of the Lord will come as a thief in the night; in the which the heavens [this is where we get the English word *uranium*] shall pass away with a great noise, and the elements shall melt with fervent heat [fire], the earth also and the works that are therein shall be burned up."

The word *element* is a Greek word that means the ABCs, the basic rudiments of the universe. The best equivalent I can give you in the English language is the word *atom*. He is saying there is going to come a time when the atoms are going to pass away. In verse 11, he says they are going to be dissolved. The word there means to loose or to melt. Then he uses the word that they will pass away with a great noise. The word there means the rushing sound of a roaring flame. He says it will melt with a fervent heat, which means a fever.

I have been told by those who understand these terms that what Simon Peter has given is an astonishingly scientifically accurate definition of a nuclear explosion. It is astonishing how close it is to modern terminology. Simon Peter was not a Ph.D. He was a Galilean fisherman. The Holy Spirit gave all this information to him. He spoke as he was moved by the Holy Spirit. Your Bible is up-to-date.

B. Saints Exhorted, 3:14-18

He closes out the letter in verses 14-18 with the Saints Exhorted. In other words, all of this is true. The end of the world is coming, the heavens and the earth are going to pass away, and the Lord is going to return. Because of that, he says in verse 14, "Wherefore, beloved, seeing that ye look for such things, be diligent that ye may be found of him in peace, without spot, and blameless." He is saying be ready. Whenever the Lord may come, be found of Him in peace. Be walking with the Lord.

Note what else he says in verse 11, "Seeing then that all these things shall be dissolved, what manner of persons ought ye to be in all holy conversation [behavior] and godliness?" It should be an incentive for us to live a holy life. It should also be an incentive for us to want to lead people to faith in Christ.

Peter tells why Jesus has not come yet, II Peter 3:9, "The Lord is not slack concerning his promise, as some men count slackness; but is longsuffering to us-ward, not willing that any should perish, but that all should come to repentance." Jesus has not come yet to give people an opportunity to be saved and to give you and me an opportunity to tell them how to be saved. If there is ever a time we ought to be faithful witnesses, if there has ever been an age when folks who know the Lord should be soul winners, it is right now. We are coming to the end of the age. The Lord is coming at any day. We are to live a holy life, and we are to tell others the Lord has tarried His coming to give them an opportunity to be saved.

He closes out this book with the letter's key word, *knowledge*? Verse 18, "But grow in grace, and in the knowledge of our Lord and Savior Jesus Christ. To him be glory both now and for ever. Amen."

Study #41
Journey through 1 John

JOURNEY THROUGH I JOHN

First John is the first of three epistles which bear the name of John, the beloved disciple. Evidently John wrote these letters toward the end of his ministry, which would have been toward the end of the first century. He probably wrote the book of the Revelation last.

John was the pastor of the church at Ephesus. He was banished to the island of Patmos, was released, and returned to Ephesus where he evidently died as an old man.

John started following the Lord as a very young man; some suggest as early as his late teens. He had been living for the Lord all through the years. He was there at the cross when Jesus was crucified, and the Lord Jesus gave His mother into his care. Tradition is John took Mary to Ephesus. John was at the resurrection and was a witness to the fact that Jesus Christ was a living Savior. Again, he had been living for the Lord since he was a young man.

The Holy Spirit used John, as the human instrument, to write five books in the New Testament: the Gospel of John; I, II, and III John; and the Revelation. It is interesting to look at these five books and see that they fall into three general categories: the Gospel of John, the Letters of John, and then the book of the Revelation.

These three letters give us a full picture of the Christian life; he deals with the Christian life in these three books. For instance, the Gospel of John has to do with salvation; it touches on the matter of salvation and it looks to our past. The Gospel of John reminds us of what Christ did for us. Christ died for us so that takes care of our past, salvation.

The primary theme in the Letters of John is sanctification. In salvation, Christ died for us; in sanctification, Christ lives in us.

The third group is the book of the Revelation and that looks forward to the future, our glorification. It is prophecy, and it has to do with the future and Christ coming for us.

The Gospel of John, Christ died for us, our salvation; the Epistles, Christ lives in us, our

Sanctification; the book of the Revelation, Christ is coming for us, our glorification. The entire Christian life is found within the scope of the writings of John in the New Testament.

Its Letter

This is one of my favorite books. This is a marvelous book for the Christian. It is a very reassuring book for God's children.

John writes in bold language. There are no in betweens; he writes in black and white. There are no shades of gray. It is either right or it's wrong, it's either true or it is false, it is either good or it is evil; there are no in betweens in John's writings.

John has a way of letting us know why he is writing. He has a way of giving us a key, which unlocks the door or tells us why he is writing. For instance, in the Gospel of John he hangs the key on the back door or towards the end of the book. In John 20:31 he tells us why he wrote the Gospel of John, "But these are written, that ye might believe that Jesus is the Christ, the Son of God; and that believing ye might have life through his name." He says I have written the book so you would know that Jesus is the Christ, you would believe in Him, and you would be saved; you would have salvation.

In the book of the Revelation, he hangs the key on the front door. In the first chapter he tells exactly why he wrote it. In Revelation 1:19, the Lord told John what to write, "Write the things which thou hast seen, and the things which are, and the things which shall be hereafter." By the way, that is the perfect outline for the book of the Revelation.

So, in the Gospel of John he hangs the key of the book on the back door. In the book of the Revelation he hangs the key on the front door in the first chapter.

In the little book of I John, he scatters the key all through the house. All along the way he will say "these things have I written that . . ." Look for that as you read I John. Note how he says throughout the book, these things have I written or I have written this in order that . . .

When you go through I John and look for those little keys along the way, you will find there are four primary reasons he wrote I John. In I John 1:4, he gives us the first reason why, "And these things write we unto you, that your joy may be full." He is writing this book that your joy may be full. One of the reasons for this book is to promote joy, that God's people might have joy. The reading of I John will bring a great deal of joy to your life.

The second purpose is in I John 2:1, "My little children, these things write I unto you, that ye sin not." The second reason he is writing is to prevent sin, to help us not to sin.

The third reason he gives is in I John 2:26, "These things have I written unto you concerning them which seduce you." He is writing about the antichrist and those people who were trying to deceive them. He is writing is to protect the saints, to protect us from those who would deceive us, who would mislead us, and who would seduce us.

The fourth and the primary reason is in I John 5:13. "These things have I written unto you that believe on the name of the Son of God, that ye may know that ye have eternal life, and that ye may believe on the name of the Son of God." The fourth and the primary reason he writes this book is in order to provide assurance, that we might have assurance of our salvation.

There is a contrast between the Gospel of John and I John. The Gospel of John was written in order that we might believe Jesus is the Christ, and believing we would have life through His name, that we might be saved. The Gospel of John is written that we might be saved. First John is written that we might know how to be sure we are saved. The Gospel, how to be saved; I John, how to be sure you are saved. There is a difference between being saved and being sure you are saved. There is a difference between possessing salvation and having the assurance of your salvation. That is the main reason the book was written though, that we might have assurance of our salvation.

Its Five Tests

The key word in John's little letter is the word *know*. You will find some form of the word *know* over 30 times in this book; in fact, it may be closer to 40 times John uses some word that has to do with knowledge or knowing as he gives these assurances.

He gives five primary assurances or tests to give yourself so you can know that you have been saved. The first test is in I John 3:9. I call this the test of Spiritual Desire. "Whosoever is born of God doth not commit sin; for his seed remaineth in him, and he cannot sin, because he is born of God." That immediately can bring a question to your mind. One of the things that you run into in going from any part of scripture into an English translation is that sometimes it is difficult to convey from one language to another the nuances of the grammar that is used.

I do not want to get too technical, but in the Greek language the tense of the verbs is very, very important. For instance, there is the aorist tense. It is a definite tense. When the Bible says, for instance, "Christ died on the cross for our sins," normally that will be the aorist tense. Where it says, "He washed us in his blood," that would be the aorist tense, which carries the idea this is something that was done definitely and it is not repeated. It is a point in time when it took place.

But there is also in the Greek language, in the verbs, what is known as the present tense. It means continuous action, something that is going on. For instance, "I leaped," that is aorist tense. I did that; that was definite. "I am walking," that is present tense; it is something that is going on. The present tense in the Greek language is something that is going on. It is something that is in the process of happening; it is continuous action.

When it says in I John 3:9, "Whosoever is born of God doth not commit sin," it is the present tense. This is a better way of translating it: "Whoever is born of God does not make a continual habit of sin." Do you see the difference? It is not saying that if you are saved, you do not ever sin again. We know better than that, so we know that is not what it is saying. Whole denominations have gotten messed up with this verse. There are denominations which teach sinless perfection. They do that on the basis of verses like this.

He is not saying that after you are saved you do not ever sin. He is saying that after you are saved, you do not make a lifestyle or a habit or a practice of it. In other words, you just don't continually desire to sin. One of the ways I know I am saved is that I don't desire to sin. It doesn't mean I do not sin, but it means I don't want to sin. I have a different desire; my spiritual desire has changed. That is what he is talking about.

That is one of the first ways to test yourself concerning the matter of your salvation. What is your relationship to sin? It is the test of Spiritual Desire.

The second test is the test of Spiritual Disposition; I John 4:7, "Beloved, let us love one another; for love is of God, and everyone that loveth is born of God, and knoweth God." Do you see the disposition there? If we are saved, we love God. Our disposition is one of love. We love the Lord; we are saved and we love the Lord.

Not only do we love the Lord, but I John 3:14 says, "We know that we have passed from death unto life, because we love the brethren." Our Spiritual Disposition is different now. We love God, and we love the brothers and the sisters. We love God's people. It is the test of Spiritual Disposition.

The third test is in I John 5:1, the test of Spiritual Discernment. "Whosoever believeth that Jesus is the Christ is born of God; and everyone that loveth him that begot loveth him also that is begotten of him." There is a Spiritual Discernment here. It is not only a desire to know the Lord and the desire to love God's people, but there is also a discernment in that we discern fellowship with God's people.

The fourth test is Spiritual Dynamic; I John 5:4, "For whatsoever is born of God overcometh the world; and this is the victory that overcometh the world, even our faith." This is the test of victory. Do we experience victory in our life as a Christian? The Bible says if we are born of God we can overcome this world. God gives us victory over the world.

The fifth test is Spiritual Deliverance; I John 5:18, "We know that whosoever is born of God sinneth not [that is present tense; does not make a habit or habitually and continually does not practice sin], but he that is begotten of God keepeth himself, and that wicked one toucheth him not." There is deliverance; we are not in the sway; we are not in the influence of Satan. We have deliverance from Satan. We are delivered from the power and the influence of Satan in our lives.

OUTLINE

Introduction, 1:1-4

- **I. Fellowship, 1:5–2:29**
  - **A. Obedience, 1:5-2:6**
  - **B. Love, 2:7-17**
  - **C. Truth, 2:18-29**
- **II. Sonship, 3–5**
  - **A. Obedience, 3:1-24**
  - **B. Love, 4:1-21**
  - **C. Truth, 5:1-21**

Introduction, 1:1-4

The first four verses might be called verses of Introduction. He starts rather interestingly. Verse 1, "That which was from the beginning, which we have heard, which we have seen with our eyes, which we have looked upon, and our hands have handled of the Word of life." John is saying Jesus is real. John is saying we were right there. We saw this with our eyes. We heard this with our ears. We touched Him with our hands. The Word of life is a reference to the Lord Jesus.

Verse 2, "For the life was manifested, and we have seen it, and bear witness, and shew unto you that eternal life, which was with the Father, and was manifested unto us." What he is saying is we want you to know this is not hearsay stuff. This is not in the realm of the mysterious as a New Age religion would be, but this is concrete and real about Jesus Christ. This is the way he introduces his letter.

John really has a two-fold division in this letter. Although it is not easy to divide up, like the book of Proverbs, this two-fold division can still be a helpful way for you to study I John.

The first division or theme is Fellowship. The key verse is I John 1:5. This division goes from I John 1:5 all the way through chapter 2. The second division is Sonship, chapters 3 through 5. The key verse is I John 4:8, "God is love." The key phrase is "born of God." He talks about Fellowship, and he talks about Sonship.

I. Fellowship, 1–2:29

Notice the repetition of this word fellowship. First John 1:3, "That which we have seen and heard declare we unto you, that ye also may have fellowship with us: and truly our fellowship is with the Father, and with his Son Jesus Christ." He mentions fellowship two times in that one verse.

Verse 6, "If we say that we have fellowship with him, and walk in darkness, we lie, and do not the truth." Verse 7, "But if we walk in the light, as he is in the light, we have fellowship one with another, and the blood of Jesus Christ his Son cleanseth us from all sin." Again, you see fellowship. Now the Greek word for fellowship is a word that you may have heard. It is the word *koinonia*. The idea is to share things in common together.

Next is Sonship, chapters 3 through 5. Note I John 3:1, "Behold, what manner of love the Father hath bestowed upon us, that we should be called the sons of God." Do you see "sons of God"? Verse 2, "Beloved, now are we the sons of God." Notice the little phrase in verse 9, "born of God." How do you become a son of God? You have to be born of God. When it uses *sons*, it is using it in the generic sense. The Bible is not an anti-woman book. It really bothers me when people make a big deal about this kind of terminology in the Bible. In human language the use of generic terms is commonly done in every area. The Bible talks about mankind, for instance. That includes the ladies. It means men and women. Mankind is a broad term. It is a shorthand in language. Instead of having to specify men and women kind, people use mankind and that includes everybody. When you see *sons of God*, it means sons and daughters of God.

How did you get into God's family? You were born of God. I am in the Vines' family. I was born into the Vines' family. I have sonship. I am in the Vines' family physically. But spiritually I also have sonship. I am in the family of God by means of a birth. That is the only way life ever occurs, by birth. You get physical life by birth. You get spiritual life by birth. You have to be born again, born from above. So in chapters 3 through 5, John talks about Sonship, about being in the family of God. Along with the phrase *sons of God*, he uses the phrase *born of God*. Note the many times you see sons of God and born of God in these three chapters. It is a relationship which is unchanging. It cannot be broken. When you are born into the family of God, you are forever born.

Being in God's family is a matter of relationship. You get in there by means of a birth. Fellowship is another matter. Nothing can take you out of God's family once you are born again, but something can take you out of God's favor. Your children are in your physical family by means of a birth. There is nothing they can do that will take them out of your family. They can displease you, they can irritate you, they can break your heart, but they are still yours. There is nothing they can do that will take them out of your family, but they can certainly be out of your favor. Your children can have a relationship with you by means of birth, but they may not have fellowship with you.

When a Christian gets out of the will of God, gets back into the world, and gets entangled in the world, that breaks the fellowship with God. You do not have anything in common with God and with other Christians at that point.

In each of these divisions John uses the same three tests to see how you are doing in your fellowship and to see how you are in your sonship, whether you are in God's family. The first division is Fellowship. God is light. If we are not walking in the light, then we are not in fellowship with God. We can get out of fellowship with God by walking in the darkness. He gives three tests for fellowship: the Obedience test, I John 1:5–2:6; the Love test, chapter 2:7-17; and the Truth test, chapter 2:18-29.

In Sonship, he goes down through the same and gives three tests for Sonship. There is the Obedience test, chapter 3:1-24. The Love test is chapter 4:1-21. The third test is the Truth test, chapter 5:1-21.

Let's look at obedience as a test of our fellowship with the Lord. Notice he talks about in chapter 1, "if we say." He says that three times. Look at verse 6, "If we say that we have fellowship with him." John's emphasis here is it is not enough to say it. If we say we have fellowship with God, but we walk in the darkness and not in the light, then we lie. Look at verse 8, "If we say." Look at verse 10, "If we say." He is saying it is not enough to say it. It has to be the real thing. It has to be true in our life. Then in I John 2:4, he changes it a little bit and says, "He that saith." Verse 6, "He that saith."

In chapter 2:7, he picks up the theme of Love and talks about our love. He talks about the fact that Jesus gave this new commandment, and the commandment is to love. Love is one of the tests of whether or not we are in fellowship with the Lord and in fellowship with one another. It is a beautiful section. Verse 8, "Again, a new commandment I write unto you, which thing is true in him and in you: because the darkness is past, and the true light now shineth." Verse 9, "He that saith he is in the light, and hateth his brother, is in darkness even until now." What he is saying is if you do not love, you are not in fellowship with the Lord because God is love. He says in verse 10, "He that loveth his brother abideth in the light." Love is one of the proofs of fellowship.

In I John 2:18, he talks about Truth. He gets into the matter of the last times and the Antichrist, singular, and many antichrists, plural. This goes all the way to the end of chapter 2.

II. Sonship, 3–5

In the Sonship section, he goes back over the same things. Chapter 3, he talks about Obedience, and that is the matter of sin in your life and not making a practice of sin. He also goes through the matter of Love for our brothers.

He picks up the matter of Love again in chapter 4. Two times in chapter 4 he says God is love. Verse 8, "God is love," and in verse 16, "God is love."

Then in chapter 5 he talks about the Truth, and he zeroes in on this whole matter of assurance, the number one way to know, to have assurance, you are saved. Note verse 11: "And this is the record." What is the record? The Word of God. The Word of God is the record "that God hath given to us eternal life, and this life is in his Son." Where do we find out about Jesus and His death on the cross for our sins? In the Word of God. You might say you were not even reading a Bible when you were saved. You maybe didn't, but whoever talked to you and told you about Jesus, where did that person find out? In the Word of God, so the Word is the record. It is the written record. God has given us a written record.

If you are married, how can you prove you are married? The only way you can absolutely prove you are married is to show the marriage license you got from the courthouse in the town where you were married. That is the only thing that will hold up in a court of law.

What is John saying? He is saying God's Word is the record, it is the written proof that God has given to us eternal life and this life is in His Son. Verse 12 says, "He that hath the Son hath life." If you have invited Jesus into your life, you have life. The last part of verse 12 says, "and he that hath not the Son of God hath not life." If you have not invited Jesus into your life, you do not have life.

Therefore, he says in verse 13, "These things have I written unto you that believe on the name of the Son of God; that ye may know that ye have eternal life, and that ye may believe on the name of the Son of God." Our feelings come and our feelings go. Our feelings are deceiving. My warrant is the Word of God. Nothing else is worth believing. You do not go by your feelings or your failures, but you go by your faith in the written Word of God.

Study #42
Jottings in II John, Jottings in III John and Judgment in Jude

JOTTINGS IN II JOHN

Second and III John tie into the first letter of John. First, II, and III John were all written, as best we know, by none other than the beloved apostle John. These two books are unusual books. They are brief books as II John has only 13 verses and III John has 14 verses, but they are rich; they have rich messages for us.

Its Readers

Note how the first verse reads because in it you have basically, in a capsule, what we are dealing with in this book. Second John 1:1 begins, "The elder unto the elect lady and her children, whom I love in the truth; and not I only, but also all they that have known the truth." We take the word *elder* to be a reference to John, meaning he is referring to himself. He begins the same way in III John: "The elder unto the well-beloved Gaius, whom I love in the truth." It is generally believed that John, the beloved disciple, is the one to whom it refers.

The question is to whom is this written? The elder is John, but it says unto the elect lady and her children. To whom does this refer? There are two views that can be taken on the matter of who these original readers were.

One of the views is that this is a symbolic way of referring to the church. We do know that the church is described in the Bible as the bride of Christ. So one of the views is that this is a reference to the church, unto the elect lady. We do know the church is known as the elect. "Her children" is a reference to her member, to her converts.

The other view is that, rather than being a symbolic representation of the church and its members, it is making reference to a literal lady, to an actual lady and to her children, a godly mother and to her children. Note the last verse, verse 13: "The children of thy elect sister greet thee." If you take the literal view, then John is writing to one lady here, and then he is making reference to her sister that he knows and the cousins of the children mentioned in verse 1.

We really do not know. We do not know just which of these views is right. I lean toward the view that he is talking to an actual lady, to a real lady, to an elect lady, that is, to a chosen lady, a saved, godly mother and her children. He is making reference to the fact that he also knows her sister and her children in verse 13. That is my personal view; and if that be true, then what you have here is a letter in the New Testament addressed specially to a lady. If this is to be taken literally, then we have a special book written to a lady.

Its Theme

The theme of this book is found also in these introductory verses, the first three verses, III John 1-3. "The elder unto the elected lady and her children, whom I love in the truth; and not I only, but also all they that have known the truth; For the truth's sake, which dwelleth in us, and shall be with us forever. Grace be with you, mercy, and peace from God the Father, and from the Lord Jesus Christ, the Son of the Father, in truth and love."

There are two words that are repeated in the first three verses of the introduction, the word *truth* and the word *love*. The word *truth* is mentioned five times in this brief letter. He makes reference to the truth, and he summarizes what he means by that in verse 9, "Whosoever transgresseth, and abideth not in the doctrine of Christ, hath not God. He that abideth in the doctrine of Christ, he hath both the Father and the Son." Verse 10, "If there come any unto you, and bring not this doctrine, receive him not into your house, neither bid him Godspeed."

The truth and this doctrine are the doctrine of Christ and are equivalent. He is talking about the same thing here. The truth to which he refers is the doctrine of Christ, the teachings of the Scripture. So truth is one of the themes, the whole body of Christian teaching.

Truth is very important to our Christian life. God works in our life to change us into the image of Christ, the likeness of Christ, by means of truth. Truth is what God uses in our minds to change us. We are to learn the truth with our mind, we are to love the truth with our hearts, and then we are to live the truth with our wills. God works on our life by means of the truth. Satan, on the other hand, works on our life by means of error. That is why it is so important for us to fill our life with the truth, and we find the truth in Scripture.

Now, the Bible is not only true, but the Bible is also the Truth. In other words, truth is that by which all other information is determined to be true or false. The Bible is the standard. The Bible is the truth. Jesus said it in John 17, "Thy word is truth." So, therefore, the Scripture becomes the touchstone, so to speak. It is the standard by which everything else is judged to be true or false.

The other word occurring in this introduction is the word *love*: "Whom I love in the truth," verse 1; verse 3, "in truth and love."

If I counted correctly, the word *love* occurs about four times in this little book. Truth and love go together. In fact, Paul put it this way in Ephesians, "speak the truth in love." So truth and love go together, and he links those two together in this book.

He deals here with apostate teachers. Let me give you a couple of definitions. Apostasy, which we see fully in the book of Jude, is teaching which goes against Scripture. It is contrary to Scripture. It departs from the teachings of Scripture, the truth. An apostate is someone who teaches apostasy.

Satan wants to get error into the life of a Christian in one of two ways. He wants to do it either in the home or he wants to do it in the church. In this book, II John, he deals with the attempt to get error into the home. That may be why he is writing this Christian mother. The man is the head of the home, but the wife is the heart of the home.

OUTLINE

Introduction, 1-3

I. Practicing the Truth, 4-6

II. Perverting the Truth, 7-11

- **A. Those Who Deceive, 7**
- **B. Those Who Destroy, 8**
- **C. Those Who Depart, 9-11**

Conclusion, 12-13

The Introduction is verses 1-3.

I. Practicing the Truth, 4-6

In the first division, John talks about truth and love. In verse 4 he says, "I rejoiced greatly that I found of thy children walking in truth, as we have received a commandment from the Father." He ran into her children, and they were walking in the truth. It is always a blessing when your children are walking in the truth.

Next he talks about love. Verse 6, "And this is love, that we walk after his commandments. This is the commandment, That, as ye have heard from the beginning, ye should walk in it." Note the word *walk*.

II. Perverting the Truth, 7-11

A. Those Who Deceive, 7

He talks about those in verse 7 who would deceive. Verse 7, "For many deceivers are entered into the world, who confess not that Jesus Christ is come in the flesh. This is a deceiver and an antichrist." The spirit of antichrist was already at work even in the New Testament day. There are deceivers who do not acknowledge Christ as the Son of God. This is especially important in the day we are living in because we are becoming such a multi-cultural nation. We have people who are coming in from many different cultures and religions. That is why so many get upset when we say Jesus Christ is the only way to heaven. It is an issue of truth. There are those who do not confess that Jesus Christ has come in the flesh, that He is the Messiah, and the only Savior of the world.

B. Those Who Destroy, 8

He talks in verse 8 about those who destroy. "Look to yourselves, that we lose not those things which we have wrought, but that we receive a full reward."

C. Those Who Depart, 9-11

Verse 9, "Whosoever transgresseth, and abideth not in the doctrine of Christ, hath not God. He that abideth in the doctrine of Christ, he hath both the Father and the Son." This is a pretty strong statement. Again, John paints in absolutes; he paints it black and white. There are no grays with John. This is one of those statements. What he is saying is those people who do not abide in the doctrine of Christ, those people who deviate from the teaching of Scripture, they do not have God. They are not saved people.

When the controversy in the Southern Baptist Convention really began to arise and we were dealing with matters of liberalism in some of our Southern Baptist schools, the big issue was Scripture. Is Scripture God's Word? I took the position then that for a person to deny the inerrancy of Scripture was pretty good evidence that the person was not saved. I was not saying that to be unkind, but I was saying it on the basis of II John 9. He makes it pretty plain.

Note what he says in verse 10, "If there come any unto you." Now we are thinking if this elect lady is a literal lady and these are her children, then we are talking about the home. If any come unto you and "bring not this doctrine"; in other words, if they do not bring the truth, the teachings about Jesus Christ according to the Scriptures; then notice what he says about it, "receive him not into your house, neither bid him God speed." Verse 11, "For he that biddeth him God speed is partaker of his evil deeds." You might think that is so harsh and so unkind. It is not harsh and it is not unkind. You have a responsibility to your family to see that nothing gets into your home that is contrary to God's Word.

Let me get specific. The Jehovah's Witnesses knock on doors. We should be knocking on doors though. The Jehovah's Witnesses deny the deity of Jesus Christ. A lot of them do their visitation during church time. They know that is when the backslidden Baptists, who are very susceptible to error, are at home. They are the folks who are not real grounded. He says specifically not to let them come into your home. I have a standard line when they come to my door. I say according to God's Word, it tells me I am not to allow you to come into my home. I am certainly not trying to be unkind, but the Bible says if you do not bring the doctrine of Christ, if you do not believe in the deity of Christ, you cannot come into my home. I also say I will be real happy to come into your home and share with you what I believe about Jesus Christ. Most of the time they do not want to do that though.

Second John is a good book. It is a very helpful book.

JOTTINGS IN III JOHN

Whereas II John was probably addressed to a lady, III John seems to be addressed to a man. His name is Gaius. Look at the first verse, "The elder unto the well-beloved Gaius, whom I love in the truth."

Now the question is who was Gaius? Three are mentioned in the New Testament. There is one from Corinth, Romans 16:23. There was another Gaius from Macedonia, Acts 19:29; and there was another Gaius from Derbe, Acts 20:4-5.

I do not know which one it is, and it may not be any of those three. One thing you do notice about him is this Gaius is a very special person because four times John calls him beloved: verse 1, "The elder unto the well-beloved Gaius"; verse 2, "Beloved"; verse 5, "Beloved"; and verse 11, "Beloved." So he is a special brother in the Lord.

Whereas II John is probably a home setting, a family setting, this is a local church setting. When I read this book I think to myself times have not changed much. We have a lot of the same problems because what John is dealing with in this book is people problems.

Three men are mentioned in this book, and that is how it is outlined. He is dealing with three men and he is dealing with people problems. We ought to ask ourselves all the time, am I a part of the problem or am I a part of the blessing in my church? I want to be a part of the blessing; I do not want to be a part of the problem in my church.

He is still talking about the matter of truth. We have talked about truth against apostasy in the home, but now he deals with it in the local church. The key word of III John is the word *witness* or some form of the word *witness*. Witness, testified; the King James Version takes the same word and translates it several different ways.

In verse 3, for instance, the word for witness is translated testified. Then in verse 6, the same word for witness is witness or have borne witness. In verse 12, it says bear record, "and ye know our record is true." To bear record, to bear witness, or to testify is all the same word. He is talking about the importance of our witness for the Lord. We witness by our words, we witness by our life, and all of us are witnesses. All Christians are witnesses. Somebody says all Christians ought to be witnesses. Well, all Christians are witnesses. We are either good ones or bad ones. We do give a testimony; we do bear record by our life, one way or the other.

OUTLINE

I. Gaius – a Commendable Christian, 1-8
II. Diotrephes – a Cantankerous Christian, 9-10
III. Demetrius – a Consistent Christian, 11-12
Conclusion, 13-14

I. Gaius – a Commendable Christian, 1-8

I call Gaius a Commendable Christian. He is the beloved Gaius, and that is the kind of Christian I want to be.

II. Diotrephes – a Cantankerous Christian, 9-10

Diotrephes shows up in verses 9 and 10. I call him a Cantankerous Christian. I have known a few Christians like Diotrephes along through the years. Look at his problem, verse 9, "I wrote unto the church: but Diotrephes, who loveth to have the preeminence among them, receiveth us not." Verse 10, "Wherefore, if I come, I will remember his deeds which he doeth, prating [that is to blow bubbles] against us with malicious words: and not content therewith, neither doth he himself receive the brethren, and forbiddeth them that would, and casteth them out of the church." Do you know his problem? Verse 9, he loves to have the preeminence. The word *preeminence* means "to be first." His problem was he wanted to be number one. He had a pride problem. Diotrephes did not have the right to be number one, and we do not have the right to be number one. Colossians 1:18 says that Jesus Christ is to have the preeminence. He is to be number one.

III. Demetrius – a Consistent Christian, 11-12

So you have Gaius, a Commendable Christian; and you have Diotrephes, a Cantankerous Christian; and then you have another good one, Demetrius, a Consistent Christian. Look at Demetrius in verses 11-12: "Beloved, follow not that which is evil, but that which is good. He that doeth good is of God: but he that doeth evil hath not seen God. Demetrius hath good report of all men, and of the truth itself: yea, and we also bear record; and ye know that our record is true." I want to be a Christian like that, to have a good report of all people and of the truth.

Then he concludes with verses 13 and 14.

JUDGMENT IN JUDE

Its Author

This book of Jude is a remarkable book. The author is Jude. Jude 1, "Jude, the servant of Jesus Christ, and brother of James." That tells us that he was a half-brother of Jesus.

Do you notice how reticent he is? He just simply refers to himself as the brother of James; he does not say he is the half brother of Jesus, but rather he says about himself that he is a servant of Jesus Christ, a slave of Jesus Christ. This shows the humility of Jude.

We do not know a lot about him. We do know he is mentioned in Mark 6:3 in the list of the half brothers of the Lord. He is mentioned again in Matthew 13:55. But other than that, that is all we really know of Jude.

Its Purpose

The purpose of this book is given to us in verse 3. He tells us in verse 3 that he set out to do one thing; and then because of circumstances that were occurring, he wound up doing another thing. He started off to write a book on one subject, but conditions were such at the time, he had to write on another subject. Verse 3, "Beloved, when I gave all diligence to write unto you of the common salvation, it was needful [a sense of inner compulsion] for me to write unto you, and exhort you that ye should earnestly contend for the faith which was once delivered unto the saints." He was going to write a little letter here about salvation, but things changed. The situation was such, the circumstances were such, that it was needful for Jude to write and exhort them to earnestly contend for *the* faith.

Notice the terminology, *the* faith which was once for all delivered unto the saints. I added two words, *for all*, because that is what the word *once* means there.

John writes about the truth. He writes about the doctrine. Jude comes along and writes about the faith. He is talking about the same thing. The truth, the doctrine, and the faith all refer to the body, the content of Christian doctrine. He is writing a letter to warn believers of false teachers.

What is false teaching? Apostasy. What are teachers called who teach false doctrine? Apostates. This is a book about apostates, to warn believers of false teachers in the church.

There are some verses that are parallel to one another in II Peter and Jude. The interesting thing is Simon Peter predicted some of these things, and by the time Jude writes these things are already on the scene.

In the midst of this, he also talks about the return of the Lord. The blessed hope of the believer is the return of the Lord. As we approach the return of the Lord, one of the characteristics, one of the things you look for, is there will be a deviation from the truth.

Look back at II Thessalonians and notice how Scripture ties together apostasy and the return of the Lord. It shows you that apostasy is one of the indications of the near return of the Lord. Second Thessalonians 2:1 says, "Now we beseech you, brethren, by the coming of our Lord Jesus Christ, and by our gathering together unto him." Verse 3, "Let no man deceive you [watch out for the apostates] by any means; for that day shall not come, except there come the falling away first [that is where we get the word apostasy], and that man of sin be revealed, the son of perdition." Apostasy is one of the indications that we are approaching the return of the Lord.

OUTLINE

I. Explanation, 1-4
- **A. Salutation, 1-2**
- **B. Subject, 3-4**

II. Exposition, 5-16
- **A. Past Analogy, 5-7**
- **B. Present Analyses, 8-13**
- **C. Prophetic Announcement, 14-16**

III. Exhortation, 17-23
- **A. Practical Theology, 17-23**
- **B. Practical Doxology, 24-25**

I. Explanation, 1-4

In the first four verses he explains why he is writing.

A. Salutation, 1-2

The Salutation is the hello, the greeting.

B. Subject, 3-4

He tells what he is writing about, the Subject. He says to "contend for the faith which was once [for all] delivered unto the saints." That means you cannot add anything to the faith. These folks who say they have a new revelation, they do not. It has been once for all delivered to the saints. When they say that, know they are not true.

Verse 4, "For there are certain men crept in unawares, who were before of old ordained to this condemnation, ungodly men, turning the grace of our God into lasciviousness, and denying the only Lord God, and our Lord Jesus Christ." He is talking specifically about these apostate teachers.

II. Exposition, 5-16

Jude goes into an exposition of the whole subject of apostasy.

A. Past Analogy, 5-7

Here he draws from the Old Testament. He talks about what happened to the children of Israel in Egypt. Then in verse 6 he talks about the angels that fell from heaven. It is fascinating scripture. He talks about the angels who apostatized. Verse 7, he talks about Sodom and Gomorrah and what happened to them. He ties it into the fall of the angels.

B. Present Analyses, 8-13

He analyzes the situation as it is occurring in his day, and by extension we can analyze the same situation today. For instance, in verse 8 he says, "Likewise also these filthy dreamers [talking about the certain men in verse 1] defile the flesh, despise dominion, and speak evil of dignities." He shows what kind of lifestyle they live and what kind of people they are. It is pretty devastating. The word pictures here are so graphic. Look at verse 11, "Woe unto them! for they have gone in the way of Cain." He is still giving Old Testament illustrations. Verse 11 continues, "and ran greedily after the error of Balaam for reward, and perished in the gainsaying of Core [Korah]." Verse 12, "These are spots in your feasts of charity, when they feast with you, feeding themselves without fear: clouds they are without water, carried about of winds; trees whose fruit withereth, without fruit, twice dead, plucked up by the roots." Verse 13, "Raging waves of the sea, foaming out their own shame; wandering stars." He keeps piling on statements about the apostates.

C. Prophetic Announcement, 14-16

Then he gives a Prophetic Announcement, verses 14-16. He goes all the way back to Enoch. Enoch was the man who walked with God. He had a testimony God-ward, but now we notice he has a testimony Man-ward. He says that Enoch made a prophecy about the return of the Lord. Verse 14, "And Enoch also, the seventh from Adam, prophesied of these, saying, Behold, the Lord cometh with ten thousands of his saints." Then he talks about when Jesus does come with His saints, the believers, He will come back to judge.

III. Exhortation, 17-25

In the third division, he exhorts a little; he preaches a little. Verse 17, "But, beloved, remember ye the words." He calls us back to the Scriptures. The best way to be prepared to handle apostasy and apostate teachers is to be prepared in the Scriptures. Remember the words "which were spoken before of the apostles of our Lord Jesus Christ." Verse 18, "How that they told you there should be mockers in the last time, who should walk after their own ungodly lusts." Go to your Bible; search the Scriptures.

A. Practical Theology, 17-23

He gives Practical Theology in verses 17-23. Verse 20, "But ye, beloved, building up yourselves on your most holy faith, praying in the Holy Spirit." Get strong in the Lord. Pray with the assistance of the Holy Spirit. Verse 21, "Keep yourselves in the love of God, looking for the mercy of our Lord Jesus Christ unto eternal life." Verses 22-23, be a soul winner. "And of some have compassion, making a difference: And others save with fear, pulling them out of the fire; hating even the garment spotted by the flesh." One of the best ways to stay close to the

Lord is to be soul winner. If you stay red hot telling people about Christ, it will make you pray more because you will encounter so many different things as you try to witness.

I am not at all suggesting that we do not learn methods of how to witness because I think we should. I have been using the Romans Road as long as I can remember. But the more you witness, the more you realize you need to pray for the Lord's help. You have to pray a lot and ask the Holy Spirit to help you as you witness to people. He says in verse 22, "And of some have compassion, making a difference: And others save with fear, pulling them out of the fire."

I do not like to preach on hell, but it is the truth. People need to know it. When I preach, I try to pull people out of the fire. When we witness, we try to pull people out of the fire.

B. Practical Doxology, 24-25

He closes out with a Practical Doxology, verses 24-25. A doxology is a place in the Bible where the writer stops and shouts for a while. You have some beautiful doxologies in the Bible, and here is one of the best of them all. "Now unto him [Jesus] that is able to keep you from falling, and to present you faultless before the presence of his glory with exceeding joy, To the only wise God our Saviour, be glory and majesty, dominion and power, both now and ever. Amen."

The Prophetical Book

Study #43
Resting in Revelation

RESTING IN REVELATION

The name for the book of the Revelation comes from the first chapter and the first verse. Revelation 1:1, "The Revelation of Jesus Christ." Though there may be a series of revelations all through the book, it is primarily the Revelation, singular, because it is an unfolding of the Lord Jesus Christ.

To reveal something is to open it up, to unfold it, to bring it to view. In the book of the Revelation we have a beautiful unfolding of our Lord Jesus Christ. The ultimate goal and purpose of a study of the book of the Revelation is that you might see Jesus more clearly and love Him more dearly.

This book is a special book in that God gives a special twofold blessing to those who will read this book and to those who will hear it Note Revelation 1:3, "Blessed is he that readeth, and they that hear the words of this prophecy, and keep those things which are written in it; for the time is at hand." The conclusion of the book, Revelation 22:7, says, "Behold, I come quickly. Blessed is he that keepeth the words of the prophecy of this book." Here is a book, at the beginning and at the conclusion, that promises a special blessing to those who will read it and to those who will keep the teachings of this book. Rather than to be a book that is avoided, it is a book to be studied and a book to read.

The book of the Revelation is the last book in our Bible. It completes the canon of Scripture, but it also climaxes the mind and counsel of God for man as revealed in the Holy Scriptures. It is a very special and very important book.

Its Background

This book has as its human author the apostle John, the beloved disciple. He became the pastor of Ephesus, and somewhere around A.D. 70 the Roman emperor Domitian (A.D. 81-96) started a wave of persecution against the church. He was a murderer, and he demanded to be worshiped as Lord God. Of course, the Christians because Jesus is Lord refused to worship Domitian. Christians were going through great persecution.

John was exiled to the island of Patmos in the Aegean Sea. It is a small island about ten miles by six miles. There was a prison camp there and John was incarcerated in that prison. I have had the opportunity to go to the island of Patmos and go into the very cave where the Holy Spirit revealed this very book to this dear old man of God, the apostle John. He evidently wrote it near the end of the century, around A.D. 95.

Its Purpose

Let's look at the purpose of this book, and there are several areas I want to discuss that will give us an overall understanding of its purpose. One of the things I want you to notice is that this book is a prophecy. Note Revelation 1:3 again, "the words of this prophecy." Several times in the Revelation it is referred to as a prophecy (1:3; 10:11; 19:10; 22:7, 10, 18, 19). So it is specifically called a prophecy

We are told how this prophecy was written. We get the clue to that in the first verse of chapter 1 where it says that God gave this Revelation of the Lord Jesus unto His servants and specifically John. He says in the last part of verse 1, "and he sent and signified it by his angel unto his servant John."

Notice the word *signified.* I want to kind of pull that word a part. He said he signified it. If you pull that word apart, you will get sign-i-fied. What he is saying is this prophecy is written by means of signs. In other words, there are symbols that are used in this book.

There are several reasons why this book was written in signs, but the primary reason was that the Christians were going through persecution. In dangerous days, sometimes God's people had to speak in symbolic language. It would be language that would be familiar to them, but it would not be significant to other people. That is what you will find in this book. For instance, symbols like the Lamb are mentioned. When I say the Lamb, you know immediately to whom I refer. I refer to the Lord Jesus because we know the verse, "Behold the Lamb of God who takes away the sin of the world" (John 3:29). But people who do not understand the symbolism of the Christian faith today or did not back in the day of John, talking about a lamb would not be significant to them.

These signs are important and their meanings are also important because they give clues to what the book is all about. Many of the signs are explained in the book itself. For instance, in this first chapter, we have a beautiful vision of the Lord Jesus. In verse 20 he begins to explain some signs or symbols he just used. For instance, he talks about seven stars, the mystery of the seven stars which John saw in Jesus' right hand. That is a reference back to verse 16, where the vision of the glorified Lord Jesus is given; verse 16, "And he had in his right hand seven stars." In verse 20, he is basically saying, I am going to tell you the meaning of that symbol and also the seven lampstands. He tells exactly what they are: "The seven stars are the angels of the seven churches; and the seven lampstands which thou sawest are the seven churches."

He tells John the seven stars are the angels, the messengers of the churches; and the seven lampstands which he saw are the seven churches. The King James Version uses the word *candlestick,* but a better word is the word *lampstand.* It is a sign, a symbol, that makes reference to the churches.

There are many places where these symbols are explained, and another one is in Revelation 4:5, "And out of the throne proceeded lightning and thunderclaps, and voices; and there were seven lamps of fire burning before the throne, which are the seven spirits of God." He tells what those seven lamps of fire represent. He says they are the seven spirits of God, that is the seven-fold manifestation of God's Holy Spirit.

Another one is in Revelation 5:8. He talks about golden bowls or vials full of odors or incense, and then he says what they are. They symbolize the prayers of the saints. So, many of the symbols are explained in the book itself.

Many of the symbols are explained in the Old Testament, or they are taken from the Old Testament. For instance, Revelation 2:7: "To him that overcometh will I give to eat of the tree of life, which is in the midst of the paradise of God." That's the use of symbols or signs that we find all the way back in the book of Genesis in the Garden of Eden.

In Revelation 2:17 he talks about the hidden manna. That is a symbol that is explained back in the Old Testament in the book of Exodus when God sent manna to the children of Israel in the wilderness and then had them take the container full of manna and place it in the tabernacle.

Another is in Revelation 2:28, "And I will give him the morning star." That ties back into a prediction in the Old Testament about a star out of Jacob. So many of these signs or symbols are explained in the book itself or they are explained in the Old Testament.

To say this book is written in signs or symbols does not mean it is unreal, that what is being dealt with here is unreal; but they are spiritual realities given in picture form, given in symbolic form. It does not mean that the truths conveyed are unreal. They are; they are very literal, but literal truth is packaged in symbolic language.

I have already indicated that one of the purposes of the book is to unveil the Lord Jesus. It is probably the main purpose. One of the keys to getting the blessing out of the book of the Revelation is when you don't know exactly what is going on in Revelation, just look for Jesus. Ask yourself, where does Jesus fit into this? How do you find the Lord in this? It sets forth the person of the Lord.

The third thing is this book is an open book; it is a revelation, it is an unveiling. Contrast that with the book of Daniel in the Old Testament. In Daniel 12:4, Daniel was told to seal up the book until the time of the end. For a long time, Daniel was a closed book, but the Revelation is an open book.

A lot of the material in this book is based on the Old Testament. We know that this book was written in Greek. The New Testament was written in the Greek language, but a lot of the thought patterns and idioms are Hebrew in nature. In fact, this book is just really saturated with Old Testament language and terminology. There are approximately 550 references to the Old Testament in this one book alone.

Another thing to notice is that numbers are used significantly here. The Jews had a whole science of numbers or the meaning of numbers. It was called Gematria. It was the symbolic meaning of numbers.

For instance, the number 7 is symbolically used in the book of the Revelation. Seven is the number of perfection. By the way, that number 7 is stamped on the material world also. There are seven notes on the musical scale, completion. When you see the number 7 in this book, it is a symbol of completion.

Another number is the number 6. Now the number 6 is the number of human failure, the number of humanity. That's why when you read the number of the beast in chapter 13, it says the number of the beast is 666. The Antichrist is a trinity of human failure, 666. So you will find numbers here that have symbolic significance

Another thing is this book is universal in nature. It covers the scope of the world and the entire future of human history.

This book is a very majestic book. It is an exalted book; it lifts your horizons and turns your vision upwards. For instance, note the majestic terminology. The word *throne* is used 44 times in these 22 chapters. It is the *throne* book, so to speak.

The words *king, kingdom,* and *rule* are used about 37 times in this book. Words like *power* and *authority* are used about 40 times in this book. You have sovereignty, you have kingdomhood, and you have majesty. Here was John exiled on an island for his faith in the Lord, and God just opens up the heavens and lets John see the throne.

One of the great messages to John was, John, regardless of what you see going on down on earth, in heaven God is still on His throne. That is the same message we derive today; regardless of what goes on in the world, always remember God is on His throne. God has not abdicated the throne of this universe.

Another thing is this book is indeed a climactic book. It climaxes the Bible and the plan and the purpose of God

There are some interesting contrasts between the first book in the Bible, Genesis, and the last book, Revelation. For instance, in Genesis we are told how heaven and earth commence; in Revelation, we are told how heaven and earth consummate. Genesis gives us the entrance of sin into the world, and Revelation gives us the exit of sin from the world.

In Genesis, we have the dawn of Satan; in Revelation, we have the doom of Satan. In Genesis, we have the entrance of death; in Revelation, we have the exit of death.

Its Interpretation

There are a number of different views concerning how the book of the Revelation is to be correctly interpreted. The first view is called the Preterest view. This is the view which says that the greatest part of the book of the Revelation was fulfilled in the first century, in the early years of the Christian faith. It says that all that you read about here has already taken place. But, remember, we are told specifically that the Revelation is a prophecy. So it is very difficult to believe that everything was fulfilled in the first century, or soon thereafter.

The second view is the Historical view. The historical view is that all of these events were fulfilled, if not in the first century during the history of the Christian church. Well, if that be true, then what value does this have for you or for me?

The third view is known as the Spiritual or the Allegorical view. That means there is no prophecy here, it is just an allegory. It is a story that just basically depicts the conflict between good and evil, and you just draw spiritual lessons from it. Of course, it is true there are spiritual lessons to be drawn, and it is true that you see the conflict between good and evil. But that does not fulfill the whole purpose of the book of the Revelation.

The fourth view, which I personally hold, is the Futurist view. This view says that this is indeed a prophecy and that from chapter 4 and on we have given to us prophecy, or prediction, of what will happen after the age of the church, after the church is raptured out of this world.

Again, John had a habit in his writing to give you a key to the understanding of his books. For instance, in the Gospel of John he hangs his key on the backdoor.

In the Letters of John, he scatters the key all through the house. In the book of the Revelation he does the same thing. He gives us a key to its meaning, and he hangs it on the front door. Is there an outline that will crack this book open for us and will show us how it is divided? There indeed is. Revelation 1:19 is the verse. Right there on the front door in the opening chapter of the book, John and the Holy Spirit give us the key and the basic outline of the book.

Revelation 1:19, "Write the things which thou hast seen, and the things which are, and the things which shall be hereafter." This is the outline. John is told what to write, and he is specifically instructed in what he is going to see. John is to write three things: Past things, things which you have seen; Present things, things which are; and the things which shall be hereafter, that is Prospective things. They are things in the future. That is exactly what you find in the book of the Revelation.

The things John had already seen refer to what he has written before that verse. Past things is in chapter 1. The things that are, he is going to write in chapters 2 and 3.

Then he said future things. Note Revelation 4:1, "After this." These are the same words used as in verse 19, "hereafter." "After this [hereafter] I looked, and behold, a door was opened in heaven; and the first voice which I heard was as it were of a trumpet, talking with me; which said, Come up hither, and I will shew thee things which must be hereafter." Notice the same words are used at the beginning of that verse and at the end of that verse, which are found also in Revelation 1:19. The Lord said to John to write the things that will be hereafter. Chapter 4:1, Hereafter and hereafter. It is as if the Holy Spirit said I want to be sure you do not miss this. So he begins the verse with hereafter, and he closes the verse with hereafter. From thereon, chapter 4 through chapter 22, he shows us things that are going to be hereafter. After what? Look at Revelation 3:22. What is the last word? Churches. What shall be hereafter? Things after the churches.

Do you see how simple it is? It is just as clear as day. It is plain as can be. To my mind, the Holy Spirit has already outlined this book for us. This is not as arbitrary as some of the outlines used in previous books.

OUTLINE

Introduction, 1:1-3

I. Past Things, 1

II. Present Things, 2–3

Seven Churches

- **A. Literal**
- **B. Historical**
- **C. Local**
- **D. Personal**

III. Prospective Things, 4–22

- **A. A Vision of Government, 4–20**
    - **1. The Beginnings of Sorrows, 4–11**
    - **2. The Beast on the Earth, 12–18**
    - **3. The Battle of Armageddon, 19–20**
- **B. A Vision of Glory, 21:1–22:5**

Conclusion, 22:6-21

Introduction, 1:1-3

The Introduction is in the first three verses of chapter 1.

I. Past Things, 1

Starting in verse 4, you have Past Things, what John called "the things thou hast seen." The focus of that chapter is on Christ. Past Things, chapter 1, Christ. You have a vision here of the resurrected, glorified Lord Jesus Christ Himself. It is beautiful. Verse 12, John turns and sees the candlesticks that represent the seven churches of Asia Minor to which he was writing. Then in the midst of those, he says in verse 13, "And in the midst of the seven candlesticks one like unto the Son of man." We know that is Jesus. Then he goes down and gives a beautiful symbolic presentation of the glorified Jesus Christ.

Keep in mind this is written in signs. Do not think when we see the Lord we are going to see His head and hair white like wool. We may see Him that way, but the point I am making is all of this has symbolic language. I do not know how it will be when we see Him. I think it was so glorious that John did not know how to describe it, and so the Holy Spirit just gives him these symbols and signs to describe in the language of man that which is indescribable. Jesus is going to be indescribable when we see Him.

II. Present Things, 2–3

The second main division, chapters 2 through 3, we are calling Present Things, the things which are. The focus in these two chapters is on the Church. You have here the seven churches. Back in Revelation 1:11-12, John was told he was to write this book and send it to the seven churches of Asia Minor. There were actually churches there.

There are several ways to study these letters to the churches. In Revelation 2:1 it says, "Unto the angel of the church of Ephesus." The word *angel* means messenger, which probably is referring to the pastor of the churches. But you notice he starts in verse 1, "Unto the angel of the church of Ephesus." Verse 8, "And unto the angel of the church in Smyrna." Verse 12, "the church at Pergamos." Verse 18, "the church at Thyatira." Then Revelation 3:1, "the church at Sardis." Verse 7, "Philadelphia"; and verse 14, "Laodicea". You have letters sent by the Lord Jesus through His messengers to these seven churches.

A. Literal

How do you interpret these seven churches? There are several different ways to study them. You can be correct in studying these churches in these different ways. I think they are all correct. First of all they were Literal churches. There were actual churches in these seven cities. On a Sunday if you were in the city of Ephesus, you could have found a group of Christian people, saved people, gathering together to worship the risen Lord Jesus Christ. They did not have buildings until about the third century, but they may have met in an outside place and they may have met in an amphitheater somewhere or they may have met in homes. These churches can be looked upon as literal, actual churches.

B. Historical

Another way to look at them is Historical. In other words, you can study these verses in terms of the entire age of the Church, from the first century until the last century when Jesus comes again, whenever that century may be. You can see here a panoramic view of the Church age and the seven stages of the age of the Church in these seven letters. For instance, the first stage is the early church, and that is represented by the church of Ephesus. One of the things that happened to them is towards the end of the first century their love for Christ began to be lost. He said they had lost their first love. You come all the way down to the seventh, and the seventh is the Laodicean church. It is the lukewarm church. If we understand this correctly, it means one of the characteristics of the churches of the last days is spiritual indifference and lethargy. This is one of the things that makes us sometimes think we may be in the last stages of the age of the Church because that is pretty characteristic of churches as you find them in the world today.

I personally take the view that you have several churches that run parallel to one another towards the end of the age. I think it is possible in these days for a church to be a Philadelphia church, a church of the open door, a church that is faithful to the Word of God. What I am saying is you can look at these seven churches as a panoramic view of the Church age, a Historical view.

C. Local

A third way of looking at these churches is to make a Local interpretation. In a local church, it is possible for one or more or all of the different identities of these seven churches to be found. In other words, in one congregation of people you may find Ephesus Christians, you may find Philadelphia Christians, you might find Laodicean Christians. Sometimes it is according to which crowd you get in at a church. The seeds of all the problems of those seven churches are just beneath the surface of a life of a church ready to grow.

D. Personal

Another way to interpret these churches is Personal. In other words, as we read those letters, take the message to the church and apply it to our own personal heart. When he talks about the church of Ephesus losing its first love, then we turn these scriptures into our own personal life and ask the Lord if that has happened to me. Use each one of these to give a personal message and challenge in our Christian life.

III. Prospective Things, 4–22

The third division is chapters 4 through 22, Prospective Things. The focus there is on the consummation, the things that shall be hereafter. There are two main divisions.

A. A Vision of Government, 4–20

Chapters 4 through 20 we call a Vision of Government. John is given a Vision of Government or the rule of the Lord and the judgments of God. God is on His throne. That is one of the keys. Chapters 4 and 5 begin with marvelous visions of God on His throne. As he looks towards the future, he wants to get us rightly related to the truth of the sovereignty of God. That is why in chapters 4 and 5, he talks about the throne.

You see all of these judgments of God. For instance, chapters 4 through 11 are the Beginnings of Sorrows. Then chapters 12 through 19, you have the Beast on the Earth and the Battle of Armageddon and those kinds of things. What can trip up Christians sometimes in getting the chronology of all of this is they fail to understand an important law of Bible interpretation. There is a law of Bible interpretation known as the law of Recurrence. It is a pattern of writing that was common at the time in which the book of the Revelation was written. In fact, it was really common to that part of the world. A writer would write about a certain event or certain period of time, and then he would come back and go over the same ground again. It was recurring. In other words, he would give you a chronological account of something, and then he would come back through that same period of time, but he would not look at it in terms of chronology, but he would look at it in terms of the great themes or great personalities. That is exactly what you find right here.

In other words, chapters 4 through 11 hang together. Then chapters 12 through 19 hang together, and they have to do with the same period of time. It is the period of time known in the Bible as the Great Tribulation or the Tribulation. Some people specify that the latter part is the Great Tribulation, but we will not go into that in this study. My point is all these chapters are dealing about the same period of time but from a different perspective. Chapters 4 through 11 give a chronology, a chronological presentation of things that will happen from the Rapture to the Revelation. He gives a time line of what will happen in this Tribulation from the time the Church is caught up to meet the Lord in the air to the Revelation when the Church comes back with the Lord to the earth. He gives the crucial events.

When he gets to chapter 12 he fills in the details, so to speak, and gives some of the main personalities. He talks about the Beast and the False Prophet, and he paints the picture of some of the key personalities. It is like an artist painting a picture. First of all he gives the overall picture, the big strokes. He gives the outline of the picture. Then he comes back and begins to fill in the details. The same law of recurrence explains Genesis 1 and 2. Genesis 1 gives the creation of the earth in terms of chronology, day one, day two, and so on. Genesis 2 gives the creation, but now he is not interested in chronological order. He is interested now in theme, in personality, so the emphasis there is on man, the creation of man. It is the law of recurrence. It is the same material from a different perspective. That is what you have in the book of the Revelation. When you read Revelation 4 through 11 and then get ready to go into chapter 12, remember you are in the same period of time but it is not chronology as much as you are looking at the different people and personalities that come into play.

B. A Vision of Glory, 21:1–22:5

Chapters 21 through Revelation 22:15 is a Vision of Glory. We are taken on a tour of the New Jerusalem.

Conclusion, 22:6-21

After he has given this beautiful vision and tour of the New Jerusalem, then he concludes the book. Notice three times in the concluding verses, the Lord Jesus says, "Behold, I come quickly." Verse 7, "Behold, I come quickly." Verse 12, "Behold, I come quickly." Verse 20, "Surely I come quickly"; to which John replies, "Amen [let it be]. Even so come, Lord Jesus."

Study #44
The Old and New Testaments at a Glance

THE OLD AND NEW TESTAMENTS AT A GLANCE

One of the things I have enjoyed through the years is gathering poems about the Bible. I have some I would like to share.

This is the greatest
Book on earth
Unparalleled it stands;
Its author God, its truth Divine,
Inspired in every word and line
Tho' writ by human hands.
This is the Living
Rock of Truth
Which all assaults defies,
O'er every stormy blast of time
It towers with majesty sublime
It lives and never dies.
This is the volume of the Cross
Its saving truth is sure;
Its doctrines pure,
its histories true,
Its Gospel old, yet ever new
Shall evermore endure.

This is another one I have used all through the years:

Though its cover is worn and the pages are torn,
And though places bear traces of tears, yet more
Precious than gold is this book worn and old
That can scatter and shatter our fears.

We have been talking about the Bible. In my library I have a set of books called the Great Books of the Western World. There are 60 volumes in this library of books, and they include the great literature of the Western world and all the great writers of the books that have affected and shaped history and have changed history.

The Bible is called the Good Book. It is made up of 66 volumes and it is a divine library.

Now in the Great Books of the Western world there are some relationships between the different authors. Some of those authors maybe knew one another; others were influenced by one another. Yet, there is no sense of cohesiveness in these great books of the Western world, but this book, which we call the Bible, is a divine library. Though it has a variety of human authors, the Bible is unique in that it has one divine author. When you take what the human authors have written, inspired by the Holy Spirit, you have a complete volume, a single book.

Some interesting facts about the Bible (King James Version) are it contains 3,566,480 letters (the King James Version). It has 810,697 words. It has 31,175 verses, and 1,189 chapters. It has 66 books, and yet it is one complete cohesive volume.

Our purpose, in this journey through the Bible, has been to really see the Bible as a whole, to get the over-all view of the Bible, and then take each of the 66 books and look at them individually and as a whole. I have used a picture as my theme for the study through this Bible survey, and I have called it a "Journey through the Bible." It is a picture of going on a journey.

Now, when you get ready to go on a journey, one of the most helpful things you can do, is to get a road map and to trace on that road map the main highways, the main roads that you want to take. It is probably helpful for you not to go into a great deal of details in your road map; just get the main highways, just get the main roads, not all of the side roads, not all of the by ways, not all the detours, but get the main roads in your mind. You can explore the side roads later, but if you are going to go on the journey you need to know what the main arteries are.

That is what I have tried to do. I have tried to give the big picture in the Bible. I have tried to show how the Bible fits together and then how each of the individual books of the Bible fit together also.

Now what you want to do is to go back and begin to fill in the details. We have had an outline for each book of the Bible. Using those road maps so to speak, I want to encourage you to go back into those books and read them. The beginning of the year is always a good time to do that. There are a variety of ways of reading through your Bible, and I have used a number of them. If you have been reading through your Bible for a number of years, there is something to be said about a variety of approaches.

Of course, one of the very best ways to begin is to just start in the beginning with Genesis 1:1 and then read. If you will read three chapters in the Old Testament a day and two chapters in the New Testament a day, you can easily read through the entire Bible in year.

Do not worry if you don't understand everything along the way as you read. If you do not know all the details, if you do not understand everything that is going on, do not worry too much about it. The Lord will help and assist you; just move on and keep looking for the main themes.

You may want to start in Genesis; you might want to start in Matthew and move that way. I encourage new Christians to begin in the New Testament. If you have never read through your Bible and if you have never read through your New Testament, start with the New Testament and just read through the New Testament. I believe there are 254 chapters in the New Testament and it is a little easier to understand.

I would encourage you, also to get a translation that might be easier to understand. The King James Version of the Bible was translated originally in 1611. That was 300-plus years ago, and words have had a tendency to change their meanings along the way. That is certainly true about the King James Bible. I would encourage you to get a paraphrase also. Paraphrases are not translations, but they are one person's attempt to give the gist of what is being said. The Living Bible, for instance, is a paraphrase; it is not a word-for-word translation.

A paraphrase is similar to do what I do. I take a verse of scripture try to paraphrase it to give the essence of it. To my mind, the most accurate of the translations is the New American Standard Bible, the NASB. Some people have a problem with the King James language. If you do, then get a new translation and read it along with your King James Bible. That will be helpful. Whatever you do, have a plan.

There are devotional books that will take you through the Bible. Christian bookstores can point you to books that will have systems of Bible reading. A lot of Bibles even have a through-the-Bible reading plan for a year.

As you read your Bible, pray and ask the Lord to help you understand and ask the Lord to help you apply its teachings and its truths to your life and to your behavior. Bible reading is a very pleasant, very enjoyable, and very wonderful experience; but sometimes it can be a painful experience. I know when I let things get in my life that ought not to be there, and then I confront those things in the Bible, that is not real pleasant. Most of us do not like to be confronted by our unchristian behavior. Sometimes it is kind of painful, and it drives you to confession and prayer and you ask the Lord to forgive you and cleanse you.

OUTLINE

OLD TESTAMENT

I. Historical (17 Books)

- **A. Pre-Canaan (5)**
  1. **Genesis**
  2. **Exodus**
  3. **Leviticus**
  4. **Numbers**
  5. **Deuteronomy**
- **B. In-Canaan (9)**
  1. **Joshua**
  2. **Judges**
  3. **Ruth**
  4. **I Samuel**
  5. **II Samuel**
  6. **I Kings**
  7. **II Kings**
  8. **I Chronicles**
  9. **II Chronicles**

- C. **Post-Canaan (3)**
  - 1. **Ezra**
  - 2. **Nehemiah**
  - 3. **Esther**

II. Poetical (5 Books)

- A. **Job**
- B. **Psalms**
- C. **Proverbs**
- D. **Ecclesiastes**
- E. **Song of Solomon**

III. Prophetical (17 Books)

- A. **Major Prophets (5)**
  - 1. **Isaiah**
  - 2. **Jeremiah**
  - 3. **Lamentations**
  - 4. **Ezekiel**
  - 5. **Daniel**
- B. **Minor Prophets (12)**
  - 1. **Hosea**
  - 2. **Joel**
  - 3. **Amos**
  - 4. **Obadiah**
  - 5. **Jonah**
  - 6. **Micah**
  - 7. **Nahum**
  - 8. **Habakkuk**
  - 9. **Zephaniah**
  - 10. **Haggai**
  - 11. **Zechariah**
  - 12. **Malachi**

There are three main divisions of the Old Testament, and I call the Old Testament the first book. That is the first book in your Bible, the Old Testament.

I. Historical

Most of this Old Testament, especially those first 17 books, has to do with the history, religion, philosophy, prophecy, hopes, and failures of a single people, the Jewish people, the Hebrew children.The Bible does an interesting thing; it starts us off in the book of Genesis with the history of the human race. Then it cuts from the human race as a whole to one race in particular, the Hebrew race, the Jewish people.

The first 17 books are books of History. You say why bother reading about the history of some nation of people I don't really care anything about? Well, the reason you do that is because God gave this history. It is not just history, it is also theology, doctrine and teaching because God's dealings with the Hebrew people teach us what kind of God God is. It shows us who God is and how He relates to His people. It sets up the system of salvation, what salvation is all about.

It is not just reading the history of a nation of a people like you would read the history of the Russians or our history. It is sacred history, and it is spiritual history. The first 17 books abound in truths and lessons for you and me.

II. Poetical

The middle books of the Old Testament are the Poetical books. Those books are books of the human heart. They address the problems of life. Some of the main problems of life are addressed. For instance, the book of Job deals with the problem of suffering, the problem of good people who have bad things happen to them. It deals with why is there evil in the world.

The book of the Psalms is a wonderful source to give you guidance and direction about all of the different kinds of problems and emotions that we experience in life. The book of Proverbs contains all these wonderful pithy principles. You get to the book of Ecclesiastes and the vanity of a life that is lived only for this world with no reference to the other world. So the Poetical books are the books that deal with the problems of the human heart, the problems of life.

III. Prophetical

The third division is the Prophetical division of the Old Testament that has to do with the prophecies that God gave. It has 17 books in it. When we think of prophecy we think primarily of something toward the future, but the books of the prophets in the Old Testament do more than just predict the future. They give God's moral and ethical teachings. When these prophets wrote and preached in their day, they had a message to their day.

Having said that, it is true that there are prophecies or predictions made in those prophetical books. We have specific prophecies about the first coming of Jesus into the world and also prophecies about the second coming of Jesus into the world.

One of the greatest ways to study the message and the meaning of Christmas is to go back to the Old Testament prophecies. I have done messages on Isaiah 9:6 for Christmas. They were *His Name Shall Be Called Wonderful, Counselor, The Mighty God, The Everlasting Father,* and *The Prince of Peace.*

What a beautiful prediction that is of Jesus. You have where Jesus would be born, predicted hundreds of years ahead of the fact; the fact that Jesus would be born of a virgin. These predictions are in the Old Testament prophecies.

Someone said that there are over 330 predictions concerning the coming of Christ in the Old Testament. They give the mathematical probabilities of all of those prophecies. In fact, a mathematician named Peter Stoner wrote a little book about it. He just took eight of the prophecies about the birth of Jesus and the mathematical probabilities of all eight of those prophecies being fulfilled in one person, the Lord Jesus Christ. The mathematical probabilities are just incredible.

You will find the first coming of Christ and, also, prophecies that were not fulfilled in His first coming, which we know will be fulfilled in His second coming.

OUTLINE

NEW TESTAMENT

I. Historical (5)
- **A. Life of Jesus**
  - **1. Matthew**
  - **2. Mark**
  - **3. Luke**
  - **4. John**
- **B. Life of the Church**
  - **1. Acts**

II. Instructional (21)
- **A. Doctrinal**
  - **1. Romans**
  - **2. I Corinthians**

3. **II Corinthians**
4. **Galatians**
5. **Ephesians**
6. **Philippians**
7. **Colossians**
8. **I Thessalonians**
9. **II Thessalonians**

B. Personal/Pastoral

1. **I Timothy**
2. **II Timothy**
3. **Titus**
4. **Philemon**

C. General

1. **Hebrews**
2. **James**
3. **I Peter**
4. **II Peter**
5. **I John**
6. **II John**
7. **III John**
8. **Jude**

III. Prophetical (1)
Revelation

The second volume or the second section of your Bible is your New Testament. We will call the Old Testament the first book and the New Testament the final book.

How many books in the Old Testament? 39. When you take three and multiply it by nine, you get 27. The New Testament, the final book, interestingly has three main divisions also.

It is very similar in its arrangement to the Old Testament books, in that the first division is what we would call the Historical section. It is five books. We are back in history again, but it is sacred history. It is spiritual history. It is just not facts, but it is also truth and doctrine. The five historical books are Matthew, Mark, Luke, John, and Acts.

I. Historical

The first four of the historical books relate primarily to Jesus, the life of our Lord. The last of those books, the book of Acts, relates primarily to the history of the Christian church. Why does the Bible begin in the New Testament by giving us these books that relate historical facts? Why do we care that Jesus went here and Jesus went there? Here is why. These books lay a foundation in historical fact for the basic truths of the Christian faith: who Jesus is, what He came to do, and what the effect is of what He came to do.

Do you remember the statement of Simon Peter in his second letter? He said, "We have not followed cunningly devised fables" (II Peter 1:16). His point is this is not a fairy tale.

Jesus said in John 14:6, "I am the way, the truth, and the life; no man cometh unto the Father, but by me." We have a faith here that is grounded in fact. These are not fairy tales as we read these gospel accounts. Christians of the future are going to have to be able to present the faith and present it in an intelligent way. They are going to have to be able to respond to the questions that come today. You are going to have to know what you believe, you are going to have to know why you believe it, and you have to be able to state it. We can't have it like it used to be anymore. It is a new day, so we had better be prepared for that and we had better prepare our young people for that.

The Gospels, the first four books, and the book of Acts lay the foundations of the gospel and the Christian church in historical fact. It is rooted to historical fact.

II. Instructional

The second major division of your New Testament is what we call Instructional. It is the great bulk of your New Testament. The Instructional section is primarily the letters. Now the letters are divided up into several different ways. Some of the letters were written by Paul to individual local churches. There are nine letters to seven churches: Romans, I and II Corinthians, Galatians, Ephesians, Philippians, Colossians, and I and II Thessalonians.

There are some letters that are personal letters; they are written to persons, individuals. In that category are I and II Timothy, Titus, and Philemon. Then there are some letters that are general in nature like the book of Hebrews.

What is the importance of the Instructional books? These books give us the basic doctrines and the ethical applications for the church corporately and Christians personally.

When we read these books, we find out what God expects the church to be and how God expects the church to conduct itself. There is a great deal of debate going on today about the church and the purpose of the church. A lot has been written, and a lot of changes are going on.

When I was a pastor, people would write and ask for a copy of our doctrinal statement. The fact of the matter is we did not have a doctrinal statement. I would just write them back and say our doctrinal statement is the New Testament. We try to go by the New Testament. I am not sure we measured up 100%, but we tried to.

The New Testament shows us what a church is intended to be, how a church is to organize itself, what a church's ministry is, and how a church is to go about that ministry. Then you come right back in these same books, and you find direction and guidance and instruction for your own personal life.

I am not Timothy; but when I read the books to Timothy, I take those truths that the Holy Spirit used Paul to write to young Timothy and I apply them to my life.

Paul wrote to Timothy to study to show yourself approved unto God, a workman who needs not to be ashamed. I apply that to my life, and you can apply it to your life. Study God's Word to show yourself approved unto God, a workman who does not need to be ashamed.

I will promise you that if you will become a daily reader and student of the Bible, it will change your life. Keep studying your Bible and get into a pattern of daily reading the Word. You do not have to read 50 chapters a day. It is the slow bee that gets the nectar from the flower. Do not worry about how much you read. It is not how much of the Bible you go through; it is how much of the Bible goes through you. Just read at a comfortable pace. If you can read a chapter a day, fine; just read what is comfortable to you. The point is, whatever you read, apply it, pray over it, and meditate over it.

I would also encourage you to memorize scripture. The finest plan I am familiar with is the Navigators. It is a great system. Memorize scriptures. Take a verse and break it down phrase by phrase. Then add a phrase and keep adding to it. Do you know what will happen? As you begin to memorize scripture and begin to put God's Word in your mind and in your heart, at key times in your life the Holy Spirit will bring to your mind and heart these scriptures. It is just like the hymns. Choruses are fine if they are biblically based, but I feel sorry for people who do not know the great hymns because at crucial times in your life these hymns will be helpful. It is the same thing about the Scriptures and even more so.

When you are going through trials and valleys in your life, if you have filled the well of your heart with scriptures, then they will come bubbling to the surface. Thy word have I hid in mine heart that I might not sin against Thee.

III. Prophetical

Now the third division of your New Testament is the Prophetical division. It is one book, the book of the Revelation. It sets forth the future from the time of the New Testament churches until the end of the age.

The arrangement of the Bible, the way these books of the Bible are arranged, is by design. I do not think you can avoid the fact, when you look at the way it is all put together, that the whole Bible is put together by divine design. God put it together.

Some years ago I saw a copy of the United States Constitution. But it was unusual in that the spacing of the letters of the words was different. I did not get it at first until I stood back and looked at the picture. When I stood back, I noticed the words had been arranged in such a way that you could see a picture of George Washington.

In Luke 24 Jesus was on the Emmaus road with two of His disciples. One of the most moving experiences I have ever had was to walk on the Emmaus road and read this passage of scripture. Jesus was raised from the dead, and these two disciples were walking from Jerusalem out to Emmaus, about seven miles. The living Lord Jesus comes and walks alongside them. Then we are told in Luke 24:27, "And beginning at Moses and all the prophets, he expounded unto them, in all the Scriptures, the things concerning himself."

I saw a picture of the Gospel of John. It had all the words in the Gospel of John. They had done those words just like they had done the words of the Constitution. When you stepped back, you could see in the arrangement a picture of the face of Jesus.

The Bible really is a picture book in that it gives us a perfect, complete picture of our Lord Jesus Christ. That is the great theme; that is the great purpose of the Bible. That is why some things are given a very minor treatment in the Bible while other things are given a major treatment in the Bible. Let me give you an example.

In the creation, it talks about the stars. How many stars are there? We know there are millions and millions and billions and billions of stars. When it talks about the creation of the stars, the Bible dismisses the stars in five words, "He made the stars also."

Yet, you come right along in that same Old Testament and run across a building in the wilderness, called the tabernacle, where the Jews worshiped in the wilderness. Did you know that the word *tabernacle* is mentioned in 50 chapters in your Bible? Do you know why? God is far more interested in creating saints than He is in creating stars. For God to create all of the stars it just took a little bit of His sand; but for God to create a saint, it took the blood of His Son.

The whole theme of the Bible is Jesus and what Jesus came into this world to do. When I cannot figure out what is going on in my Bible, one of the main questions I ask is where is Jesus in all of this? When you can find Jesus and see something about Jesus in it, then it begins to clear up.

I want to leave you with this poem:

I find my Lord in the Bible
Wherever I choose to look.
He is the theme of the Bible,
The center and heart of the Book.
He's the Rose of Sharon,
He is the Lily fair.
Wherever I open my Bible
The Lord of the Book is there.

Wonderful journey, isn't it? The journey through the Bible.

Companion series on CD by Dr. Jerry Vines

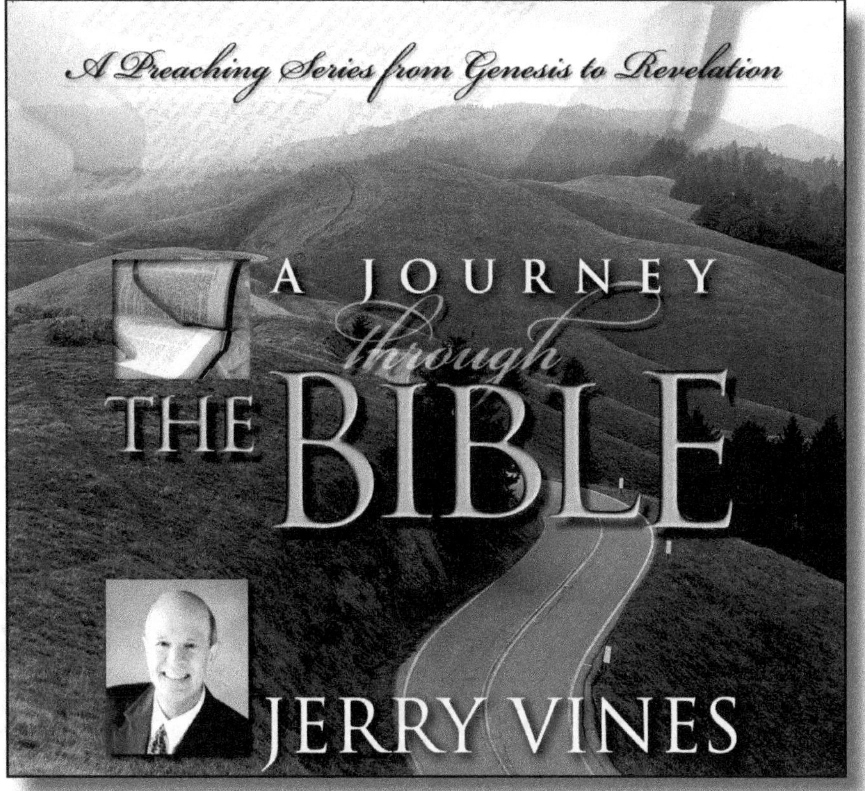

To order more copies of this series, in print or on CD, visit JerryVines.com

CPSIA information can be obtained
at www.ICGtesting.com
Printed in the USA
LVHW010935180322
713540LV00005B/7

9 780982 656174